B.

GETTING STARTED WITH
RHODODENDRONS AND AZALEAS

D0052943

GETTING STARTED WITH RHODODENDRONS AND AZALEAS

by J. HAROLD CLARKE

TIMBER PRESS
Portland, Oregon
1982
in cooperation with
THE AMERICAN HORTICULTURAL SOCIETY

Copyright © 1968 by J. Harold Clarke
All rights reserved.
Printed in the United States of America

Reprint edition published by TIMBER PRESS, 1982

Library of Congress Cataloging in Publication Data

Clarke, J. Harold (Joy Harold), 1899-
    Getting started with rhododendrons and azaleas.

    (The Timber Press horticultural reprint series)
    Reprint. Originally published: 1st ed. Garden City,
N.Y.: Doubleday, 1960.
    Includes index.
    1. Rhododendron. 2. Azalea. 3. Rhododendron—
Varieties. 4. Azalea—Varieties. I. Title. II. Series.
[SB413.R47C55   1982]   635.9'3362   82-16995
ISBN 0-917304-30-6

Contents

PART ONE: RHODODENDRONS AND AZALEAS; THEIR ORIGIN, USES, AND SPECIAL REQUIREMENTS.

1. Where Rhododendrons Came from and How They Got Here.   **15**
Botanically, azaleas are rhododendrons; species native to North America; largest number of species from Asia; many from high altitudes; early botanical collections; the plant explorers; introductions by the U.S.D.A.

2. How Rhododendrons Differ from Other Plants.   **24**
Shallow rooted; require acid soil; role of symbiotic fungi; use nitrogen in ammonium form; closely related plants.

3. Garden Use of Rhododendrons and Azaleas.   **28**
Tall trees to prostrate dwarfs; for the small garden; landscape uses; unexcelled border plants; for mass planting; color harmony; fragrance; beautiful foliage; companion plants; in the rock garden.

4. Climate as Affecting Rhododendrons and Azaleas.   **47**
Wide variation in hardiness; effect of low temperatures; effect of high temperatures; moisture requirements; shade is important; modifying the climate; winter protection.

5. Soil Requirements.   **57**
Importance of soil knowledge; soil texture; importance of organic matter; drainage; improving heavy soils, light soils; chemical elements in soils; biological problems; soil acidity.

PART TWO: METHODS OF CULTURE, FERTILIZING, AND PEST CONTROL.

Varieties and species; seedling plants; collected plants; horticultural varieties; group varieties; American Rhododendron Society Code of Nomenclature; hardiness ratings; quality ratings; where to purchase plants; acclimatization; nursery stock; when to plant; how to plant; use of planters.

Lath-house culture; what to do in alkaline soils; degree of acidity required; acid fertilizers; fertilizers for the essential nutrients; forms of nitrogen; organic fertilizers; phosphorus, potassium, magnesium, the minor elements; cultivation not desirable; weed control; mulch, advantages and disadvantages; pruning; watering; care of gift plants; moving large plants.

Why the beginner may be interested; seed propagation; care of seedlings; layering; grafting; types of grafts; budding; cuttings; use of hormones; mist propagation; the Nearing frame.

No special control needed in some areas; types of insect pests; how insects are controlled; specific pests and their control; physiological troubles; girdling; abnormal leaf color; leaf drop; specific diseases and control measures; useful fungicides; moles and rabbits.

PART THREE: SPECIES AND VARIETIES FOR GARDEN USE.

How species are determined; how species plants may be obtained; selected forms; why grow the species; how the species are classified; descriptions of species which make good garden plants.

Named selections of species; hybrid varieties; how varieties are

List of Illustrations

First group of pictures facing page 24

Rhododendrons flank a garden gate
Azaleas soften walk lines
Rhododendrons peep through garden fence
White azaleas for accent on shady lawn
Specimen 'Bow Bells' effectively used
Steep hillside covered with azaleas
Low-growing varieties under windows
Rhododendrons with woven board fence
'Mrs. E. C. Stirling' graces stone steps
Informal rhododendrons by a formal pool
R. *carolinianum* in the shrub border
Rock wall holds dwarf rhododendrons
Large 'Cynthia' well located
Rhododendrons in scale with dwelling
Deciduous and evergreen azalea border
Yellow azaleas top yew hedge

Second group of pictures facing page 96

Polyethylene-covered frames over seedlings
Spotted rhododendron seedlings
Making a rhododendron cutting
Wounding the cutting
Completed cutting ready for hormone dip
How a saddle graft is made
The saddle graft completed
'Naomi' trained to a single trunk
Rooted cuttings ready for the lath house
'A. Bedford' two years from cuttings
Flower bud compared with vegetative bud
An 'Antoon van Welie' liner

Preface to the Timber Press Edition

Garden books may sometimes be thought of as timeless, complete and correct fifty years ago, the same today. However, the last two or three decades have seen a number of changes so it seems desirable to update a few items although most of the material in the first edition of *Getting Started With Rhododendrons and Azaleas* is still basic garden information.

THE USE OF PESTICIDES

Many developments have occurred in the field of pest control, some good, some not so good. Fortunately rhododendrons and azaleas, in most areas, are relatively free of pests and thrive without benefit of chemical sprays. However, in some areas pest control is necessary to produce healthy, high quality plants. A few years ago Congress effectively removed a number of the most valuable pesticides, including lindane and DDT, from the hands of home gardeners. Only selected pesticides can be legally used, and these only against specified pests, on specified plants, at the rate and time of application printed on the labels. Fortunately, there now seems to be a trend towards permitting a little greater leeway for home gardeners. As a general rule the gardener may safely purchase and use, according to the labels on the containers, any materials displayed by legitimate dealers, as dealers are quite conscious of the regulations with which they are bound to conform.

Chemical weedkillers will seldom be needed as rhododendrons and azaleas are usually best grown with a mulch which will restrict weed growth, or at least cause the weeds to develop very shallow root systems. Such weeds may be pulled about as rapidly as they can be spot sprayed with a herbicide. A few, such as Canada thistle, quack grass, and horse tail, if well established, may require chemical treatment for eradication. If you haven't used herbicides please get specific advice before starting, as many of the weed-killers will injure garden plants if used incorrectly.

Biological control of pests, such as providing predatory insects to control other insects, or the growing of certain companion plants to repel insects or prevent diseases has found limited application but is probably oversold. The most important biological control is, undoubtedly, the use of varieties which have some genetic resistance to certain important diseases or insects. The idea that plants will be more insect- and disease-free if grown without chemical fertilizers appears to be without basis in scientific fact.

Increase in the popularity of rhododendrons in areas of high temperature and relatively moist soil is the result, in large part, of recognition that failure of plants was often caused by root rot fungus *Phytophthora cinnamomi*. By providing good drainage the growth of this root rot fungus is usually retarded. Planting in raised beds, up to 12 inches above the normal ground level has proven to be very helpful in preventing *Phytophthora*. In most southern states, unless the soil is very well drained, raised beds are almost essential.

PROPAGATION

There have been some changes in methods of propagation. Most spectacular has been the development of tissue culture, under laboratory conditions, now being tested extensively on a commercial scale by a number of nurseries. This is worth knowing about but should be tried by the home gardener only if he has had some experience in propagation and wants to try any new methods which come along.

Some comments should be made about propagation by cuttings, by far the most important method at the present time. The time of taking cuttings, as suggested in the first edition of this book was Aug. to Oct. That is good but the trend is toward earlier dates when possible, June in the Northwest for early growing and maturing varieties. The key to good rooting of the deciduous azaleas seems to be taking the cuttings very early, while they are still very soft; they may flop over when first put into the rooting medium but will gradually straighten up.

A good, easily available disinfectant for cuttings as they are being made is Clorox, 1 part to 20 parts water. Cuttings may be dropped into a container of this solution as they are made, and given a quick dip, or they may be left in for several minutes without damage to the cuttings. The Clorox solution should be made up fresh after 3 or 4 hours.

In Holland and Belgium many nurseries are putting flats of azalea cuttings into outside cold frames, or on greenhouse benches, and laying sheets of polyethylene directly onto the cuttings. This seems to minimize drying out and does not require support for the plastic. If this method is tried by the beginner on a small scale, such as one flat of cuttings, care should be taken to wrap the plastic under the flat so moisture will be retained. It would be advisable to spray with captan, before covering, to prevent gray mold.

As indicated, we did have good results with rooting in straight peat, and with continuous mist, but now suggest a mixture such as 80% perlite or sawdust and 20% sphagnum peat. Other similar mixtures are being used, nearly all of which contain a small amount of peat. Intermittent mist is preferred over constant mist as it uses less water and there is less danger of waterlogging the propagating medium.

The propagator may wish to put his rooted cuttings into a peat bed or, more likely, into 3 or 4 in. plastic pots, which can then be plunged into peat or soil. Careful watering is necessary in either case. Some propagators root their cuttings directly into small pots or plastic bands which largely eliminates damage to roots as cuttings are removed from a cutting bed.

Some 25 years ago most rhododendrons were grown in the field, then dug and burlapped for market. That has changed because of difficulty in getting burlap and the development of containerization. The use of pulp pots has increased recently, although at this writing various types of plastic pots still dominate the market. Either may be used by the beginning rhododendron propagator. In England, black plastic bags are commonly used and may well be tried by the home gardener. They do not look as trim and neat in the garden center but plants seem to grow as well in them as pots.

At one time rhododendrons and azaleas were sized more or less vaguely by height and width of plant and often, if in containers, by the size of the container. The standard way now is by diameter of plant. If you see what you buy there is no problem. However, if you are reading a newspaper advertisement for a 15 – 18 rhododendron the plant should measure between 15 and 18 inches in width, bud to bud.

SOME CULTURAL SUGGESTIONS

A good form of nitrogen for rhododendrons and azaleas, not previously mentioned, is ammonium phosphate, useful in soils deficient in phosphorus. Both N and P are readily available to the plants. Since nitrogen may leach out of the soil more or less rapidly depending on type of nitrogen fertilizer used, rainfall, temperature and soil type, additional applications really should be made based on the color of the leaves and general growth response of the plant.

As stated, dolomite may be used to correct magnesium deficiency where the soil is very acid to begin with. It is of interest that dolomite has seemed to improve the growth and color of plants in certain parts of the Northwest where no visible symptoms of magnesium deficiency were found. These soils are usually in the pH4.5 to pH5.5 range.

CHANGES IN RATINGS

The quality and hardiness ratings developed by the American Rhododendron Society have proven very useful but there has been change here also. The familiar quality ratings, X to XXX, have been changed to 1 to 5 and are applied to both plant and flower, written as 1/1 to 5/5. A very poor seedling might even rate 0 for plant or flower or both. A rating of 4/1, for example, indicates an above average flower on a poor plant. Hardiness is now officially rated in degrees F, but the old H-1 to H-7 will probably be seen in catalogs for some time.

As new and more adaptable varieties are produced and new methods of culture and pest control are reported the area considered suitable for rhododendrons and azaleas has increased until now only very cold and inhospitable locations are considered off limits to outdoor planting.

The size and importance of rhododendron and azalea organizations has increased along with the number and distribution of gardeners specializing in these plants. Since the original edition of this book the number of chapters of The American Rhododendron Society has increased from 18 to 46. The A.R.S. has a well organized Seed Exchange. The Rhododendron Species Foundation has a very promising rhododendron species collection in a 25 acre garden at the Weyerhauser headquarters near Tacoma, Wash. Various A.R.S. chapters and some unrelated groups have established display gardens, publish news letters and, in general, promote rhododendrons and azaleas as desirable garden plants in their communities. Beginners should, wherever possible, take advantage of such sources of information.

CHOICE OF VARIETIES VERY IMPORTANT

The greatest improvement in the rhododendron and azalea field has undoubtedly been the creation and distribution of new varieties, which are not only more attractive in plant and flower, but also more resistant to extremes of heat and cold, to pests, and to various unfavorable soil and weather conditions. Most of those listed in this book are still good garden varieties and relatively easy to grow. However, if I were to revise those lists in detail many newer varieties would be included. But then five years later still newer ones will have become available, for the breeders, and especially American breeders, have been very active in recent years. Some of the best new varieties are still in short supply, and not tried out in a wide range of soils and climates, so I'm not going to revise the lists in detail.

There are, however, a few which, for various reasons, I would omit from some of the lists, including — 'Charles Dickens', poor color and size of flower, 'Atrosanguineum', poor color, 'Goldsworth Yellow', flower doesn't open wide, 'Mme. de Bruin', brittle twigs, 'Mrs. P.D. Williams', poor root system, (Loderi G) 'King George', a beautiful variety but finicky and will grow too large for any but very large gardens, 'Lady Chamberlin', beautiful, but named clones not free flowering, 'Canary', poor plant, usually yellowish leaves.

When looking for superior varieties to replace the above, local rhododendron enthusiasts would probably be the best source of information. During recent years certain very useful groups of new varieties have emerged. In the east selections from the Dexter group, and those from Gable and from several other eastern breeders are much superior to the ''old hardies''. Hybrids of *R. yakusimanum*, from many breeders, are promising as compact, hardy dwarfs in both East and West. Listing all the very good new varieties would be a monumental task, of more interest to the fancier than the beginner.

One new group known as the Malesian rhododendrons is interesting gardeners in coastal and southern California. The many species of this tropical group include unusual colors and forms. Unfortunately, these species are tender and useful for outdoor growing only where the climate is practically frost free.

Exploring for new species of rhododendrons and azaleas is still going on and additional forms of known species or entirely new ones are sure to be found.

The botanical classification of rhododendron species is now being given great consideration with the trend being toward a system proposed by Dr. H. Sleumer and away from the Series concept previously in vogue. However, serious beginners should become familiar with the Series grouping as many will be making use of it for a long time to come.

BOOKS

A number of new and useful books have appeared since the list on page 259 was prepared. I can't name them all but the following at least should be included.

Van Veen, Ted. *Rhododendrons in America*. Sweeny, Krist, and Dimm.

Leach, David. *Rhododendrons of the World*. Scribner.

Cox, Peter. *Dwarf Rhododendrons*. Macmillan.

ACKNOWLEDGMENTS

The number of those to whom I, at this time, owe a debt of gratitude is legion.

To plant hunters who risked life and liberty to bring, from far away valleys and uncharted mountain ranges, the plants which have enriched our gardens and provided the basis for many friendships—

To the breeders of long ago, and even to this day, who have labored so devotedly to improve on nature's finest—

To the nurserymen and others who have scattered this genus so widely, the treasured findings of the plant hunters and the culmination of each breeder's efforts—

To the scientists who have helped to solve the myriad problems of culture and classification—

To the writers of other years and other lands, as well as our own, who have collected, tabulated, explained, and organized countless bits of information into what we proudly call the literature of rhododendrons—

To all of these I am grateful, for without any one of these groups there would not be the interest there is today nor any place for a book such as this.

The number of individuals who have helped me acquire information about azaleas and rhododendrons is very great. Nearly all are members of the American Rhododendron Society. The willingness of the officers and members of the Portland chapter, and of several other chapters, to share their knowledge and their plant material has been greatly appreciated. There are several whom I would like to name, but each name calls to mind another, almost equally worthy of special mention, so there would be too long a list. I am grateful to them all.

And to my family which, as always, has been understanding and forbearing during a period of special effort, my grateful thanks.

J.H.C.

Introduction

Not every garden-minded person in the fifty states of the U.S.A. can grow rhododendrons or azaleas—but almost everyone can. At the present time the general culture of these delightful plants is largely confined to the eastern seaboard from Boston south, the Gulf states, and the Pacfic Coast states, especially from central California north. Much of the remainder of the country has been considered "off limits," to rhododendrons especially, and to a certain extent to azaleas. It is true that much of the Great Plains, the Rocky Mountain area, and some of the Middle West does not offer ideal growing conditions, and many varieties could not be grown outside at all. However in a good part of this region, and especially in protected gardens, it should be possible to grow certain varieties with reasonable satisfaction. It will be more difficult, of course, than in areas where rhododendrons are especially well adapted.

Where soil and climatic conditions are relatively unfavorable, the gardener will have to follow certain practices of soil preparation, watering, mulching, and possibly winter protection. There are rather widely scattered gardens where rhododendrons are now being grown with considerable success in spite of very unfavorable environment. I have never run onto gardens which have abandoned rhododendrons after the gardener made a real effort to provide satisfactory conditions for them. I hope that what is said in this book will enable many more people personally to enjoy the beauty of the multiform varieties and species of this very large genus, and people who are already growing rhododendrons to grow them better and in greater variety.

METHODS OF GROWING EMPHASIZED

The emphasis in this book will be primarily on how to grow the plants, with just enough discussion of varieties and species to enable the beginner to make a start with those plants which give the greatest promise of successful growth. Classification and discussion of the various species and varieties is naturally a very important phase of the whole subject of rhododendron growing, and is of interest especially to the advanced amateur. This is inevitable in a plant group as large as the genus *Rhododendron* which, because of its size and intrinsic garden value, lends itself so well to the study and enthusiasm of the plant "collector." The genus is surpassed in intricacy and complexity of nomenclature and classification only by orchids, among garden plants.

Rhododendrons differ in their basic requirements from many other garden plants, as will be brought out in a later chapter. A knowledge of these differences should be quite helpful in enabling the gardener to give them the care and culture they prefer, and is absolutely necessary for the gardener in those regions where growing conditions are somewhat unfavorable for this particular plant group.

Interest in rhododendrons and azaleas is increasing, and spreading rather rapidly into new areas. The farther it spreads the less likely it is that the plants will find growing conditions exactly to their liking, hence the need to stress culture for those gardeners who are just beginning.

In the areas where rhododendrons have been grown for close to a hundred years, they have not become as numerous in gardens, or as widely grown as many other shrubs, because of their peculiar requirements. As new gardeners develop, it will be important for them to hear something of the rhododendron story before attempting to grow them. This may come from experienced gardener neighbors or from the printed page. It is hoped that this book will be helpful in this particular field.

BOOKS ABOUT RHODODENDRONS

It has been the better part of a century since the first American book on rhododendrons was published. This is a little-known volume entitled *The Rhododendron and American Plants,* by E. S. Rand, published in 1871. It is remarkable how accurate this book is, as viewed by modern standards, in many of the phases of rhododendron culture. If it had been generally available to the gardening public all these years, the rhododendron picture nationally might be somewhat different.

Since the book by Rand was published, there have been several volumes printed, in this country and abroad, on rhododendrons or azaleas or on both together. Some are quite recent, and most of them are very good. More books in this field are slated to appear in the future. Of the fairly recent books, at least one is out of print. Most of the books about rhododendrons and azaleas have been written primarily for the advanced amateur, with major emphasis, in many cases, on the intricacies of botanical classification, so important in a genus as large as this. The justification for this book lies in the hope that it will reach the uninitiated, and that it will stimulate interest in gardening with rhododendrons and azaleas—an interest which, in many cases, may lead to the reading of other books more complete and advanced than this one.

Some form of rhododendron may be found growing as a native from the sands of Florida to beyond the Arctic Circle. Wide areas in that span, of course, have no native rhododendrons. However, this great range would seem to justify our feeling that much of the area so encompassed can sustain reasonably satisfactory growth of certain rhododendrons and azaleas, for those gardeners who are willing to learn their requirements and do the few little extra things needed to make them satisfied with their growing conditions.

WHO IS A BEGINNER?

This book is slanted toward the beginner with rhododendrons and azaleas, and not necessarily the beginning gardener. There are many fine gardens in this land of ours which contain no rhododendrons or azaleas. They are located mostly in those parts of the country not usually considered as ideal for these plants, although there are many even in good rhododendron country.

We are thinking of the beginner, then, in terms of one who has had some garden experience, who perhaps does some little reading in garden magazines, but who has had little or no experience with that great plant family, the Ericaceae, or Heath family, to which rhododendrons and azaleas belong. Or perhaps the gardener has tried to grow some of these plants with indifferent success. If a few rhododendrons or azaleas, or both, have been tried, and they have languished and died, or have not made good growth and the wonderful show at blossoming time that the gardener has been led to expect, perhaps we can help to locate the trouble and make suggestions as to its correction.

It is my feeling that the American gardener is generally a person of considerable knowledge and with ability to understand most of the technical points of gardening. Even the young couple starting their first home and garden bring to bear on the problem a level of scientific education and general knowledge, obtained from school and from their reading, which is unprecedented. No longer can garden writers give very definite and arbitrary instructions as to methods of growing plants, unless those instructions are in agreement with the general scientific standard of the day. Gardeners, like Americans in every other occupation and hobby, are looking for the reasons behind the instructions, so that they can come to their own conclusions and perhaps modify their methods to fit their own specific conditions. We hope, therefore, to appeal to the gardener's interest in how plants grow and why they do well or poorly, and give suggestions which, though based on scientific experiments, are readily understandable, since we realize that the beginner with rhododendrons may be, and very likely is, a gardener of long standing.

Part One

ORIGIN, PECULIARITIES,
AND REQUIREMENTS OF
RHODODENDRONS AND AZALEAS

CHAPTER 1

Where Rhododendrons Came From and How They Got Here

At the very beginning we may as well emphasize the fact that rhododendrons and azaleas are very closely related—so close, in fact, that botanists now place both types of plants in the same genus. Some botanists in years past did consider azaleas to be in a separate genus, and so we may occasionally see, in older publications, a two-word term of which the first is Azalea and the second the species name, as *Azalea nudiflora*. The botanical name for this azalea now is *Rhododendron nudiflorum*. We will in this book, of course, go along with modern usage and call them all rhododendrons. In most cases—where we are discussing culture, for instance—we will simply use the word "rhododendron" to indicate both rhododendrons and azaleas. In some ways azaleas seem to be somewhat more adaptable to unfavorable conditions, and may be grown more easily than other rhododendrons in certain places where conditions are less than optimum. Where these differences as to culture or garden use exist, and seem to be important, we will try to bring them out.

SPECIES AND VARIETIES

Most readers will know that the word "species" is used to designate each readily distinguishable type of plant as it is found in nature. Closely related species are arranged in a larger group known as a "genus." The species will normally "come true" when grown from seeds, as that is the way it has maintained its identity over the centuries, in the wild. However, species are often found which are very similar—so similar, in fact, that they will hybridize easily in nature, and so botanists may be confronted with natural hybrids as well as "good" species, which is one reason botanical names are occasionally changed.

Two terms which will be used frequently in the following pages are "species" and "variety." The former, as we have seen, refers to a group in nature, such as *R. carolinianum,* which will breed true, although each seedling will be at least a tiny bit different from every other one. By "variety" is meant horticultural variety: plants grown from cuttings, layers, or by grafts from one individual plant supposedly superior in one or more ways, enough so to justify its propagation and usually its naming as a variety. So 'Pink Pearl' rhododendron is a variety, and every 'Pink Pearl' plant is actually a part of the original seedling and genetically identical with it.

Some writers use the term "cultivar" in place of variety, as botanists use the latter term somewhat differently, to refer to a subgroup within a species. The term variety, however, has been so long used in horticultural literature that I prefer it, and feel that my readers will recognize it as a very familar and readily understood term.

The list of azalea species includes some seventy or more, and is usually referred to as the azalea "series" within the very large rhododendron genus, which is made up of some eight hundred different species. With so large a group of plants it is not surprising that the distribution in nature is very wide. In fact it might be said that the distribution is world-wide, except that almost all are found in the Northern Hemisphere.

RHODODENDRONS NATIVE TO NORTH AMERICA

In North America we have *R. lapponicum* in the arctic regions, where it is widely distributed. This hardy little plant may be found in much of the tundra region surrounding the Pole, and extending southward into the tree-supporting zone as well. In Florida there is a native species, *R. chapmanii,* which grows on the sand dunes under conditions usually considered fatal for rhododendrons. In the Southeast there are three important species which are found in large numbers, especially in the Blue Ridge Mountains. *R. carolinianum* and its near relative *R. minus* are prevalent on the lower hills and adjacent parts of the coastal plain. Great hillsides are covered with *R. catawbiense,* especially in North Carolina, growing in full sun up to elevations of close to 6000 feet. In the same area and extending much farther north, running into Southern New England and even into Maine and Quebec, is *R. maximum,* the Rose Bay.

In addition to the above there are many species of rhododendrons of the azalea series in the Southeast. This territory is usually taken to include the area east of the Mississippi and north to Washington,

D.C., although several azalea species extend much farther north. These azaleas are not the ones that are commonly found in the famous "azalea gardens" in the Southeast, those being imports from Europe made many years ago. That is not to say that the native azaleas are not, in many cases, very fine garden subjects. They are, however, daintier and less spectacular, and probably more refined in their general appearance and atmosphere than the more gaudy varieties of the florist trade and of the large azalea gardens. These native eastern azaleas constitute a rather complicated group botanically, as they generally hybridize quite freely in nature. It is not our purpose to discuss in detail the characteristics, distribution, and genetics of such plant groups, except where it may be of some use to the gardener getting started in this field. Brief discussions of certain ones suggested for garden use will be found in Chapter 12.

In the Northwest, *R. macrophyllum* is found in many areas along the seacoast, along the western side of Puget Sound, on Mount Hood, and on certain other highlands. Another species, *R. albiflorum,* is found only in the mountains of the Northwest, extending east as far as Colorado and north into British Columbia. So far this species has been of interest because of hardiness and rather unusual native habitat, rather than garden value. In the Northwest also *R. occidentale,* the native Oregon azalea, extends along the coast from the Columbia River south to certain isolated locations in the southern part of California. It is at its best in central and southern Oregon and northern California. This deciduous species is frequently found in western gardens, but it is of general importance also because of the part it played in the development of some of our best garden azaleas.

EUROPEAN AND ASIATIC RHODODENDRON SPECIES

In Europe there are few native species. *R. luteum,* a bright yellow, deciduous azalea has garden value in the milder climates and has been used extensively, especially in Holland, as an understock for grafting named varieties of deciduous azaleas. It has also been used for breeding purposes.

The Alpine rose, *R. ferrugineum,* and its near relatives are found in the higher mountains of southern Europe but have not been used extensively in gardens. England is overrun, in many localities, with

R. ponticum, to such an extent that one might naturally consider it to be a native there. However, it was introduced from southeastern Europe and Asia Minor, and has simply become naturalized and spread so exuberantly that it is somewhat of a weed in a few places.

By far the greatest number of known rhododendron species come from Asia, particularly the Himalayan region and the highlands surrounding it. These lower ranges and foothills lie in northern India and western China. A number of species have been found in Burma, Assam, and southern and southeastern China, but the wealth of rhododendrons of possible garden value is apparently not as great there as it is farther west in the highlands. Japan and other islands off the coast of Asia have also added to the treasure of garden rhododendrons.

If we were to mention here all the potentially important species from Asia and give them the space they may well deserve, comparable to the comments made about American and European types, many pages would be required. We hope the reader will become interested enough to read some of the stirring tales of the search, by that hardy breed the plant explorer, for more and different species—to add to botanical knowledge, it's true, but to beautify our gardens certainly. In those accounts geographical location, elevation, and general environmental characteristics are set forth. This information is of value to the gardener, and especially to the rhododendron fancier and collector. For the beginner, however, a knowledge of where and under what conditions a few American and European species grow in natural stands may convey useful information, whereas similar facts about species from far-off western China would be much harder to translate into something usable. So for the moment we will pass over that great group of the finest of rhododendron species, but a number will be considered for specific garden uses in Chapter 10.

One other important rhododendron locality might be mentioned, the East Indies, where a group of tender species is sometimes spoken of as the Javanicum Rhododendrons. These are too tender for any but tropical countries, as they are apparently injured or killed by a touch of frost. They may have certain characteristics which will eventually be valuable in breeding, but up to this time they are somewhat of a novelty in the temperate zone, appearing usually, if at all, in the tropical houses of botanical gardens.

OUR CULTIVATED TYPES—A BLEND OF EAST AND WEST

It might be said, in general terms, that the cultivated varieties at present grown in the eastern states are largely hybrids between native American species and some of the Asiatic types. On the West Coast most of the varieties being generally grown and considered as the most satisfactory are hybrids between different species of Asiatic origin, although occasionally a variety is found which includes one of the eastern American species in its parentage. The reason, of course, is that the American species have qualities of hardiness not found in the Asiatic types, and on the East Coast hardiness is a much more important factor than it is on the West Coast.

HARDINESS AN IMPORTANT FACTOR

We should perhaps not generalize too much about the hardiness of American, as compared to the Asiatic, species. Some of the Asiatics are fairly hardy, but many of them are quite astonishingly tender. I say astonishingly because some were discovered at high elevations, up to ten to fourteen thousand feet, at or above timber line, where very low temperatures occur during the winter. Apparently these tender species are so located, in rather protected places in the mountains, that they are covered with snow before really severe winter weather sets in, and are able to survive because of the insulating blanket of snow, which stays in place all winter. It is a common observation that a continuous cover of snow is a good protection for rhododendrons in this country. The problem in our gardens usually is that the snow does not stay on until the end of winter. The plants may be protected for a considerable period, but are not covered by enough snowfall, or they are uncovered by high winds, which permits the plants to receive the full effect of low temperatures.

On the other hand, some of the species collected in localities where conditions are quite tropical sometimes display a considerable amount of hardiness. These observations are probably of little value to the beginning rhododendron grower except to indicate that one cannot always make a general statement of hardiness based on the geographic origin of the parents of a particular variety. It has to be observed under trying conditions in order to be sure of its hardiness, regardless of its parentage.

Some of the semitropical rhododendrons are epiphytes, growing on other trees rather than in the soil. These particular species, however, when grown in this country, either in the conservatory or, in some cases, out of doors, are able to thrive in soil just like other varieties. In other words they may grow as epiphytes in their native habitat, but are not necessarily restricted to that method of growth, and in fact could not survive as epiphytes under the cooler and drier conditions existing in the United States.

If we were restricted to our native American rhododendron species, aside from the azaleas, we would have some vigorous-growing, fairly attractive-leafed, hardy shrubs, but the flowers would be relatively small and mostly in a color range of somewhat bluish pinks, best described as magenta, although with some fairly good pinks and a very few whites. We would be almost entirely lacking in the dwarf types now being found so desirable for use on the small lot, or with the ranch-type house with lots of glass, and windows close to the ground.

THE PLANT EXPLORERS

The bringing into this country of the more spectacular and varied types from Asia is a very interesting and romantic story. Practically none was brought directly from its native home into North America. Seeds were collected by men especially fitted by training and experience to be plant explorers, and sent mostly to England, but to some extent also to Germany, Holland, and other European countries. In those countries they were grown, studied, and hybridized, and the resulting horticultural varieties were eventually imported into North America. Somewhat later many of the species themselves were also brought into this hemisphere by advanced amateurs who liked them for their native beauty, elegant forms, and unusual colors.

The collecting of the Asiatic species dates back only a little over a hundred years. The first collections were made, in general, by people who were primarily botanists. In fact some of them collected dried specimens of the flowers and felt that they had done their duty when these were adequately described, correctly labeled, and established in a herbarium in some European university. Even the botanists, however, were thrilled by the size, color, and beauty of many of the species. Since rhododendron seeds are very small, light in weight, and retain their powers of germination fairly well, at least for a year or so, it was logical for the botanical collectors to send seeds to the old country. In many cases these went not only to botanical gardens but also to private individuals who were especially interested.

The first introductions of the Asiatic species were more or less incidental, but late in the nineteenth century certain English estate owners, men of wealth as well as keen gardeners, became interested in financing expeditions, the main purpose of which was the actual procurement of new plants for garden use.

Obtaining seeds, of the Asiatic varieties particularly, often involved a very long journey. Starting from England, the expedition, outfitted for a year or more of exploration, would go by ship to some important Asiatic port, and from there possibly ascend a river for some hundreds of miles, after which the journey became an overland trip by horseback or on foot. Some of the species we now accept rather casually were brought out from valleys high in the Himalaya foothills which, in some cases, meant the crossing of several passes with elevations close to 12,000 feet. Naturally the summer season, when collecting could be done, was very short. Everything had to be timed to a fine point. If the expedition was slow in getting out it could be fatal, because there was usually little natural food in the distant valleys. Everything had to be carried in, and survival during the winter would be extremely difficult, if not impossible. This meant that the project had to be well equipped to provide the necessary horses, bearers, and servants of all types to see that the expedition moved and had a reasonably permanent camp for headquarters. All this was in addition to special provisions for collecting seeds of promising plants, and the herbarium specimens to go with them, so they could be properly identified if previously collected, and described and named if species new to botanical science.

Such expeditions usually went out under the auspices of a botanic garden or a group such as the Royal Horticultural Society, but financed, wholly or in part, by private individuals. It was understood, of course, that these private individuals would share in the seeds which were sent back. That is why we find so many old species plants in certain English gardens today; they are the direct result of these explorations.

A number of books have been written about these trips, both by the explorers themselves and by others, and I could not do justice to any of them here by attempting to outline their accomplishments. It should at least be mentioned, however, that among the outstanding names in connection with these early importations are Hooker, Farrer, Fortune, Forrest, Kingdon-Ward, Rock, Ludlow and Sherriff, and Wilson. Persons at all interested in plants will find exciting reading in accounts of these explorations "on the roof of the world."

In addition to these plantsmen, there were others, such as missionaries, government surveyors, and just plain travelers, who became interested in rhododendrons quite incidentally, and sent back seeds of things which took their fancy. The English explorers were by no means the only ones, as early French, German, and Russian travelers, missionaries, and botanists all contributed to some degree.

WHAT OF THE FUTURE?

The height of the collecting effort occurred during the early part of this century, at a time when venturesome souls could be found to make the trips and wealthy individuals could be found to finance them. At the present time practically no work is going on in this field, or is even in the planning stage. Unsettled conditions in western China preclude exploring in much of the most promising areas. It might be thought that these remote mountains and valleys have been so thoroughly explored that nothing new may be expected. From the accounts of the explorers themselves one can readily see that the vastness and difficulty of access of these high mountain valleys make it almost impossible for a few people completely to exhaust their botanical treasures. Undoubtedly many things are yet to be found, possibly not so much in the way of new species as new and better garden forms of species already known to science.

Unfortunately the current financial situation, particularly in the English-speaking world, is not such as to encourage more such expensive expeditions' being financed by one individual. Certainly we are not likely to see again as many as three or four expeditions under way at once, the expenses of which were largely borne by one individual.

PLANT INTRODUCTION BY THE U.S.D.A.

At the present time the United States Department of Agriculture has plant explorers working occasionally in different parts of the world. They are mostly interested in what might be called "economic plants"—that is, crop plants, forage plants, or those which may be used for new chemical compounds or drugs—rather than in ornamentals. However, some ornamental plants, including rhododendrons and azaleas, are being brought in, especially from Japan. Nursery lists from many countries are scanned, and material listed is introduced to this country. Botanic gardens and private collections in other countries will no doubt yield occasional new types, and certainly many new varieties, for American gardens.

VAST AMOUNT OF MATERIAL NOW AVAILABLE TO PLANT BREEDERS

It is interesting to speculate on what may yet be introduced, especially as to quality rather than quantity of new species, although introduction will undoubtedly be slow until international tensions have been relieved. Actually this situation is no great blow to the rhododendron world. There have been listed, and presumably brought into the western world, some eight or nine hundred species of rhododendrons, including azaleas. This provides a tremendous reservoir of breeding material for the hybridizers. Considering it mathematically, the making of all possible crosses between individual species is something that is not likely to occur for many, many years, if ever. In other words, the breeders have available more material than they can fully exploit in the foreseeable future. As crosses are made and new hybrids produced, the amount of potential breeding material will actually increase. This is not to deny that there are still lacking certain important qualities, which may eventually be found in as yet undiscovered new species. We shall all be looking forward to the day when the foothills of the Himalayas may again be invaded by the peaceful expeditions of plant exploration.

The preceding discussion may seem a bit pointless to the gardener deciding whether or not to invest in his, or her, first rhododendron plant. Most gardeners, however, have an interest in their plants which goes somewhat beyond mere physical appearance, and rhododendrons or azaleas may easily become a fascinating hobby which extends beyond mere collecting of varieties, or species, to an interest in the origins and natural habitats of the various types. Perhaps this very brief account may encourage further reading in a most interesting field.

CHAPTER 2

How Rhododendrons Differ from Other Plants

There was a time when it was thought that various kinds of plants differed greatly in their requirements as to soil conditions and soil fertility. Experiments during the past two or three decades have indicated that most plants require essentially the same nutrient elements, and that the same fertilizer program is satisfactory for almost all. The trend has been to think of fertilizing as being the addition of those elements which are lacking, or deficient, in a particular soil. If your garden soil is deficient in phosphorus, then practically all plants will benefit from the application of phosphorus. In other words we are fertilizing the soil, bringing it up to where it should be for optimum plant growth, rather than fertilizing on the basis of individual plant requirements. In general this has worked out to the advantage of the average home gardener, who is usually concerned with a great variety of plants.

With rhodendrons and azaleas, however, we do have a group of plants which differ in several respects from most common garden plants, be they fruits, vegetables, or ornamentals. Gardeners who have come to the conclusion that using plenty of lime and a complete fertilizer is good for any garden subject may find themselves puzzled by the fact that rhododendrons or azaleas have not responded as they had expected. This is due to certain inherent physiological differences which possibly occur also in other members of the Heath family, the Ericaceae, to which rhododendrons and azaleas belong.

THEY ARE SHALLOW-ROOTED

In the first place rhododendrons and azaleas are extremely shallow-rooted. This means that it is not ordinarily practicable to cultivate them to control weeds. From the standpoint of good plant growth, a system of permanent mulch is far superior to cultivation. As we shall see later, in Chapter 7, there are certain drawbacks to the use of mulch, at least under certain climatic conditions, so the gardener will have to give some thought to his own conditions and make the

Rhododendrons are ideal for flanking a garden gate.

Azaleas of various types break the hard, straight line of a concrete walk.

Utilitarian straight lines of a wooden railing are softened by these rhododendrons peeping through.

White azaleas stand out as an accent mark on shaded lawn.

Single specimen of 'Bow Bells' rhododendron, used effectively at entrance.

Hillside, too steep to mow, covered with azaleas and perennials to the sidewalk line.

Low-growing varieties are a must for planting in front of low windows.

Rhododendrons combine well with a woven-board fence.

'Mrs. E. C. Stirling' on the right graces stone steps.

The pleasant informality of rhododendrons lends charm to a somewhat formal
pool in this Seattle garden.

The graceful and rather low-growing *R. carolinianum* can be used in many.ways in the shrub border.

An informal lava rock wall wide enough to provide interesting pockets for dwarf rhododendrons.

Large plant of 'Cynthia,' at left, ties house intimately into the landscape.

Effective use of rhododendrons in proper scale with house and lawn area.

Deciduous and evergreen azalea border outlines a bit of fine-quality lawn.

Bright yellow azaleas blaze above a clipped yew hedge.

decision for himself. The roots, under mulch, will frequently grow out of the soil into the mulching material. Varieties differ, of course, but as a group these plants spread their roots mostly within a very few inches of the surface. Furthermore the roots are quite fine and fibrous, and in cultivating or hoeing about the plants, the roots might be severed without the gardener's being aware that he was doing any damage.

This shallow rooting is something which should be remembered when the weather becomes dry during the summer. Other shrubs, with roots extending two or three feet into the ground, may show little evidence of being damaged by drought when rhododendrons, with their roots all in the drier surface soil, might be suffering.

REQUIRE ACID SOIL

Another way rhododendrons differ from most plants is that they prefer an acid soil. So many of the usual garden plants, particularly the vegetables, do appreciate lime and, where the soil is quite acid, require it for normal growth, that many gardeners have followed the practice of using lime frequently to bring their soil almost to the neutral point. As most gardeners know, the neutral point is indicated on the pH scale as pH 7. Rhododendrons and azaleas will make their best growth at around pH 4.5 to pH 5.5. Where the reaction, or degree of acidity, approaches the neutral point or goes even beyond it to the alkaline condition, these plants will express their displeasure by making poor growth, remaining rather yellowish in foliage color, and actually dying in many cases. It is true that many other types of plants will tolerate rather acid soil, but few detest lime as do rhododendrons.

The third way in which these plants differ from many others is that they do not usually have root hairs, those minute, single-celled appendages near the root tips which function as the moisture-absorbing organs of the plant. The absorption of moisture and nutrients is, to some extent, directly through the fine, fibrous roots rather than through root hairs. This makes rather essential a great mass of these very fine, fibrous roots. Presumably this lack of root hairs may be one reason they must have fairly ample moisture during the summer months.

Minute, threadlike hyphae, or strands of fungus growth, have been found to be nearly always present in and around the small roots of rhododendrons. These fungi are called mycorhiza, and presumably live symbiotically with the plants; that is, they help them take in water and nutrients from the surrounding soil. This is probably a factor in the absence of root hairs, as seedlings may have root hairs until the mycorhiza "infest" them. Certainly we do not know as much as we should about this mysterious fungus-rhododendron relationship. Blueberries, which also belong to the family Ericaceae, also have mycorhiza, and the relationship has been studied, but without definite conclusions as to the function of each partner in this unusual relationship. We may simply conclude, therefore, that it is probably one of the several factors in making rhododendrons differ from many other plants in their cultural requirement.

REQUIRE NITROGEN IN AMMONIUM FORM

Another point of difference is that rhododendrons and azaleas use their nitrogen in the ammonium form rather than in nitrate form. In certain areas in the East and South, nitrate of soda and calcium nitrate and, more recently, ammonium nitrate have been the usual sources of nitrogen for direct use, or to go into mixed fertilizers. Experiments with azaleas at Oregon State College indicated that nitrate nitrogen was not directly available to the plants, and furthermore that it seemed to have some undesirable effects bordering on toxicity. It is possible that the nitrogen content of a soil in which rhododendrons and azaleas are growing could be maintained at a sufficiently high point by the use of nitrate, as a certain amount of it would be changed over, rather slowly but continuously, to the ammonium form by the action of soil microorganisms. Direct application of nitrogen in the form of ammonium sulfate or urea, which becomes available in ammonium form, has usually given superior results.

We see, then, that these plants differ from most garden subjects in being acid-loving, shallow-rooted, without root hairs but with friendly fungi in the roots, and in using nitrogen in ammonium form rather than the nitrate form. These peculiarities and the lack of knowledge concerning them have undoubtedly been responsible for many garden failures. In most cases, of course, the failures were associated with natural conditions which were unfavorable. That is, the soil was naturally alkaline, or nitrogen was present largely in the nitrate form, or the soil tended to dry out rather rapidly.

In Chapters 3 and 4, on climate and soil requirements, these idiosyncrasies will be discussed and specific methods of providing the conditions preferred by the plants will be given.

RELATED PLANTS

The family to which rhododendrons belong, namely the Ericaceae, or Heath family, includes many other ornamental plants and some crop plants, particularly blueberries and cranberries. Among the ornamental plants are the heathers, mountain laurel, pernettya, pieris, ledum, menziesia, kalmiopsis, leucothoë, gaultheria, arbutus, kinnikinnik, andromeda, and others. Many of these are known to be rather shallow-rooted and to prefer an acid soil, although there are some exceptions. Whether they all use nitrogen in the ammonium form is still unknown, except in the case of the blueberry, where that has been found to be true. Presumably, from certain observations, it is also true with cranberries.

Certainly there is evidence that various members of the Heath family require somewhat the same cultural conditions as rhododendrons. Many of the ornamental members of the family make good companion plants for rhododendrons because of their type of growth, flowering habits, foliage pattern, and other characteristics. If they also require the same growing conditions, as is apparently true for many of them at least, then there is an additional reason for using them as companion plants. Where soils are somewhat unfavorable for rhododendrons and special beds have to be made up with proper characteristics, then some of the other plants of the Heath family might well be included in the specially treated soil. Where rhododendrons naturally grow freely and well, these other Ericaceous plants are usually found rather commonly in the gardens of the area and may be confidently selected as companion plants.

An understanding of the peculiar requirements of rhododendrons will undoubtedly be a factor in their continued spread to areas where they may formerly have seemed very difficult to grow. This expansion has been proceeding rather rapidly during recent years, and may be expected to continue until we see at least some rhododendrons or azaleas in most of the different sections of the country. An additional factor, of course, in this expansion will be the development of hardier varieties for states having extremely low winter temperatures, and possibly of varieties having greater tolerance for hot, dry summers and alkaline soil.

CHAPTER 3

Garden Use of Rhododendrons and Azaleas

The genus *Rhododendron* includes not only a tremendous number of species, as previously stated, but also an extremely wide range of plant types. There are species which, in their native habitat in China, reach a height of 80 to 90 feet, with trunks 2 feet and more in diameter, good-sized trees by any standard. Granted, it will take a long time to grow a tree of this size, possibly two hundred years, where conditions are favorable. Where they are less than favorable, such an ultimate height will never be achieved.

There is a question whether any rhododendron will ever reach a height of 90 feet in this country, but a height of perhaps 40 or 50 feet is certainly not out of the question where conditions are exceptionally good. I have seen rhododendrons in England reaching a height reliably estimated at 65 feet, with many other specimens up to 40 feet or more. These English rhododendrons were old, some over 100 years. They were very striking and very beautiful, and in a setting of other trees and broad expanses of lawn with borders of smaller rhododendrons and other shrubs to help the giants melt into the landscape, the general effect was very pleasing.

Whether we could grow rhododendrons to 65 feet in this country I do not know. Conditions would have to be nearly ideal with no unseasonable killing freezes for 100 to 150 years. Few people now design gardens on that gargantuan scale or plant for posterity that far in the future. Our eldest sons do not expect to continue at the old family homestead and then see their own grandson continue the tradition. As a nation, we are on the move, young people looking for a larger house or older looking for a smaller one. More gardeners now are looking for smaller shrubs than for larger ones.

SIZE AT TEN YEARS OF AGE

The American Rhododendron Society has initiated the practice of estimating height at ten years, which permits comparisons to be made. Most varieties grow fairly rapidly the first few years, and by the age of ten have settled down to put most of their energy into blossoming and relatively little into extended growth, and so one would not be far wrong to consider the size at ten years as at least 75 per cent of the maximum. At the end of that time one could prune to keep the plants from increasing in size, could remove them and plant a better variety, could move them to a more suitable place, or could remove adjacent plants and let the rhododendrons continue to grow. This last alternative depends on their location's being satisfactory, not too close to the house or in front of low windows.

From plants which will reach gigantic size let us turn to the other extreme. There are many low-growing, or dwarf, species which lend themselves exceptionally well to garden use. Some, such as *R. prostratum* and a few other species, are actually creepers, reaching only 5 or 6 inches in height, while spreading over an area perhaps 2 or 3 feet in width. Many of these creeping types were originally found in the wild, growing in high mountain valleys where strong winds and relatively unfavorable conditions prevented any type of plant from growing much beyond the low, bush size and form. In fact quite a few of the rhododendron species grow above the tree line. This can refer both to altitude and latitude. *R. lapponicum,* growing in northern Canada beyond the Arctic Circle and beyond the normal tree line, forms a low shrublet some 3 inches in height. In spite of their small size, these arctic inhabitants sometimes live to a great age. It has been reported that some plants have been found with stems as large as a broomstick which, when cut, indicated an age of between 300 and 400 years.

Most species are intermediate between the tall, treelike forms and the low, creeping types, the complete range from small trees to large, medium and small shrubs down to the very low, creeping types being well covered.

The great variation in this group of plants, as we shall see later, involves not only the size and general type of bush, but practically every other character, especially the obvious ones of leaves and flowers. A rather large portion of the species are evergreen, but a number of the azalea species and some of the rhododendrons are deciduous. Some are semideciduous, holding only a portion of their leaves over winter. Almost without exception, however, they do have one thing in common, and that is a decorative quality found in few other genera. True, some species and varieties are more attractive than others, but

I know of no other genus of woody plants which includes such a wide range of altogether delightful and useful garden plants.

FOR GENERAL LANDSCAPE USE

One of the first questions that might occur to the beginner at this stage is, "How about the special treatments which are needed to make rhododendrons grow satisfactorily? Will that not restrict or eliminate the garden use of many types which might be very fine where conditions are favorable?" The answer is, of course, that the more nearly general conditions are favorable, and the less special treatments have to be provided, the freer the use that can be made of these plants in the landscape. The gardener is fortunate who lives where conditions are so favorable, as they are in certain parts of the country, that rhododendrons can be used for almost any landscape purpose just as freely as one would use any other ornamental woody plant.

For purposes of discussing this subject, garden use, perhaps we should just assume that conditions are favorable. If they are not, then the extent of use will depend quite largely on how much modification of soil and general environment has to be accomplished before the plants can be successfully grown. Obviously if one in a generally unfavorable locality wants to make the necessary effort to prepare a large area properly, then rhododendrons could be rather freely used. So let us at this point consider garden use without restricting our thoughts too much by a consideration of special requirements. Later, in the chapters on climate and soil requirements, the various factors will have to be dovetailed to provide the best solution. In some cases the solution may be a completely free use of these plants, and in other cases climatic hazards may be so great, and the requirements for soil modification may be so exacting, that only two or three plants can be accommodated, and those in planters or built-up beds.

SUITABLE FOR THE SMALL GARDEN

An important factor affecting garden use of any ornamental material is the size of the area to be planted. Obviously in the very small garden some of the large-growing varieties and species would either be out of place, or a very few plants would pre-empt and dominate most of the available space. The most spectacular use of rhododendrons is on the large estate, where there is unlimited space, many different types of soil and exposures, and many types of garden pictures to be designed. Few of us have such unlimited facilities, and it is reassuring to know that rhododendrons and azaleas can be used just as effectively on the very small lot. The effect produced is one of different scale, but the general picture may be, in miniature, very much like that on some of the larger estates.

In evaluating garden use of these shrubs, the most important factor to many people is the amount and quality of the bloom. In general they are unexcelled for size and beauty of flower, and the freedom with which the flowers are borne. Most of them hold their flowers for a relatively long time, unless conditions during the blooming season are very unfavorable.

Those who become really interested in rhododendrons find that they are, or at least may be, very attractive the year round. This means that the gardener should know how to keep the foliage a good, healthy green, and relatively free from insect or disease blemishes. Many varieties, if well grown, can be extremely attractive twelve months each year, with fine flowers, beautiful leaves, and shapely bush.

An important thing to emphasize is that these, or any other plants, should be used in such a way as to get the most out of them. This means the proper use of each variety, as well as selecting varieties which will be at their best under the conditions furnished. Adequate space for the plant to develop its natural and usually graceful form, so that it may be well clothed with leaves to the ground level or to a proper hem line, is necessary for the maximum fulfillment of its capabilities. Fortunately rhododendrons may be moved rather easily and, where set too close together, they may be spaced out with very little setback to the plants, if the moving is properly done.

LANDSCAPE USES

With very few exceptions rhododendrons and azaleas can fulfill most of the functions which any woody plants perform in the landscape. They do not produce brightly colored berries for the benefit of the birds. Neither are they ideally suited for use as a windbreak, although with reasonable care some kinds may function as such. Certainly where winds are a problem and windbreaks are really needed, they should be provided for the rhododendrons rather than expecting the rhododendrons themselves to be a windbreak. Another garden function for which rhododendrons are hardly adapted, in this country at least, is providing shade. True, some of the rapidly growing types within a man's lifetime might reach a height of 20 or 25 feet, but in most cases they would do better shaded than shading.

AS SPECIMEN PLANTS

Among other landscape uses, we still find some place for specimen plants. In general, specimen plants, on the small grounds at least, are somewhat out of favor. Too often they tend to clutter up the lawn area with little islands of plants which do not add to the general landscape picture. Usually shrubs are placed, and preferably so, in borders or groups, so that one is conscious of a pleasing general effect rather than of a miscellaneous collection of individual specimens. However where there is sufficient space, rhododendrons make wonderful specimens, as many varieties will produce broad, well-rounded, and well-filled-out plants. The leaves and, in season, the flowers are borne in good condition from the ground clear to the top.

The impression of one good, large plant, from a little distance, may be that of a group of plants with some large specimens in the center surrounded by smaller plants, and still smaller ones around those, in the best landscape tradition. This effect may be heightened dramatically by setting three to five plants of the same variety or species rather close together and encouraging them to grow up in one mass. In certain English gardens I have seen what appeared to be magnificent single specimens which, on careful examination, proved to be clumps of several individuals. However, few other plants are capable of producing as nice single specimens as certain rhododendrons or azaleas, because of their spreading habit of growth.

In selecting plants to be used as specimens, there must be great care as to choice of variety or species. In the border, any little fault of a plant may be hidden by actual cover of the adjoining plants or by the fact that they are such as to draw one's attention to their own beauty rather than permit it to wander to the faults of the plant in question. When a shrub is in a conspicuous place by itself, it is like an individual seated on a platform with people staring from the audience. Any little displacement of the necktie or unusual wrinkle in the clothing is quite obvious.

My own inclination is to avoid the use of specimen plants almost entirely, except perhaps in semi-isolated spots in the border, where one has the opportunity to see a plant develop naturally and un-crowded, but so closely associated with other plants that it is re-garded more as a part of the picture than as a picture in itself. Some may question the definition of the term "specimen plant." I have been using it as meaning individual plants in the lawn, growing untouched by other woody plants. Presumably many border plants might be considered as specimens, even in the rock garden, where the low-growing rhododendrons make themselves so beautifully at home. Even among the rocks, many plants will grow uncrowded and almost untouched by other plants, so in one sense they could be considered as specimen plants. However, the emphasis is on the rock garden as a whole, and not on the one individual plant.

RHODODENDRONS AND AZALEAS IN THE BORDER

Most of our landscape planting of shrubs these days is done in borders—fairly wide beds, usually adjacent to a boundary line, a fence or a wall, a building or a walk or, in the large landscape or park, surrounded by lawn areas of suitable size. The usual and obvi-ous thing is to place the larger-growing material at the back with intermediate shrubs near the center, and low-growing ones in the front. This is varied in infinite ways to avoid the appearance of monotony. The arranging of plants in an unnatural, straight-line pat-tern is most carefully avoided so they may show off their natural beauty of form and color in an arrangement as nearly natural as possible.

One would suppose that straight-line planting of shrubs had gone out with the horse and buggy. But just a few years ago I saw an ambitious state-highway planting, covering several miles, where each large group of shrubs was laid out in "orchard formation." And within the last couple of years the custodian of a nearby school lifted the plants of a naturalistic rhododendron border and reset them in straight lines "so he could get a lawn mower through." There are places where straight lines are unavoidable or even desirable, as in certain formal plantings, but for most rhododendron or azalea bor-ders—no!

The border may often include bulbs, perennials, and small trees as well as shrubs. The purpose is to provide a continuous and attractive over-all picture, leading the eye around the garden and usually to some central object of interest such as a house or a view of the mountains or a lake, or some garden ornament, or a particularly nice group of plants. This is where rhododendrons and azaleas are at their best. The great variety of sizes, shapes, colors, and seasons permits their use as tall background, and as intermediate and foreground plants so that one might produce an extremely varied and very interesting border using nothing but rhododendrons. Many people might feel that some variation in kind of plant is desirable. This may be simply a psychological idea that such variety is necessary, even though the other plants used may look almost as much like rhododendrons as do some other rhododendron species or varieties. At any rate the most interesting borders I have seen have been interspersed with other types of plants.

One could talk almost indefinitely about the details of using woody plants in the border. Their charm lies in their almost infinite variety and the definitely limitless patterns of arrangement that are possible. The wonder of it all is that, so subtly do nature's jigsaw pieces fall in place, borders featuring rhododendrons and azaleas are usually beautiful even when designed by a novice or, more frequently, when they are not really "designed" at all. Such being the case I will refrain from presenting a "do-it-yourself" border kit, a plan with numbers to designate where each plant goes, you to secure the plants and set them in the designated spots. Rather would I have you picture the border in your mind's eye, as you have dreamed of it, and then wish for you the determination to study the descriptions of a few varieties and to order the plants which seem most nearly to meet your specifications. It would be better, of course, to write down the specifications, just as a matter of orderly procedure. If you can't find varieties to fit the specifications, a rhododendron nurseryman will be glad to help you.

Visits to established gardens, where you can see different varieties in bloom, will be of immense help in making your own selections. Published descriptions and recommended lists for various uses, as given in later chapters, will have to suffice if you have no opportunity to see plantings of the desired type in other gardens. The quality ratings should not be overlooked. Varieties rated xxxx or xxx will, on the average, be the most beautiful, although when those rated xx or x are included in suggested lists, there is a reason. It may be greater hardiness, or vigor, or some other character which is important enough to offset some lack of perfection of flower and general appearance.

Borders may function as screens to increase privacy, or to frame a garden picture, or simply as a place to house a collection of rhododendron species or varieties. Most of us do not analyze the situation too deeply from the esthetic and psychological standpoint, but simply realize that we like to have a border of shrubs and other plant material in certain parts of our garden. There may be some who do not care for the ordinary border planting, because we find an occasional lawn peppered with individual specimen plants, sometimes in straight rows, sometimes just wherever there seemed to be an open space at the time the gardener had the urge to plant. Frustrating, to the man who pushes the lawn mower!

FOR SCREENS AND HEDGES

Screen planting is a phase of landscaping to accomplish a definite purpose. Depending on the height of the view which needs to be screened out, rhododendrons may be used successfully. Certainly they do not grow as fast as some other shrubs and trees which might be preferable where a particularly obnoxious view must be screened out as rapidly as possible. However, some of the free-growing types will make a sizable screen planting in a reasonably short time, and the evergreen leaves make it effective throughout the year. I have seen screens of *R. ponticum* some 10 feet high, with glossy, rich green foliage which completely blotted out all view of what was on the other side. They had been sheared, on one side at least, which accomplished the dual objective of making the screen more dense and preventing its obstructing a driveway.

Nearly every kind of shrub has been used somewhere, sometime, as a hedge, and our own favorite plants are no exception to the rule. Of course where hedges are used as fences to exclude animals or trespassers, then a more rugged or thorny type may be desirable. But most modern hedges are decorative rather than utilitarian, and for such, many kinds of rhododendrons may be used successfully. In most cases I would not recommend shearing them to get the very close, tight effect of well-sheared privet or box, but they do make nice, naturalistic hedges. Varieties may be selected that are upright or spreading, depending on the type of hedge desired.

Azaleas are often used as edging plants, or what amounts to a low, naturalistic hedge to enclose a planting of larger shrubs. The large shrubs, of course, might be anything, such as some of the larger rhododendrons. There are a number of dwarf rhododendrons which would make very fine low hedge plants. What they have to recommend them is a pleasant evergreen appearance, rather slow growth and, if unsheared, as they should be, a delightful show of flowers in season. *R. racemosum* can make a very nice, low-growing, somewhat spreading, naturalistic hedge which is tough enough to survive occasional accidental brushes with the neighborhood children.

AS ACCENT PLANTS

As accent plants, either rhododendrons or azaleas are superb. Varieties are available with flower colors so vivid, be they red, or pink, or pure white, that they stand out very clearly. The real problem sometimes is to provide an accent which is controllable and which does not stand out too boldly. Many of us have seen large border plantings of rather somber plant material, where one or two rhododendron or azalea specimens, properly placed and in full bloom, have produced a delightful effect. It is almost as if the whole border were in bloom. As a matter of fact, one or two individual plants, blooming under such circumstances, can often be appreciated even more than if they were in a mass planting.

FOR MASS PLANTING

Azaleas, particularly, lend themselves very well to mass planting. I believe they are so used, to some extent at least, in many Japanese gardens, instead of a number of different varieties planted together, to make a very bright and coherent, rather than a somewhat disturbing, picture. A half-dozen or a dozen plants of one variety will provide a sheet of bloom which in some cases may be much more effective than the multicolored result of a collection of several varieties. Many American gardeners seem concerned about the individual plant more than the over-all theme or feeling. He, or she, likes variety in the garden, is perhaps something of a collector. Nurserymen very frequently hear "Oh I have one of those, let's get something different."

On the larger estates mass plantings are used very effectively to cover large areas and to produce certain effects. No other woody plants will give the spectacular mass effect that one may see in a well-designed planting of either azaleas or rhododendrons. For this purpose azaleas have certain advantages, as they cover themselves so completely with flowers. Some rhododendron varieties are almost as spectacular, but in my opinion nothing makes such a blaze of color as a large mass of blooming azaleas. The individual flower may not be as outstandingly attractive as that of some rhododendron species or variety, but in such large masses of color the individual flower may never even be visualized by the onlooker. With many rhododendrons, and of course with some azaleas also, the flowers have a grace and charming attractiveness that cause us to look within the mass of bloom to separate out and enjoy the single blossom.

Aside from the use of mass plantings, we have the general landscape problem of color in the garden. Rhododendrons and azaleas provide a very wide range of both brilliant and subdued colors. The one weakness, perhaps, is in the blues, although we do have so-called blue rhododendrons. Many of those are somewhat suffused with pink to give more of a magenta than a true blue color. Certainly we do not as yet have the blue of the forget-me-not or gentian. Occasionally new blue varieties are introduced, and certainly the breeders have not yet reached the limit of improvement as far as color is concerned. There are very delightful pinks, reds, yellows, and whites with almost all intermediate shades, including various forms of spotting and blotching.

PLANTING FOR COLOR HARMONY

From the standpoint of color combinations, the individual gardener probably has personal convictions and should by all means cater to his own individual taste, for he is the one to enjoy the garden, or otherwise. If the gardener has no particular likes or dislikes or, on the other hand, very radical tastes, or preferences for color combinations that no one else can stand, then perhaps he should do some reading on that particular subject, or ask for help from his gardening friends. Rhododendron colors seldom clash, partly because they are displayed against a background of green, and because they usually tend to blend well with each other.

The subject of color harmony is a field in which I claim no great proficiency. To my mind, nature's colors clash very infrequently. It is usually when we are faced with very crude, man-made colors, either dyes or paints, or some varieties of certain plants which have exceptionally strong colors, that we are likely to have a problem of clashing colors in the garden. It is certainly true that we can make a more attractive picture in the border by being especially careful how the colors are combined, but this depends on whether we have good color sense and sensitivity.

There are some combinations which everyone seems to like. Yellows and blues together usually seem to satisfy. White flowers or green foliage seem to soften and blend other colors which might tend to clash if very close together. Grays, either of gray-leafed plants, or of stone, or weathered wood, serve to soften harsher colors. Strong colors—reds, yellows, blues, whites—if mixed at random may not actually clash but will look very "spotty" rather than blend into a pleasing, unified garden picture. Some mauve- and magenta-colored rhododendrons may look rather muddy if growing near bright, clear reds but very pleasing if grouped together, somewhat in the background, and especially if in front of evergreens or scattered in the edge of open woodland.

Rhododendron fanciers often arrange their plants to use the size and general contour and the foliage of the plant effectively, without worrying too much about its color, although there are some exceptions where the color must definitely be considered. I have seen many color combinations of rhododendrons, and have been unable to recall any that I considered absolutely undesirable. Perhaps the color of azaleas should be watched somewhat more critically because of the great mass of flowers which practically hide the foliage and give the impression, at a little distance, of a solid sheet of color. Such a display is more likely to clash, with a color which does not blend well, than would be the case if the same color were on flowers a bit more scattered over the plant and separated by relatively large masses of green leaves.

I have seen some mass plantings of azaleas where a few odd plants of a contrasting color were accidentally included in what was supposed to be a drift of one variety. The effect was jarring to me, not because of clashing colors but because the pattern was not pleasing; the odd plants seemed so obviously out of place.

CHECK COLORS AT PLANTING TIME

Fortunately rhododendrons may be moved while they are in full bloom. As a matter of fact, in many areas that is when most of the plants are sold. These plants are balled and burlapped, or in some cases in cans. They do not have to be planted immediately, provided they have been kept well watered and are in good condition. This permits the gardener to set them on top of the soil, where he thinks they should be planted, so he can observe the general effect before actually doing the planting. If the color combination seems to be a little less than satisfactory, the plant may be moved around until the most desirable place for it is found. This should be done promptly, and the plants set in the ground as soon as the best arrangement has been determined. Even then, if it turns out to be a mistake the plant can be dug and moved again without any serious consequences. This is especially easy to do if the burlap has been left on the ball.

Some other kinds of shrubs do not offer much of a problem, so far as color harmony is concerned, because they have such a short period of bloom. Any one species or variety of rhododendron, on the other hand, has a fairly long blossoming period, although this depends a great deal on seasonal growing conditions. Slight shade and ample water, with temperatures not too high, are conducive to long retention of the blossoms in good, fresh condition. The blooming season in a particular border may be extended for a relatively long time by planting some of the earlier-flowering varieties, as well as midseason and late ones. Some varieties even tend to bloom a little in the fall, although the flowers are usually not quite as large and well formed as on the same plants in the spring.

PLANTING FOR FRAGRANCE IN THE GARDEN

Fragrance in the garden is not usually considered as something to be expected from rhododendrons or azaleas. However, there are a number of types which do have considerable fragrance. There is one, 'Odoratum,' which can scent the entire garden area almost as would a clump of lilies. This azaleodendron (a cross between an azalea and a rhododendron) has an insignificant flower of rather small size and not very striking color, but it certainly is fragrant. There are a number of others, both species and hybrids, which are fragrant if one takes the trouble to sniff the individual flower, but which do not perfume the air. In general, rhododendron fanciers do not pay too much attention to fragrance, accepting any that is found as an unexpected bonus.

A number of species, especially some of the dwarfs, have leaves that are quite aromatic. If they are crushed in the hand, one gets a very strong odor of a pleasant, spicy nature. Some have such strong foliage odor that simply walking through a group of plants will stir up enough to be plainly discernible.

UTILIZE THE BEAUTY OF THE LEAVES

We have mentioned the fact that the evergreen leaves of many rhododendrons are beautiful and attractive the year round. A great deal of thought should be given to the foliage, as one must look at it twelve months in the year, whereas the flowers are usually present for only three to five weeks. In other words when choosing varieties, we should be thinking about the over-all appearance of the plant during the eleven-month period just as much as we think about the show produced during the one-month blooming season.

There are a number of rhododendrons which are grown primarily for their leaf characters, including some of the so-called large-leafed species coming from western China and the Himalayan region. Some have extremely spectacular leaves, ranging in length up to 2 feet, and 6 inches in width. *R. sinogrande,* for instance, has large, beautiful leaves which are extremely striking, but unfortunately it is not a very hardy species. A group of these growing in the background, or in an opening in a woody area, will give quite an exotic, tropical effect. Most of the large-leafed varieties have flowers that, while attractive, are somewhat less spectacular than most of the varieties with which we are more familiar. There are some intermediate types which have quite large leaves and also large, beautiful flowers.

Another leaf character, in addition to large size, which is appreciated by many rhododendron growers is the indumentum, or woolly felt, found on the underside of the leaves of certain species and varieties. In some cases this may be a rich brown in color, with the appearance of a fine quality suede. In other cases it is pure white, resembling very fine wool. True, these characters are partially hidden, unless one takes the trouble to turn over a leaf; or one may see a little of it if a breeze moves the leaves about. Rhododendron fanciers are accustomed to examining the undersides of the leaves of such varieties, and take pleasure in pointing out the character of the indumentum to the uninitiated visitor.

We do not often think of rhododendrons for autumn coloration, but there are some deciduous azaleas which display autumn colors as brilliant as will be found in almost any group of plants. These colors run from yellow to red to purple—in short, practically all of the so-called autumn colors. Most of the true rhododendrons do not have such autumn colors, remaining about the same shade of green throughout summer and winter. However there are some of the small ones, particularly in the *R. sanguineum* group, which have very definitely strong maroon to purplish-colored leaves in fall and winter, but green leaves in summer. Some of these are quite brilliant in their autumn and winter colors, which are retained all winter, whereas the deciduous azalea leaves are shed during early winter.

COMPANION PLANTS

The garden use and effectiveness of any group of plants such as this will be affected materially by the choice of plants to be used with them. It would be a most ardent hobbiest who would refuse to grow anything but rhododendrons. I have not yet found one quite that enthusiastic, particularly as most of them realize that the charms of the rhododendrons themselves can be emphasized and accentuated by proper use of companion plants.

TREES TO USE WITH RHODODENDRONS

Trees of some kind are almost essential at some place in every garden, to give height to the landscape composition and to provide shade for garden visitors, as well as to provide some shade for plants such as rhododendrons. It is true that rhododendrons may be, and often are, located on the north side of the house, but space there is usually quite limited, so we must rely on trees or artificial shade structures such as a lath house.

In selecting kinds of trees to use with rhododendrons, we should first consider whether the trees' characteristics are what we want. Do they have the size, shape, general appearance, and other qualities that we would want in the trees themselves, for our particular garden use? If they do, then all we have to consider is their relationship to rhododendrons, and whether the latter will in any way be unfavorably affected. If the trees are to be used to provide shade for the rhododendrons, their general form, color, and type of leaf are not usually of primary importance, provided they are acceptable in the general landscape plan.

The density of the foliage is important, as most rhododendrons do not like extremely low, dense shade. A well-grown specimen of Norway maple, for instance, would provide shade that is too dense for satisfactory growth of rhododendrons directly underneath. A rather open, dappled shade is most desirable, such as might be provided by a relatively open-growing specimen of honey locust, or small trees such as laburnum, and many others. Somewhat denser trees may be spaced farther apart to permit intermittent sun, or to provide shade for a few hours in midday, with sun during morning and late afternoon.

Azaleas, as a general rule, are somewhat more sun-tolerant than other types of rhododendrons. In the Northwest many varieties will do well in full sun if well supplied with moisture during the summer. Where hot weather and low humidity prevail for long periods of time, some shade is very desirable. Even in the Northwest a very hot, dry day during bloom may brown the flowers that are in full sun, and greatly shorten the blossoming season.

DEEP-ROOTING TREES WITH SHALLOW-ROOTED RHODODENDRONS

It has been mentioned that rhododendrons are quite shallow-rooted, and it follows that they are particularly susceptible to drought because of that fact. Some trees conveniently send down taproots and draw most of their water and quite a bit of their plant food from the lower soil levels where rhododendron roots never penetrate. Other kinds send out many of their roots at the same level as the rhododendrons and, being more vigorous and aggressive, may thrive to the detriment of the latter. I have made up special beds for rhododendrons near spruce trees. The soil is light sand, tends to become very dry in the summer, and is naturally lacking in fertility. When such beds are made up with some peat moss, or other organic matter, and fertilizer, and are watered during the summer, conditions become ideal for invasion by the spruce roots. After a few years the whole bed is almost a solid mass of tree roots, and even heavy applications of fertilizer and ample water seem to be used by the trees at the expense of the rhododendrons. Ideal trees, then, would be those with rather sparse, or open, shade and with deep roots which are not too aggressive. Where one can use a legume, such as the honey locust, it has an added advantage in that the available nitrogen is not depleted so rapidly.

The lighter-colored varieties, especially, show up wonderfully well when viewed against a background of evergreen trees. If the trees are fairly deep-rooted, the rhododendrons can be effectively planted near or among the trees at the edge of a grove. How far back into the woods one would want to go with rhododendrons or azaleas would depend on the density of the stand of trees, as well as their tendency to compete for water and nutrients. I have seen some very nice plantings in rather open stands of pine.

OTHER SHRUBS AS COMPANION PLANTS

There are many kinds of shrubs which will combine happily with rhododendrons or azaleas in a group planting. This is not to say, however, that companion shrubs are always needed. When one thinks of the availability of hundreds of different varieties and species, of all sizes, seasons, and almost all colors, it is obvious that a great deal of variety can be obtained, if desired, just by using different kinds of rhododendrons. Most gardeners probably will like to work in some other plant material. Perhaps we might compare it to our daily diet and say that we would get tired of having steak every day.

Things to consider in selecting companion shrubs would be their general appearance, color, blooming season, and adaptability to conditions which are also favorable to rhododendrons. From the standpoint of soil requirements, special consideration should be given to ericaceous plants. These would usually require rather acid soil and good drainage in winter but ample moisture in summer, conditions required by rhododendrons. In this group of plants of the Heath family some excellent shrubs are available, including kalmia or mountain laurel, the various types of pieris, including the ones usually sold as andromedas, the pernettyas, the heathers, and a number of others. When using these terms in the plural, I simply call attention to the fact that there are different species or varieties available, and that space does not permit a detailed discussion of these and the specific characteristics and uses of each type.

CONIFERS AS COMPANION PLANTS

The use of the various low-growing conifers with rhododendrons involves the mixing of broad-leafed and narrow-leafed evergreen material. There is no inherent objection to this, although of course there will be great contrast in texture. In general I would prefer a grouping of broad-leafed evergreens and a separate grouping, perhaps nearby, of the conifers. The variegated forms, or those which are extremely unusual in character—such as the very narrow, columnar types, and the very low, spreading types—or those which are best seen as specimen plants trimmed to a globular or definitely conic shape, must be used expertly, if at all, as they hardly seem at home with rhododendrons. The latter plants are rather free-growing, often irregular in shape, and seldom lend themselves to geometrical forms.

The advisability of using deciduous shrubs adjacent to or intermingled with rhododendrons and azaleas will depend somewhat upon the time of year that the garden is to be most enjoyed. If it is a year-round garden, where the gardener will be walking and enjoying the plantings during the winter months, deciduous material will have to be used with considerable care. A deciduous shrub growing in a bank of rhododendrons may look perfectly at home during the summer, but there may be an unsightly gap, with bare ground visible, during the winter. Sometimes the contrast is rather startling when one recalls the summer appearance. If deciduous azaleas are indiscriminately mixed with evergreen types there may be rather annoying patches of bare ground during the winter. On the other hand, if the deciduous varieties are grouped so that a particular border or hillside is completely covered during the summer and completely bare of leaves during the winter, the effect is not so startling.

I have seen deciduous azaleas used in the foreground of borders containing evergreen material. During the blossoming season they stood out very prominently, but during the winter only the bare twigs were present, so that one saw the evergreen material back of them as a unit, and the lack of leaves on the plants in the foreground did not appear unsightly. This lack of any distracting or unpleasant effect resulted from the fact that the part of the border which was evergreen had been designed to be complete in itself, when viewed through the leafless plants. Such arrangement, where possible, would seem to be much better than random mingling of evergreen and deciduous plant material.

BULBS MAY BE INTERPLANTED

Many bulbous plants are well adapted for use with almost any type of shrubbery which does not bloom at the same time as the bulbs. The bulbs bring color and variety to the garden while the shrubs are just getting their spring growth under way. Evergreen rhododendrons will eventually form such a thick umbrella of leaves that the bulbous plants may be shaded out or unseen, even if they do survive and bloom. However, bulbs around the front of the border may be very attractive. They should preferably be used in small groups and in some variety, rather than having a long string of very yellow daffodils or very red tulips precisely outlining the border. Of course if the emphasis in the garden is on formality, then the definite border outline may be more in place.

The usual custom is to secure fairly small plants of rhododendrons or azaleas and to space them, in anticipation of increased size, farther apart than they would be if planted to occupy the whole area at once. Some gardeners set the plants close together and then plan on thinning them out or moving them, as they begin to crowd. However, spacing them out to their final distance and interplanting with bulbs of various types has sometimes been a happy solution. One of the most fascinating garden pictures I recall, from an English garden, is of rhododendrons growing in fairly moist land with tall lilies displaying their blossoms far above the shrubs. The bulbous plants do not seem to compete to an undersirable extent with the rhododendrons, and as the shrubs grow, the bulbs will gradually be shaded out, or they can be dug and moved. Small shrubs or perennials used for interplanting in this way may tend to increase in growth as the rhododendrons do, and eventually give them something of a battle for survival, unless the interplants are kept under control.

Various types of perennials may be used if thought is given to the possibility of too much aggressiveness. In most cases, the best gardening effects will probably be secured by planting rhododendrons or azaleas in groups, with other areas for perennials. This does not mean that one should not use available space between rhododendron plants for certain selected perennials or annuals, if they are chosen with an eye to their effectiveness, and compatibility with the general rhododendron character and color.

RHODODENDRONS IN THE ROCK GARDEN

When one considers dwarf rhododendrons or azaleas in the rock garden or in a special border, the problem of interplanting becomes one of considerable complexity and finesse. Some of the finest rock gardens in the world have rhododendrons featured very effectively, and they are also interplanted with other plants which require the same general growing conditions. The growing of rock garden plants is a very highly developed and intricate phase of gardening, if one goes at it in a serious mood. There are literally hundreds of desirable rock garden plants, each of which may require something special by way of drainage or exposure or winter protection, or any one of several environmental factors.

The confirmed rock garden enthusiast may already have certain species of rhododendrons in mind for use in his plantings. Too often the confirmed rhododendron enthusiast may know little or nothing about other rock garden plants. This is a field in which I have had no special experience. I would simply say that if you do plan to grow some of the dwarf rhododendrons in a rock garden, then by all means study other rock garden plants to associate with them, and begin with a few of the easier ones which are fairly sure to grow well for you. Do avoid, however, bringing into such a planting the ordinary annuals and perennials, which will probably grow like weeds and look like them, too, among the dwarf, spreading, and slow-growing shrubs. Some other dwarf shrubs, belonging to the Heath family, which combine well with dwarf rhododendrons, are *Andromeda polifolia,* the dwarf pernettyas, and some of the dwarf gaultherias.

Some suggestions as to rhododendrons for the rock garden are given in Chapter 14. They may range from the very small-leafed, low, spreading species such as *R. radicans* or *R. sargentianum,* which clamber up and down over the stones, to somewhat larger and more upright forms which serve as accent points. Among the latter type, which would have to be used with great restraint, would be such varieties as 'Racil,' 'Sapphire,' and the dwarfer forms of *R. racemosum.*

CHAPTER 4

Climate As Affecting Rhododendrons and Azaleas

A lack of understanding of climatic requirements of these plants, by a portion of the gardening public has had two unfortunate results. A few people have purchased plants and tried to grow them under conditions that were unsuitable. In some cases the conditions could probably have been modified, but as they existed at the time, they were unsuitable, and the plants languished, and some eventually died. The other unfortunate situation, which affected more people than the first, is that many have refrained from growing rhododendrons because they mistakenly thought that their climatic conditions precluded any success whatsoever with this particular group of plants. In some cases where there were failures, the proper choice of varieties might have given good results without specific climatic modifications, and in other cases, with some climatic modification many additional varieties could have been grown.

One of the important factors and often the deciding factor for success or failure is hardiness of individual varieties, a characteristic which varies greatly. Some species will be injured at the slightest touch of frost, whereas others will survive, uninjured, −25°F. or even colder. Fortunately ratings which indicate minimum temperatures that varieties and species may be expected to withstand have been prepared and are discussed in Chapter 6. Enough to say, at this point, that any garden which does not normally experience temperatures less than −25° can grow at least some types of rhododendrons successfully, if the other factors are favorable.

Minimum temperatures, to be expected in midwinter, are not the only climatic factors which the gardener must consider as affecting these or any other garden plants. Minimum temperature is one of the more important factors, but there are others, as we shall see.

SPRING FROSTS
Many types of rhododendrons start growth very early in the spring,

and some bloom extremely early, or even during midwinter in the milder climates. These plants are easily started into growth by a little warm weather, and then may be injured by frosts just barely below the freezing point. Our own location is one where frosts may occur during a long period in fall and spring. We are located on a narrow peninsula extending between Willapa Bay and the Pacific Ocean, in the very southwestern corner of the state of Washington. The winters are relatively mild and some growth may continue almost all winter. Then as the varieties begin to bloom in the spring, occasional frosts may burn back the new shoots or wither the expanding petals of the earlier-blooming varieties. Sometimes the damage is more serious, as we have had rather hardy varieties completely killed by a few degrees of frost, occurring too late in the spring—apparently just when those particular varieties were at their most susceptible stage.

Most gardeners will know their own situation so far as frosts are concerned or, if not, some thought and study should be devoted to it. It is a well-known fact that cold air tends to settle into low pockets, and so we say that there is "poor air drainage" in those low areas from which the cold air cannot readily flow. Plants a few feet higher in elevation may be completely untouched when those in such a pocket may be badly frost-damaged. It is not at all unusual to find frost injury on the lower parts of a tall-growing shrub but none on the upper branches. Such temperature stratification of the air occurs on still nights. If freezing occurs during a windy night, the cold air is mixed with the warm and there will be almost as much, or sometimes more, damage at somewhat higher elevations as in the frost pockets. Since most spring frosts occur during quiet nights, the early-growing and early-blooming rhododendrons and azaleas, at least, should be left out of such frost pockets, if at all possible, and planted where there is adequate air drainage.

LOW WINTER TEMPERATURE

A rather baffling situation sometimes occurs where there are apparently no specific frost hazards, temperatures are not extremely low, and yet the plants seem to be too frequently winter-injured. This is often associated with rapid changes in temperature, and may occur at any time during the winter. If the temperature falls steadily in the autumn and remains rather low during the winter, then comes up steadily in the spring, conditions are most favorable for successful overwintering of these or any other garden plants. If, however, during any part of the winter there are periods of relatively warm weather, followed rather suddenly by periods of very cold weather, the chances of injury are considerably greater. Experiments with other plants have indicated that these periods of high temperature actually result in a more tender condition of the plant tissues. If the temperature falls fairly steadily and not too rapidly for a few days, then the plants become relatively more hardy. They may alternate in actual hardiness several times during the winter, as warm periods alternate with cold periods. This is no doubt one reason an area may be considered rather unsuitable for rhododendrons, and even "too cold," whereas another area having about the same minimum temperatures but less fluctuations may be deemed relatively favorable.

EFFECT OF HIGH SUMMER TEMPERATURE

Another important consideration is high summer temperatures. Although some of the rhododendrons we grow came from semitropical countries, they were usually found at rather high altitudes and in regions of heavy fogs and relatively high humidity. High temperature and low humidity are extremely trying to these plants. Somewhat the same situation prevails here as just discussed with respect to fluctuations of winter temperature. If the maximum summer temperature rises rather uniformly in the early summer and it remains fairly hot during the summer, there will be less damage than if there are periods of cool, moist weather during the summer, followed, rather quickly, by hot, dry weather. In some cases failure with rhododendrons which had been attributed to low winter temperature may in all probability have been caused by high summer temperature, especially if the humidity was low.

EFFECT OF WINDS

Air movement is another important factor of climate. Strong winds, at times when humidity is low, may cause considerable damage to rhododendrons, resulting in marginal burning of leaves and, if they occur during the winter, in injury which probably would not have occurred at the same temperature if the winds had not been so severe. Strong winds, of course, may cause direct breakage of branches and whipping off of leaves. This is particularly true with some varieties which have rather large leaves and brittle twigs, easily split off. It is almost always advisable to protect rhododendrons and azaleas from prevailing winds if they are of any consequence at all. Perhaps we should say "bad" rather than "prevailing" winds. In our own case winds from the east are not so very frequent, but at least once each summer we will have very hot, dry winds from that direction, and each winter a few days of strong east wind that is very cold. Some protection against east winds, therefore, is very desirable even though they are not prevailing.

ADEQUATE MOISTURE NEEDED

Moisture or rainfall is, next to temperature, perhaps the most important component of climate affecting plants. It is not so much the amount of rainfall which needs to be emphasized, but rather soil moisture and air moisture content, or humidity. Even with low rainfall during any particular period, it should be possible to keep rhododendrons in good condition by irrigation, if sufficient water is available. The problem of low humidity is more difficult to solve. Something can be accomplished by sheltering the plants from drying winds and giving them partial shade. Where extremely low humidity is likely to be prevalent for several days, sprinkling the foliage during the heat of the day may be essential. These plants seldom suffer from excessive humidity, although certain diseases may be more prevalent under such conditions.

LIGHT INTENSITY

Another environmental factor, which is a phase of climate, is the amount and quality of sunlight. As previously stated, many rhododendron species are native to areas where there are frequent high fogs and long rainy seasons. Almost all rhododendrons and azaleas will appreciate having some shade and not being subjected to continuous direct sunlight. This is essential in regions where temperatures are rather high, sunlight intense, and humidity low. Varieties differ, but I know of none which does prefer full sun in regions where the light is likely to be very intense. In the Pacific Northwest certain varieties fail to set flower buds freely unless they are in almost full sunlight. Even here they may be severely damaged in periods of intense light and low humidity, unless the proper precautions are taken.

CLIMATE MAY BE MODIFIED

To speak of modifying the climate seems rather farfetched, and perhaps like something out of science fiction. However, a few years ago landscape architects and horticultural scientists began to consider the modification of climate from a scientific standpoint and came to the conclusion that actually a great deal could be done to accomplish that end by using ordinary common sense in the making of plantings, with respect to their general location, size, arrangement, and composition.

The proper use of windbreaks certainly does affect the climate of a particular garden. It may help greatly to prevent actual wind damage, to prevent cold injury, and to prevent burning by very dry, hot winds. The partial blocking of air movement from any direction from which strong winds are likely to come, either summer or winter, will probably be beneficial to rhododendrons, provided the windbreaks do not form frost pockets.

There are many problems of type, size, and location to be solved in connection with windbreaks. Probably the most satisfactory type would be a high picket or board fence, so designed that the air could move slowly through it and not be diverted over it, which might cause a turbulent effect on the lee side, usually resulting in protection for some areas and little protection for others. Such a picket windbreak, unlike trees or hedges, will not grow out of scale, and it will not compete with the plants for water and plant food. For the very small garden, such a windbreak, if one is needed, may be very useful and even attractive. In the larger gardens, the use of trees or tall growing shrubs as natural windbreaks has an advantage from the standpoint of economy and general appearance.

In England and some continental European countries, stone or brick walls are used very frequently as garden features. They provide privacy and also serve very satisfactorily as windbreaks. They also provide a background for planting and a support for climbing vines, often resulting in very beautiful garden effects.

SHADE IS IMPORTANT

The providing of shade, or reducing it in any way, also affects climate by causing a definite temperature difference. The temperature in full sun may be as much as 15° or 20° higher than in the shade, often the margin of safety with sun-sensitive plants.

Rhododendrons seem to prefer a broken shade, or one which does not decrease light intensity too much. Plants may be set on the north side of an object which casts a shadow—as, for instance, the north side of a house or the north side of a very dense tree—in such a way that they will get full light from the north and some sun during early morning or late afternoon. In other cases trees which are not so dense may be scattered through the garden and provide intermittent shade. The choice of shade trees has already been discussed briefly under the heading of companion plants. It is worth re-emphasizing that trees with a deep root system with relatively few surface-feeding roots are much to be preferred. Some of the oaks, for instance, will get their moisture from a depth of several feet, leaving most of that in the surface soil for lawn or rhododendrons, or whatever other small plants may be growing underneath their branches.

The nature of the soil, for instance a shallow hardpan, may cause even taprooted trees to form most of their roots near the surface. Rather than name specific trees as being satisfactory under all conditions, therefore, we prefer to bring the problem to the attention of the gardener, who will use his knowledge of local trees and of local soil conditions to work out the best possible solution. It may be necessary, and not at all impossible, to live with already established, and more or less indispensable, shallow-rooted trees. That will simply mean more careful attention to watering and feeding, and possibly occasional cutting of tree roots around a rhododendron border, or even the introduction of a barrier of sheet metal or polyethylene. Such a barrier is not likely to exclude tree roots completely, but should retard their invasion if deep enough.

One of the best methods of providing shade, from the strictly technical standpoint, is the man-made lath house, as this can be designed to give any percentage of shade desired. Perhaps the most frequently seen is one which provides about 50 per cent wood or metal and 50 per cent space. Cross members and thickness of lath must also be considered in determining the total effective amount of shade. Exactly 50–50 spacing will give considerably less than 50 per cent of sunlight because of the thickness of the lath and the supporting members. We use 1×4-inch cedar for covering lath houses, with

50 per cent space on the sides, and 5-inch space to 4-inch wood on the tops.

In many gardens, especially in zones of high summer temperatures, vine-covered pergolas or lath-covered structures are important garden features from the standpoint of providing shade for the gardener's comfort. Such structures can easily and satisfactorily be constructed to shade a patio or outdoor living room or, primarily, to provide a favorable climate for shade-loving plants such as rhododendrons. Whether such a structure is unsightly or not depends somewhat on the specific reason for constructing the lath house—that is, whether it is to be entirely utilitarian or to be an important part of the garden picture. If the latter, then the possibilities of making it attractive are almost limitless, as only the builder's imagination and the materials available will be limiting factors.

MODIFYING THE CLIMATE WITH WATER

The provision of water by surface irrigation or overhead sprinklers is another important method of modifying the climate. Greater modification will be achieved by sprinklers, as the air temperature and humidity will be affected as well as the amount of moisture available to the roots.

Most gardeners now make use of irrigation, at least occasionally, for other garden plants, and know how to handle the water effectively. It should be pointed out, however, that rhododendrons, because of their shallow rooting, may begin to suffer when three or four inches of the top soil has dried out; whereas other, deeper-rooting plants may be able to go on without apparent harm for many days.

Mention has already been made of the possibility of "burning," or browning, of rhododendron leaves in very hot weather. One way to avoid this is to keep the leaves wet by sprinkling during the period of high temperature. In extremely hot, dry climates this may give rise to various problems, such as the waterlogging of the soil from excessive sprinkling and the accumulation of alkaline salts from water that is high in such materials. I visited one well-known azalea garden a few years ago which had just experienced a period of ten days with daily maximum temperatures above 100°. During that time the sprinklers were run continuously during the heat of the day, and the plants came through beautifully.

The idea that one should not sprinkle in full sun is certainly not entirely correct. Most commercial florists, vegetable growers, and nurserymen find that they have to sprinkle when the plants need water, regardless of whether or not the sun is shining. In many cases they pay little attention to the sun, but turn the sprinklers on when the water is needed. The experience has been that continuous sprinkling during very hot, dry days will usually prevent burning, which would otherwise occur. In the Northwest practically all commercial cranberry acreage is equipped with sprinklers, which are turned on whenever the temperature rises to a predetermined danger point.

The idea that droplets of water may act as tiny lenses and focus the sunlight to cause burning is, in my opinion, not borne out by the facts. Such droplets seldom occur on the waxy rhododendron leaves, but if they were present, and if the sun were strong enough to cause such burning, the droplets would undoubtedly evaporate before any serious damage by this lens effect could occur. Where the moisture is not in droplets but a continuous film, obviously there would be no such magnifying effect. My guess is that most burning attributed to watering while the sun is shining brightly probably occurred either before or after the sprinkling, was visible only at a later date, and was erroneously blamed on the sprinkling.

MIST NOZZLES MIGHT BE USED

In areas where very high temperature and low humidity are likely to prevail for a long period, the use of mist nozzles similar to those used in propagating greenhouses might possibly be considered. These discharge a very limited amount of water in very fine droplets, some running as low as one gallon per hour per nozzle, if used at a fairly high pressure. Such mist, if discharged under a lath house, would certainly tend to maintain a fairly high humidity and to keep the temperature relatively low, even though the mist nozzles were spaced some distance apart. I would not care to suggest any specific spacing, as it would vary so much with the type of nozzle and with the climatic conditions to be considered. Certainly a competent mist-nozzle salesman in the general locality should be able to provide data which would be helpful in indicating whether the use of mist is practical under local conditions. The alkalinity of the water and its salt content would be important factors in determining practicability.

WINTER PROTECTION

In northern localities winter temperatures are likely to be low enough, and the danger of actual cold injury or of desiccation of the tissues sufficient to indicate the value of some winter protection to varieties of marginal hardiness. This may take the form of surrounding or actually covering the plant with a burlap-covered frame, or with a cage of wire netting which may be filled with leaves or evergreen boughs. The effect is to modify somewhat the minimum temperature, unless that minimum is maintained rather steadily over a period of several hours. If there is a drop to a minimum temperature, lasting only an hour or two, as very commonly happens, it will usually not get as cold within the protecting material as it does outside. Furthermore such winter protection acts as a shield against strong winds, which is very helpful. It also tends to prevent rapid freezing and rapid thawing, which are conducive to injury to plants on the borderline of hardiness. Actually a temporary windbreak to prevent strong, cold, and drying winds from directly striking the plants may be sufficient winter protection in some gardens where the varieties have been selected for hardiness to match the local climate.

Winter protection in general is something that we would all like to avoid if possible. I know of no winter-protective material which is as attractive as the plants would be if the material were not used, but it is sometimes necessary to sacrifice winter appearance for appearance the next spring and summer. Fortunately there are many, many gardens in all the milder areas where no winter protection is needed.

Dwarf rhododendrons lend themselves fairly well to protection with evergreen boughs or a loose mulch of some type. To be avoided, under most conditions, would be a deep mulch, over the entire plant, of leaves or any other material which would mat down during the winter, especially when wet, to exclude air and possibly increase the likelihood of some damage from fungus attack.

MOVING PLANTS INTO A PROTECTED PLACE

The ultimate in winter protection is to move the plants into an adequately lighted, cold cellar, or some other type of weather-defying structure during the severe weather. Rhododendrons move rather easily, and so may be dug and moved in, with a good ball of soil, and then moved out in early spring without appreciably checking the normal growth of the plant. If the more tender varieties and species are desired in northern gardens, it would probably be best to grow them in large wooden boxes or tubs of some kind which could more readily be moved in and out. Some growers have provided dugouts covered with hotbed sash or, in some cases, with a plastic material or even a canvas or brush cover. It is not necessary to have such a storage cellar completely frost-free for most varieties. Those which would stand −5° outside should stand that in a shelter such as this because, if properly shaded, the temperature would fluctuate much less rapidly than it does outside.

The growing of shrubs in planters or containers of various types has not been developed as much in this country as it has in some others where soil and weather conditions make such methods almost essential in the growing of any ornamental plants. Rhododendrons properly grown in attractive boxes, tubs, or other containers might be used around the patio or in other selected spots around the home to provide a variety and changeability in the garden which we often desire and seldom achieve. In some public places rather large rhododendrons are being successfully grown in boxes of soil, which can be moved about as desired. If the shrubs are too tender for the local climate, this moving may involve putting them in a protected place or even inside the house to miss the worst of the winter weather.

The use of mulch will be considered in the chapter on how to care for the plants, but it also provides a method of modifying the climate to a certain extent. The retention of moisture and the insulating effect of the mulch may help to offset unfavorable climatic conditions, although under some conditions that same insulating effect may be a factor in causing increased damage from frost.

There are undoubtedly other ways of modifying the climate that will occur to the reader. The genuine gardener, who has a natural feeling for the particular requirements of his plants, can often grow them satisfactorily in localities where others would think of them as impossible.

CHAPTER 5

Soil Requirements

It is quite generally known that rhododendrons and azaleas require an acid soil. However that is not all of the soil knowledge one needs to grow these plants satisfactorily. Of course in ideal soils the plants may do very well in spite of a gardener who may be entirely ignorant of soil condition and soil requirements. It is when the plants do not grow well, and the leaves are too small, or pale, or are burned at the edges, or the plant simply refuses to grow at all, that one begins to wonder about the soil. Symptoms such as these might be caused by poor or unfavorable soil, but, on the other hand, they might be the result of insect or disease attack, or of injury by cold weather. The gardener who has no trouble getting the perfect type of growth that he desires, relatively large leaves, good color, and plentiful bloom presumably has no soil problem. Unfortunately there are few places where such ideal conditions exist, and for the great majority of gardeners some knowledge of soil conditions will be very useful, if not essential.

Soils are actually very complex and extremely variable. They differ in their physical make-up, that is, the size of the soil particles, and in their chemical composition. Further than that, the soil is filled with countless forms of plant life, from the ultramicroscopic up through the bacteria, fungi, algae, and finally the higher plants, which are the ones we usually see because they grow partly above ground. Any soil scientist will admit that there are still many, many things we do not know about soils, particularly the biological content and how it affects the growth of crop plants.

SOIL KNOWLEDGE IS VALUABLE

The gardener who may want to grow two or three rhododendrons or a half dozen azaleas may have little interest in becoming learned in the ways of the soil. If these plants grow well under his conditions, then he should consider himself fortunate, and might understandably skip this chapter. Perhaps, however, he is one who is inclined to worry, and think that rhododendrons may be very difficult, even though most other garden plants grow very well for him. Actually where most other plants do grow freely, rhododendrons, if the climate is favorable, will usually do well also, with a few possible exceptions.

Most garden plants do not require as acid a soil as do rhododendrons. However a soil test to determine the relative acidity or pH, as it is usually written, is relatively simple to make, and small do-it-yourself kits are available. In some areas the county agricultural agent will be able to make the test, or will send the soil sample to the state college. There will be a small charge for this service in some states; in other states it is given free. Fertilizer dealers often maintain a soil laboratory for making such tests. If the pH is relatively favorable for rhododendrons, and other garden plants are growing well, then the chances are very good that the rhododendrons will be satisfied with the soil conditions in general. Sometimes a gardener may feel that his plants are growing satisfactorily because he has never seen, or noticed, the growth obtained on better soils. For him, and perhaps for most people, a little thoughtful reading about soils may give useful ideas for a more critical evaluation and possibly some improvement.

Knowledge of soils is important, at some time or another, for everyone who grows plants, unless he is extremely fortunate. The farmer and the professional gardener who raise fruits, vegetables, or farm crops on acreage large or small almost always have soil problems to consider. It may be the selecting of the best soil of their available acreage for a particular crop. If they do not have a satisfactory soil, then they must consider methods of modifying what they have to make it more suitable for the crop they wish to grow. The average home gardener, especially in the city, does not usually have enough land available so that a search for the best soil for a particular plant would be fruitful. He does have the problem, however, of deciding whether or not his soil is at all suitable for the plant he wants to set out, and if it is not good enough, but might be improved, then he needs to know how to go about making such improvement.

SIZE OF SOIL PARTICLES

The physical nature of a particular soil is the logical thing to consider first, as it can be estimated reasonably well without any particular laboratory equipment. The terms "heavy" and "light," as applied to soils, refer to the texture of the soil, or the size of the particles. Those made up of very fine particles are called clays or heavy soils, and the ones with coarse particles, the lighter soils, are called sand, or in the case of very coarse particles, gravel. The following table gives the terms soil scientists associate with soils of certain particle sizes:

TABLE NO. I

NAME	DIAMETER OF PARTICLES IN MILLIMETERS
Gravel	2.0 and larger
Coarse Sand	2.0 to 0.2
Fine Sand	0.2 to 0.02
Silt	0.02 to 0.002
Clay	0.002 and smaller

Another term commonly used to describe soils is loam. Loam soil contains 20 to 50 per cent sand, 20 to 50 per cent silt, and 30 per cent or less clay. If there is relatively more sand or more clay, then it is called sandy loam or clay loam.

Soils made up of very fine particles, that is the clays, since they have a very large number of particles per unit of volume also have a very large particle surface. It is common observation that these clay soils absorb and hold a relatively large quantity of water, and that they dry out much more slowly than a coarse soil. In regions where there is a considerable amount of rainfall during the winter, such soils are likely to become waterlogged or saturated to such an extent that very little oxygen can get into the soil. Oxygen is necessary for survival and normal growth of roots of most kinds of plants. The waterlogged clay soil, therefore, may cause dying of the roots of many kinds of plants.

The lighter soils, made up of a fairly large proportion of sand or gravel, are well drained, but they dry out very quickly. Water from rains or irrigation goes through them rapidly and, of course, will take with it much of the soluble plant foods which may be present. This will result in plants indicating a lack of nutrients, particularly nitrogen, much more rapidly in sandy soil than they would if growing in clay.

It is obvious that both the very light and the very heavy soils have some advantages and some disadvantages. As might be expected, the intermediate type of soil—that is, the loam or sandy loam—is superior for a great many types of plants, and rhododendrons and azaleas are no exception. If one were to name an ideal soil for these plants, it would be a medium sandy loam, well supplied with organic matter.

IMPORTANCE OF ORGANIC MATTER

Plant residues in the soil, either from plants naturally growing there or brought in in the form of manure, mulching material, sawdust, or compost of any kind, have a definite effect on the physical nature of the soil as well as on its chemical make-up. Abundance of these residues, known collectively as organic matter, normally results in the soil's being somewhat looser, or more porous, especially in clay soils, and hence able to provide a more adequate supply of oxygen for the roots. It also permits more rapid penetration of rain, more rapid leaching through of free water, but a longer retention of some moisture.

Rhododendrons seem to prefer a soil with a high content of organic matter, although this is not absolutely essential, especially in light soils with adequate moisture. In their native habitat, many species of rhododendron have been collected from high mountain areas where the organic matter is probably rather meager. The fact that, under cultivation, they do seem to prefer a large amount of organic matter may mean that our soils, in some way, are not entirely suited to their needs, and that the organic matter does alter their characteristics in a direction which the rhododendrons like.

IMPORTANCE OF GOOD DRAINAGE

Another physical factor to be considered in evaluating a soil is drainage or, to put it another way, the amount of water that collects and is held in the soil from one rainy period to another. Poor drainage results in a relatively high water table, and low oxygen supply to the plant roots. Rapid or excessive drainage means that the plants may be suffering for lack of water when other plants in a heavier, less well-drained soil may have an ample supply. However during periods of extremely wet weather, the coarse soil may dry out fast enough so that the plants will not be injured, whereas they might be seriously injured or killed on poorly drained soils.

Drainage depends not only on soil texture, but on the ability of water to escape. A hillside may be of fairly heavy clay, but surplus water either runs off the surface or tends to drain out rather readily through springs or other underground channels. On level areas the same type of soil may remain much more highly saturated and be much less satisfactory for growing the kind of plants which require fairly good drainage. Even light, sandy soils may be underlain by an impervious hardpan, or they may be so low, in relation to the water table, that they are essentially poorly drained in spite of their relatively coarse texture.

METHODS OF IMPROVING SOILS

The average gardener, wanting to plant a few rhododendrons about his home, may have some choice in selecting a desirable kind of soil, but is more often concerned with evaluating what he has and determining how to improve it. Soils that are too heavy may, rather obviously, be improved by adding sand. However this is usually somewhat expensive, and is certainly a laborious process. A little sand scattered over the surface is of no value at all. At least two to four inches of sand would need to be applied over the surface and worked in to make enough improvement to be worth while, and few gardeners will find it desirable to improve a very large area of heavy soil in this way. Somewhat the same results can be secured by incorporating organic matter, the amount of improvement depending on the extent of the operation. Materials such as peat moss, sawdust, planer shavings, peanut hulls, corn stalks, straw, or compost of any kind will tend to loosen a heavy soil. True, they will not last indefinitely, as will sand. On the other hand they have additional values: they add some plant nutrients, and apparently provide a better root climate for rhododendrons and many other plants than would be true if the same soil were lightened with sand.

The poor "growing" qualities of a particularly heavy soil may be due as much to poor drainage as anything else. The installing of tile drains in such a heavy soil should tend to improve its plant growing ability materially. But there is a problem of topography. On flat areas where there is no place to drain, there is certainly no object to putting in tile, although where a drainage outlet can be provided it will undoubtedly be useful. A line of 4-inch drain tile every 20 feet, with an adequate outlet, even in heavy, soggy soil will give good results.

The heavier soils are usually more fertile than the lighter types because the nutrients inherently present in the soil, or resulting from application of fertilizer or decay of plant material tend to remain fixed rather near to the point where they become available, whereas, in the lighter soils, they tend to be leached farther down into the subsoil, or away with the drainage water. For shallow-rooted rhododendrons this leaching may well take a significant portion of the nutrients beyond the reach of the roots.

IMPROVING THE LIGHT SOILS

Light soils are usually more easily improved than heavy soils. As a matter of fact a great many plants prefer a relatively light soil, if the water and nutrient supply can be maintained at an adequate level. The few plants which seem to prefer dense, poorly drained soils may have roots with a lower oxygen requirement than most. An obvious way to improve a soil that is too light and sandy is to add clay. Here again there is a problem of supply: where there is a great deal of light, sandy soil, clay may be scarce, and vice versa. Furthermore, the bringing in of the clay and mixing it with the soil is an expensive and backbreaking job.

Strangely enough, organic matter can be used to improve light as well as heavy soils. In the light soils it will tend to hold moisture and nutrients, and hence, so far as the plants are concerned, drying out is less rapid. The sand particles may lose their moisture, but the organic matter has soaked it up, and the plant rootlets are able to get it from the moist organic particles. The type of organic matter to use to improve light soils is determined most often by local supply. Where peanut hulls are available, they would be useful; where crushed corncobs are available, they would be fine. In our own locality we would have great difficulty in obtaining either, except at great expense. However, we can obtain sawdust at a reasonable cost, and it works very well. Some materials, such as a legume hay, for instance, would decay very rapidly and, over a relatively long period, would not be as desirable as something like peat moss or sawdust, which would persist and continue to improve the soil condition. That does not mean that legume hay would not be a good soil improver, but it certainly would not last. It would provide more nutrients, especially nitrogen, than would the sawdust, and the rapid breakdown in the soil would make what nutrients it does contain rapidly available to the plants.

Practically, one can handle soils which are very light without actually improving their physical quality simply by adding adequate nutrients in the form of fertilizers and seeing that the moisture supply is maintained at an adequate level by irrigation. This corrects the principal faults of the overly light soil, namely the rapid drying out and rapid loss of nutrients. Mulching of light soils is also very useful, as it helps maintain soil moisture. A mulch of a desirable form of organic matter also tends to improve the fertility of the soil, and, as it is eventually worked in, it will help to improve its texture.

ORGANIC MATTER AND NITROGEN

The use of organic matter as a soil improver has been stressed for both heavy and light soils. It is also evident that this will also influence the fertility of the soil to the extent that the organic matter adds mineral nutrients or nitrogen. In the case of a legume hay, for instance, used either as a mulch or plowed under, there will be a rather rapid release of nitrogen which, in some cases, might even cause too rapid and lush a growth, or definite plant injury.

With non-legume hay or straw or other dry organic matter, such as sawdust, used as a mulch or worked in, there will eventually be an addition of some mineral nutrients. On the other hand there will be an almost immediate lessening of the amount of nitrogen available to the plants growing in the treated soil. For many years this was not understood, and it was commonly stated that sawdust, or other dry organic matter, would "poison" the soil. Some said that it made it too acid for the plants. More recent investigations indicate that sawdust does not increase the acidity of the soil, but may even change it a little toward the neutral side. However, when sawdust is incorporated into the soil, or the bottom of a layer of sawdust mulch comes in contact with moist soil, it soon starts to decay. The decay is brought about by certain soil microorganisms which require nitrogen and minerals to live and multiply, much the same as do higher plants.

When there is a large amount of sawdust or similar material on or in the soil, and it starts to decay, the number of these microorganisms increases very rapidly because of the abundance of food supply— this same organic matter. As they increase in numbers so rapidly, their requirement for nitrogen to build up protein in their own bodies increases in proportion. They can obtain the nitrogen only from the surrounding soil, just as do the roots of whatever garden plant is being grown. The result is a temporary shortage of nitrogen, which may cause yellowish leaves and very slow growth of the rhododendrons, azaleas, or whatever plants are being grown. This shortage is temporary, because the microorganisms will eventually die, and the nitrogen which they have tied up in their bodies will again be released for plant use, perhaps a few months or a year later. The gardener, however, should be on the alert and add additional nitrogen fertilizer where such mulching is done. This will be discussed further in Chapter 7.

CHEMICAL ELEMENTS IN THE SOIL

It has been stressed that the soil is very complex from both a physical and a chemical standpoint. Practically all of the known chemical elements may be found in the soil, either as its natural components, or dissolved in the soil solution, or in the soil atmosphere between the soil particles. Although this would seem to present an infinitely complicated problem, we can simplify it by stating that, from the standpoint of plant growth, we are concerned with two types of elements. First there are those which provide nutrient material—or fertility, as we might express it—for the plants, elements which the plants take in and use in some way. These will be discussed in more detail in Chapter 7.

The second group of elements with which we are concerned are those which are not necessarily nutrients, but which may cause damage to the plants. They are called toxic materials. Actually some of the nutrient elements may be highly toxic if present in large quantities, but are essential for plant growth in very minute quantities. The toxic elements include such things as sodium, which tends to produce alkalinity and in large quantities is quite toxic to plants. There are other toxic elements in some soils, such as aluminum, and even excessive amounts of the common fertilizer elements. With rhododendrons the principal problem would seem to be with those elements which tend to make the soil more alkaline. Whether these elements are actually poisonous to the roots of the plants, or whether they simply make the soil less acid and hence less favorable for plant growth is sometimes difficult to say. However, soil acidity, or pH, is much easier to determine than the chemical composition of the soil or the amount of any single element. A pH reading will give at least an indication as to whether conditions are favorable, so that some remedial steps may be taken if necessary.

SOME BIOLOGICAL PROBLEMS

The biological nature of the soil is probably understood much less clearly than its physical and chemical attributes. In the first place we do not know, with any degree of completeness, just what living organisms are in the soil. Some are so minute that they differ not at all in size and appearance, but only in the way they live and the way they may, or may not, attack plants and cause disease symptoms. Many of the organisms are beneficial. We have already mentioned their function in the decay of organic material. If they were not present in the soil, the debris from higher plants would accumulate indefinitely, and that of course would be disastrous. Other microorganisms are at least partially responsible for the breakdown of soil particles into their chemical constituents, thus releasing minerals in their elemental form so that plants may utilize them.

Some microorganisms are harmful to, and others have directly beneficial effects on higher plants. Sometimes these beneficial effects occur over a rather wide range of plants, but in other cases there is a specific relationship between two particular types of plants, one a microscopic one and the other larger, such as a shrub or tree. Such mutually beneficial relationships are called symbiotic relationships, or symbiosis.

The ericaceous plants, to which rhododendrons belong, have long been noted for an apparent symbiotic relationship with certain fungi. This was worked out with blueberries many years ago, and it has been believed that blueberries would not grow normally without these fungi in the roots. Since the blueberry plants do not have root hairs, at least when the fungi are present, it was thought that the strands of the fungi functioned in the same way as the root hairs. This is a difficult thing to study, as it is almost impossible to secure plants without the fungi in the roots so that a comparison could be made.

We do know, of course, that certain legumes, such as clovers, will make poor growth unless they are inoculated with the bacteria which live symbiotically in the nodules on the roots. Whether the relationship between the microorganisms known as mycorhiza and rhododendrons is as direct and obligatory as this, we do not yet have sufficient data to indicate. In the propagation of rhododendrons, however, it is evident that the well being of young plants—that is, young seedlings or newly rooted cuttings—is certainly affected by microorganisms. These plants are easily damaged or killed by certain fungi which may first kill the roots, or the tissues at the crown of the plant, resulting in what is usually termed "damping off." In other cases certain seedlings, or rooted cuttings, will grow much more rapidly than others, giving the impression, at least, that a favorable symbiotic relationship has been set up.

There is not very much we can do about this situation, except to try to control the microorganisms which may be harmful and to provide the soil conditions which seem to be most favorable for the growth of the plants. Whether such conditions are actually most suitable for the plants, or for the mycorhiza, or least suitable for the harmful microorganisms, it is sometimes difficult to say. This whole problem of microorganisms and ericaceous plants should provide good material for further scientific research.

SOIL ACIDITY

Most gardeners are somewhat familiar with the pH scale which indicates the relative acidity—pH 7 is neutral, figures higher than 7 are on the alkaline side, and lower than 7 on the acid side. Many horticultural crops prefer the soil somewhat acid, and rhododendrons and azaleas, for the most part at least, prefer it quite acid—that is, around pH 4.0 to pH 5.5 or even pH 6.0.

The acidity of soils is normally associated with the climate—that is, with the amount of rainfall. With a high rainfall, the soils are usually acid; with very low rainfall, they tend to be alkaline because salts accumulate to cause alkalinity, and are not leached out. There is a large intermediate area where rainfall is moderate and where soil acidity seems to be affected more by the original chemical composition of the soil than by the rainfall. In such areas, soils that are quite acid may be found fairly close—that is, within 100 yards or even closer to soils which are neutral or fairly alkaline, close enough together so that the rainfall is practically the same. In such areas, soil tests are of especial value. In our own area of high rainfall and sandy soils, we are quite sure of finding the soil very acid wherever we sample it.

The foregoing has been written in an effort to give the gardener a little idea of soil problems, soil variation, and how certain unfavorable soil conditions might be corrected. This will be carried further, especially from the practical standpoint, in Chapter 7 where fertilizers and acid-forming methods are discussed in more detail.

Part Two

METHODS OF CULTURE,
FERTILIZING,
AND PEST CONTROL

CHAPTER 6

Obtaining the Plants and Setting Them Out

As with most other ornamental plants, the first thing to consider when purchasing rhododendrons or azaleas is choice of variety, or species. Although most beginners will probably start with hybrids, some of the species rhododendrons make very fine garden plants, and they will be discussed in some detail in Chapter 10.

The species are usually grown from seed, although some good forms of a few species have been selected and are reproduced by cuttings. The securing of asexually propagated plants, of course, is the only way one can be sure of their exact characteristics. Some species have, over the centuries, become so uniform in nature that they reproduce themselves quite true to type from seed. They seem to cross-pollinate very rarely, and so open- or chance-pollinated seed gives rather uniform seedlings. Other species are variable in nature, and may even be described botanically as having flowers of several colors, as white, rosy-white, or purple. Most of the species seedlings now available in the nursery trade were grown from seed secured from some botanic garden or large collection, where the opportunity for cross-pollination was very good, and so it is not surprising that the seedlings occasionally show evidence of its having occurred.

Most nurserymen, who raise species from seed, indicate that the plants are seedlings, and that one cannot guarantee the character of the bloom until it is seen. Those who purchase species rhododendrons are often rather advanced amateurs, who know in general what the species should be, and who frequently go to the nursery to see the plants in bloom before buying them, certainly the most satisfactory way to buy.

"JUST SEEDLINGS" TO BE AVOIDED

Advertisements not infrequently appear listing "Rhododendrons" without any variety name at all. In small type we may see the word "seedlings," and perhaps in larger type the names of the varieties from which the seed was taken. Usually the seedlings of these named varieties are extremely variable and one cannot, with any assurance, predict their color, size, or general desirability. This is partly because the pollen parent of the seedling is seldom known. Even where it is known, two hybrids crossed together are bound to give offspring showing a considerable amount of variation. It is true that occasional seedlings may produce very fine plants, perhaps even better than the parent plant, but for every such superior individual there will be hundreds, or thousands, which are inferior.

One does not ordinarily purchase just a rose, or just a seedling dahlia, without having any idea as to when it will bloom, or what its color will be, or whether it is of any value at all. The breeders have been hard at work for many years to provide plants which have more and larger flowers, more fragrance, better color, more resistance to disease, flowering at unusual times, and a host of other improved characters. When we buy an unnamed seedling, unless we can see it in bloom, we, in effect, throw all this in the discard and go back to where the breeders started many years ago.

The great appeal of the seedlings of hybrid rhododendrons is their price. They are frequently advertised at prices so low that it is obviously impossible for cutting grown, or grafted, plants of named varieties to compete with them on a price basis. I once had a chat with the garden editor of a prominent Eastern newspaper which was carrying large ads featuring these rhododendrons at a few cents each. The photographs were enlarged so that it was very difficult to tell the size of the plant, although in some cases that did appear in small type. These were seedlings, germinated in flats, transplanted to plant bands, and sold directly in the bands just as one would sell cabbage or tomato plants. From the pictures these appeared to be nice little plants, although quite small, and probably a fairly good percentage of them would survive if growing conditions were good. The garden editor's comment, when queried about the advertising, was that at least a few of them would grow, and people would thus become interested in rhododendrons, and would later purchase named varieties. That was quite possibly true in some cases, although in many others I am afraid the poor survival, and poor quality of the seedlings after they bloomed, would cause the gardener to become less inclined to purchase other rhododendrons.

COLLECTED PLANTS
Another type occasionally advertised, but more frequently seen on

peddlers' trucks in some localities, is the plant collected from the wild. There are collectors who make a business of going through the wild stands of rhododendrons on the Pacific Coast and in the Appalachian area, digging up small plants, frequently without much of a root ball, and retailing them for a dollar or so apiece. Some of these plants are fairly nice, and if they have an adequate root system and have not dried out too much during the process of digging, transporting, and selling, they may eventually make fairly nice bushes. The flowers, of course, will be the same size and color as those of the wild plants, which is fine, if that is what the gardener wants.

However, there are so many superior things from the standpoint of size, color, and general attractiveness, that the use of collected rhododendrons is confined almost entirely to those who definitely want mass plantings of the wild species, or to those who are making their first rhododendron purchase, and who perhaps do not know about the improved varieties. In some cases the attitude is that a rhododendron is a rhododendron, and that they have a chance, even with these collected plants, of getting some with large, attractive, brightly colored flowers better than those in the wild, which of course does not occur.

The gardener who lives near a natural stand of rhododendrons may be tempted to do his own collecting. The difficulty lies in finding nice seedling plants, small enough to be easily and successfully transplanted. If there are many of them, some collector will probably have gone over the area and dug up the best ones. There is often a temptation to give up looking for the ideal-sized, small plants, and try to move some of the larger ones. These may have been broken down or burned over, and perhaps have a small top but a large stump and root system.

It is usually difficult to dig large plants in the wild and move them satisfactorily. I have heard gardeners in the Southeast tell of moving plants out of the mountains, saying that they would remain alive for two or three years, and then a good many of them would die. Others might eventually develop fairly good bushes after a number of years. In our own part of the country we see quite a few plants of our native *R. macrophyllum* which were moved many years ago, and which have made large and reasonably attractive bushes, but many that were moved failed to survive. The moving of any kind of plant of large size is always a difficult and doubtful job. It is even more so with rhododendrons in the wild which, if moved without an adequate ball of soil, are pretty much doomed to failure.

HORTICULTURAL VARIETIES

In order to have a variety that you know will bloom at a certain time and have a flower of known size and color, it is necessary to see the plant in bloom, or to purchase plants which have been grown from cuttings, layers, or grafts taken from the desired variety. Lists of such desirable varieties for different types of growing conditions are given in later chapters. Even here, however, there is a hidden hazard, which is not frequently brought out in nursery catalogs. This is a very unfortunate practice of giving a name to a group of seedlings from a particular cross, and not to an individually selected plant.

As most gardeners know, woody garden plants in this country are normally propagated asexually—that is, by budding, grafting, cuttings, or layers, so that each plant so propagated is really a part of the original plant and, barring very infrequent mutations, is identical with it. If you purchase a Peace rose, or a Delicious apple, or an Elberta peach, you will expect to get a plant which will be identical with one of the same name which your neighbor might purchase. Plants propagated in this way are said to be clones; that is, each one is actually a part of the original, selected plant.

THE GROUP VARIETIES

The rhododendron varieties originating in Holland, and to some extent in other countries, have normally been propagated as clones. However, a number of years ago, English breeders began to use group names for large lots of seedlings of the same cross. This practice probably stemmed from the custom of giving Latin names to natural hybrids found in the wild. According to botanical custom, once such a name is given to a natural hybrid, additional findings of the same parentage must be given the same name. Some of the breeders, being perhaps more familiar with botanical than with horticultural practice, adopted this method of giving a name to all of the progeny (hybrids) of a particular cross. The next step was to set up a stud book, under the auspices of the Royal Horticultural Society, registering names for each cross. Breeders who made the same cross at a later date were then expected to use the name which had already been given by the first person who made it.

At first the crosses were between species, and so the seedlings were primary hybrids, similar to those found in the wild, and giving a botanical name to all the progeny of a particular cross probably seemed the logical thing to do. Later, crosses between a species and a hybrid were registered, then between registered hybrids, then between a hybrid and an unknown variety, essentially just open-pollinated seedlings of a hybrid. The stud book did have value in indicating what crosses between different species had been successfully made, and was of historical value in indicating who first made the cross. The unfortunate thing was that these seedlings were then sold under the group name. If the group names had been confined to use by the breeders, simply for their convenience, to indicate a particular group of seedlings, no harm would have been done. However, seedlings got into the nursery trade under the group name, and many were brought to this country.

This method of naming presumably did not appear undesirable to the English breeders, because they were familiar with the system and knew what was indicated by a particular name. The American gardener, on the other hand, being accustomed to woody shrubs sold as clones, was often disappointed and disgusted to find that he had purchased a seedling, and that it was different from a plant of the same name seen at a show, or in some other garden. A few American breeders, following the English system, also named group varieties. There is an advantage, from the standpoint of the breeder, as it provides a name by which he can sell his seedlings, but the gardener, who wants a specific form of plant, then could obtain it only by actually seeing the seedling in bloom.

Any rhododendron cross will usually produce some individuals which are reasonably good, or even superior, and others which are very definitely inferior. The stud-book system provides for the naming of superior clones within the groups. Thus we have clone 'King George' in the group Loderi, properly written (Loderi G.) 'King George.' This imposes the burden of remembering two names, rather than one, which is sufficient for most other kinds of plants. It is insufficient to remember the name 'King George' because there is already a red clone by that name in the nursery trade. If one asked for Rhododendron 'King George,' therefore, he might either get the red clone, or the really magnificent white 'King George' of the Loderi group.

AMERICAN RHODODENDRON SOCIETY CODE OF NOMENCLATURE

Several years ago the American Rhododendron Society drew up a code of nomenclature for the guidance of American breeders, most of whom have co-operated in conforming to its provisions. According to this code, group names are not to be used. Any seedlings not receiving a clonal name should be sold as unnamed seedlings or, if desired, with the parentage indicated by formula—as, for instance, 'Pink Pearl' x 'Britannia.'

In the A.R.S. publication *Rhododendrons 1956*, the group varieties are marked with a "G" to distinguish them from the clonal varieties. More recently the Royal Horticultural Society of England has also taken a stand that the group names are superfluous, and is actually registering only clones. It should be pointed out that, in some cases, even though a group name was given, only one clone was ever propagated and distributed. However, the fact that the name and the cross were published in the stud book was, under the old English system, warning to future breeders to give the same name to seedlings of the same cross.

This repudiation of the system of group naming should give reasonable assurance that only clones will be named in the future. However, there are many well-known varieties in the nursery trade which are actually group names, such as 'Elizabeth,' 'May Day,' 'David,' 'Fabia,' 'Cornubia,' 'Cilpinense,' and many others. A number of these are actually in the trade in more than one form. Your 'Elizabeth,' for instance, may be different (a sister seedling) from one you see in a show or in someone else's garden. Confusing! But if you know how rhododendrons have been named, it may help you avoid some of the pitfalls.

HOW VARIETY ADAPTABILITY MAY BE INDICATED

Recommended variety lists for specific localities are of considerable value, but they are not completely foolproof. This is particularly true in hilly country, where the temperature and general climate may vary a great deal within a short distance. Zone maps which indicate the average minimum temperatures of rather large areas are useful. This system of indicating plant adaptability was developed by Prof. Rehder of the Arnold Arboretum a number of years ago. The United

States was divided into zones, and plants were described as being "adapted to Zone 6," or whichever the zone might be. This was of some help to the gardener in avoiding plants not hardy enough for his particular zone. However, in hilly country, the climate at the top of the hill or on the plateau might be in one zone, so far as plant adaptability is concerned, and in a different zone at the bottom of the valley, and all within a distance of a mile or so. Obviously it is impossible to construct maps on a scale large enough to show all these local differences, even if they were known. More recently a plant-hardiness zone map, in considerably greater detail, has been developed by Dr. Henry Skinner, Director of the National Arboretum, in co-operation with the American Horticultural Council. Even this, however, will not give all the information needed to help the gardener who may be in a particularly cold—or a particularly favorable —place within a certain zone.

THE A.R.S. HARDINESS RATINGS

One way of giving the desired information as to adaptability would be to indicate in degrees the minimum temperature a plant could experience and still survive. Nurserymen, or anyone else, would probably hesitate to indicate an actual figure, even if it could be determined scientifically, as hardiness of a particular plant varies so greatly, depending on the growth condition of the plant, time of year, and other factors. The American Rhododendron Society has attempted to help in solving this problem by establishing a system of hardiness ratings. The classes are at intervals of 10 degrees, as it was felt that anything smaller would be difficult to determine and somewhat misleading. The ratings indicate the minimum temperature which a particular variety, when reasonably well matured, may be expected to survive during midwinter without damage to leaf, flower, or stem. It is realized that cold spells early or late in the season, rapid fluctuation of temperature, or unusual softness of growth will result in damage at a considerably higher temperature than indicated by the ratings. However, these ratings do provide the gardener with an opportunity of learning which varieties are relatively quite hardy, which are quite tender, and which are in various intermediate grades.

The symbol H–1 indicates that the variety should be hardy to −25°. These varieties should grow in southern New York and southern

New England. H–2, hardy to –15°; H–3, hardy to –5°. This group should be fairly hardy around Philadelphia. H–4, hardy to +5°; H–5, hardy to +15°. These should be fairly hardy during most winters in the Portland and Seattle areas. H–6, hardy to +25°; H–7, hardy to +32°.

DETERMINE YOUR OWN MINIMUM TEMPERATURE

These hardiness ratings, it will be realized, are rather crude, but they have been used with reasonable success. If you do not know the minimum temperature likely to occur in your garden, it would be advisable to do a little experimenting. Place a maximum-minimum thermometer or, if you do not have one, any accurate household thermometer in your garden where you expect to plant rhododendrons, the coldest nights you can find, and read it after midnight. You may not hit the lowest temperature which may be expected over a series of winters, but you will have a figure which you can compare with reports usually available from a local weather station, in the newspaper, or over the radio. If your garden runs consistently colder than the minimum reported by the weather observer, and according to local weather records the lowest likely to be encountered is –10°, then you can estimate that in your garden you might have to expect –15°, or whatever the differential may be.

Of course these minimum temperatures occur only during occasional, very cold winters. Whether you want to gamble on not having a real test winter for several years will depend on how much you are interested in trying certain varieties which might not be hardy during such a winter. As a beginner, it would be advisable to stick to those varieties whose ratings indicate they are hardy enough to survive the coldest weather you are likely to experience.

A rhododendron fancier may be willing to try a very desirable variety even though the chances are that it might last only five years. If it bloomed for three of those five years, he might feel that his original purchase price was justified. When a test winter does come, it may not damage the plant so severely but what it will recover and again perform satisfactorily. It is not my feeling that one should necessarily stick to varieties so hardy that they may be expected to grow, uninjured by cold, for the next hundred years. It is true that old rhododendrons may make very beautiful and very large plants. On the other hand, gardeners frequently want to redesign their garden and move existing plants, or eliminate certain varieties and replace them with newer and superior introductions. Under such conditions a life expectancy of a relatively few years may be enough to justify trying a particular variety.

QUALITY RATINGS

Hardiness is an important factor, of course, but just as important in choosing a variety, and in some ways more so, is the general quality of the plant and flower. Most of us would not care to bother with a rhododendron, no matter how hardy, if it is not really attractive. In order to give the beginner, and any other prospective purchaser, a basis for choosing varieties, the American Rhododendron Society has set up a system of quality ratings based on 0 for the ones not worth planting, x for the next best, up to xxxx for the finest variety. This is based on plant characters, flower characters, and general desirability. Hardiness is not considered, as there is a separate hardiness rating, described in the preceding paragraphs.

It is sometimes difficult to tell whether a xxxx rating has been based primarily on the flower or on the bush, or both. Some well-qualified people, helping to develop the ratings, might give the flower a great deal of importance, while others might consider the plant characters as extremely important. In order to develop more meaningful ratings, the American Rhododendron Society is working on the use of a dual rating, to be expressed as a fraction. A variety rating of 3/4 would, therefore, mean a blossom rating of 3, or xxx, and a plant rating of 4. If it were written as 3/0, it would mean that the blossom rated 3, but the plant was so poor that it was not even worthy of x. This system is a little more difficult to develop, but once ratings are established they should be of more value than where flower and bush characters are indicated by one combined symbol. These A.R.S. quality ratings, as published, are based on observations and opinions of a large number of growers, sorted out by a committee, and the "official" rating finally established that best fits the general opinion of the variety. Such ratings are always subject to revision as more information becomes available.

It should not be thought that ratings form the only basis for choice of varieties. Experience of other gardeners in your neighborhood should be given great weight. If you see a variety in a show or in another garden and like it, there is no reason you should not plant it, even though its quality rating is low. But if you are considering purchase of a variety from a catalogue, the rating can be very useful, and should be given careful consideration.

WHERE TO PURCHASE PLANTS

After one determines the varieties or species he wishes to include in his garden, the next question is where is the best place to secure the plants. This will obviously depend a great deal on the things desired. Some rare varieties and species are obtainable only from a few rhododendron and azalea specialists. Others are quite common, and are handled by retail outlets over wide areas. The best place to secure any rhododendron plants, just as it is the best place to secure any nursery stock, is from a nearby grower. This will make it possible to see the plants at their best and decide for yourself whether they are of the quality you wish. Furthermore, there will be a minimum transportation charge, and a minimum of time that the plants will be out of the ground. The same plants going through a wholesaler and a retail outlet cannot help but suffer just a little bit from drying out, overexposure to sun, breakage of buds, and the normal wear and tear inevitable when plants are moved around a great deal.

Nurseries which actually propagate rhododendrons or azaleas are not very numerous, however, and so most gardeners will have to buy from a local retailer, or by mail. This is not to imply that a good retail nurseryman, who buys all of his stock, may not have excellent quality if he buys carefully and takes good care of the plants. You can judge that, to a considerable extent, by the appearance of the nursery. Are the plants heeled in, in a bed of peat or sawdust, or are the root balls simply standing exposed on the ground, or on a concrete slab? Do the leaves stand up alive and green and have a fresh appearance? Possibly you may not know exactly how the leaves of a particular rhododendron variety should look. Some are normally rather pale green, and others tend to hold their leaves in a drooping position. If you do not know the varieties, you can be guided somewhat by the other plants with which you are familiar. If they all appear to be in first-class condition, it indicates that the nurseryman is a careful operator, and probably his rhododendrons will be good also.

WHAT ABOUT ACCLIMATIZATION?

The question often arises as to the value of acclimatization of nursery plants. Sometimes nurseries in the North advertise that their plants are exceptionally hardy because they have been grown under severe northern conditions. Hardiness depends on two things: the heredity or genetic make-up of the particular variety, and the conditions under which the individual plant has been grown, especially the amounts of water and nitrogen available. Ordinarily plants do not become acclimated simply because of the latitude in which they are grown. Any good grower can get his plants into a relatively mature condition by winter, so that they will be about as hardy as can be expected for any particular variety.

If one buys from a nearby grower, the plants are most likely to be in a growth condition normal for that particular locality. If I were buying from a distance, for fall planting, I would prefer to obtain plants from my own latitude or farther north. For spring planting, it would make practically no difference where the plants came from, so far as acclimatization is concerned. Plants grown in the North may not be dug, because of soil conditions, until after a southern gardener would like to have them planted. On the other hand, plants from the South, shipped North, if received at the proper time for planting, may be somewhat advanced in growth. Since rhododendrons and azaleas are always dug with a ball of soil, they may be shipped when actively growing much more safely than could bare root plants although, of course, dormant plants are to be preferred. After one growing season in your garden, the plants should be as well adjusted to your conditions as they will ever be.

HOW NURSERY PLANTS ARE GRADED

Nursery stock of rhododendrons and azaleas is graded according to height, and sometimes according to width of the plant. Usually the sprawly types, such as some of the evergreen azaleas, are graded by width. The taller-growing plants are graded by height, with the requirement that they have a width commensurate with the height to make a good, reasonably bushy plant. The measurements, of course, are from the ends of the branches and not the tips of leaves, which may extend out beyond. It is a good idea to note sizes, whenever the opportunity offers, so you will know what is meant by a 12–15 or a 15–18 plant. You may sometime want to order one which you cannot personally examine.

RHODODENDRONS RELATIVELY EASY TO MOVE

Rhododendrons may be more easily moved, at any time of the year, than most plants. They are always dug, or should be, with a ball of soil, which is relatively easy, as the very fibrous root system tends to hold the soil tightly in a reasonably small, compact ball. The size of the plant which can be moved is limited only by the space in which it is to be planted, and the amount of money the purchaser desires to spend doing the job. Suggestions for moving larger plants will be given in the next chapter.

The average homeowner will usually be interested in small plants. In fact some may go to the extreme and purchase rooted cuttings, or very small liners, from propagating nurseries. This is undoubtedly the cheapest way to get a start with a particular variety, but it is not one that I would recommend to the beginner. In the first place, it will take quite a while for such a small plant to become large enough to be of any value in the landscape. In the second place, and much more serious, rooted cuttings and small liner plants have a definitely poorer chance of survival.

Rhododendrons of the usual retail sizes may be transplanted with every assurance that they will grow, if the plants are in good condition and they are treated as they should be. On the other hand, rooted cuttings and liners, usually grown in straight peat moss, seem to be much more susceptible to damping off and other fungus troubles while they are becoming established in soil than are the older, established plants. The small plants would be more satisfactory for the advanced amateur, who may have a lath house in which to grow them on, or who at least knows a good deal about taking care of them, than for the beginner. Some nurseries list what they call lath-house plants. These are usually known in the nursery trade as fall liners, or one-year liners. They are plants which were set in the lath house as liners about June 1 and grown until fall or the following spring. They are established in soil and, if well grown, are relatively sturdy little plants which have a good chance of survival but which will take a year or two longer to bloom than the larger nursery grades. My suggestion for the beginner, and for the advanced amateur as well, would be to purchase plants grading about 12 to 15 inches, without flower buds, or 15 to 18 inches, usually with flower buds. Plants of this size are less expensive than larger ones, they usually stand transplanting well, and are ready to bloom immediately or within a year, so that one can really begin to enjoy them.

NURSERY STOCK AT THE SUPERMARKET

Within recent years these and other ornamental plants have been added to the extensive list of items handled by many markets and supermarkets. The competitive atmosphere has encouraged the operators to look for cheaper and cheaper nursery stock, so plants could be advertised at "sensationally low" prices, and some I have seen quoted were really that. And so we have seen smaller and smaller rhododendron plants offered. But impulse buyers at the supermarkets, usually not knowing the varieties by name, purchase mostly while the plants are in bloom, so the markets must have budded plants, but very small ones. The result is that suppliers have had to find ways of getting flower buds on plants of liner size—and it can be done, with some varieties at least, by partial or controlled starvation. The varieties which refuse to form flower buds at this tender age are not favored by this particular trade. The main objection to these plants, dwarfed to get flower buds, is that they are in poor condition to start off in the garden with good vigorous growth, and may not bloom again for two or three years. A vigorous young plant without flower buds will very likely become established more quickly, make better growth, and give a better show of blooms the following year.

With azaleas there is probably less likelihood of very small plants' failing to grow than is true of some varieties of rhododendron. However even with azaleas I would suggest plants of at least 6 to 8 inches in diameter as being more satisfactory than smaller ones. Plants of a little larger size, perhaps in the 10 to 12 or 12 to 15-inch grades, would be even better if they have a good ball of soil. Too often flats of rooted cuttings are offered at very cheap prices, and the quality of the plants is pretty well indicated by the price tag.

So far we have not said anything about plants in cans. Evergreen azaleas, especially the smaller-growing varieties, seem to grow quite well in gallon cans, or in larger ones for that matter, and so I would consider them of equal value to balled and burlapped stock. However, the buyer must be somewhat critical of the quality of the plant itself. I have seen azaleas carried over from one season to the next in cans, and they did not look very good because they had not been fed or properly watered. If they had been balled and burlapped and "heeled in" in sawdust or peat, the roots would have grown out through the burlap and the plants would probably have looked better than canned stock. At this time the opinion of nurserymen with whom I have talked, and who are good growers, is that they would prefer rhododendrons balled and burlapped rather than in cans. My guess is that certain varieties, especially the dwarfer ones, will prove relatively well adapted to can culture and that many will be handled in that way. Most of the larger-growing varieties, and certainly large plants, will probably continue to be balled. Certain markets are set up to handle only plants in cans, and they will, no doubt, demand rhododendrons that way. The gardener would be well advised to buy only such plants in cans as are well established. Sometimes liners are "canned up" and sold immediately, in which case the soil is likely to drop away at planting because it is not yet held together by the roots.

TIME TO PLANT
The best time to plant, in many localities, is early spring. In the South, or wherever spring weather is likely to be rather warm and dry, and where winter weather is not too cold, windy, and dry, fall planting may be superior to spring planting. Actually, on a country-wide basis, planting of rhododendrons and azaleas during blossoming time is probably more frequent than any other. This is not because it is necessarily the best time to move the plant, but because the purchaser can see what the flower looks like. Since the plants are balled, and should have been heeled in in a bin of peat or moist sawdust, they can be moved reasonably well while in full bloom. In our own locality, where summers are rather cool but dry, we move plants successfully at any time of the year. However, if someone wishes to take plants into a drier and hotter climate east of the mountains, we do not like to see them moved during midsummer.

PREPARING THE SOIL
Since the soil, in many areas, is not naturally very favorable for rhododendrons, careful and adequate preparation is more important than it is for most other hardy shrubs. Where the soil is well

drained, acid, and contains a reasonable amount of organic matter, rhododendrons or azaleas may be planted just as simply and easily, and with as little extra care, as one would use to plant any woody shrub. However where drainage may be rather poor, or where the soil may not be quite acid enough, or where it is very low in fertility, a great deal of care should be used in its preparation for planting.

Where growing conditions are quite favorable, the size of hole dug need be only large enough to hold comfortably all of the root ball. If unfavorable, and the soil needs to be improved by adding organic matter, then the hole will have to be larger. It might be said that the more unfavorable the conditions are, the greater the amount of soil which should be prepared, and the larger the hole must be dug to receive it. Where conditions are not very favorable, it will be advisable to dig a hole two or three times the diameter of the root ball This should be filled in around the roots with whatever is needed to improve the soil, such as peat moss, old sawdust, or leaf mold to increase the organic matter, or just a more favorable soil, or a compost which has been acidified by the addition of sulfur, in areas where the soil is alkaline. Where organic matter is added, it should usually be mixed with soil rather than just poured into the hole. Heavy clay may be improved by incorporating sand as well as organic matter. If the soil is poorly drained, then drainage must be taken care of by tiling, if at all possible.

Where conditions are quite unfavorable, especially where the soil is low, heavy, and poorly drained, it may be desirable to consider raised beds. I have had correspondence with gardeners who have been unable to keep rhododendrons alive in their gardens when planted in the soil, even though they used peat moss and leaf mold in large quantities. However when a raised bed was built on top of the soil, and made up pretty largely of peat moss or of peat moss, old sawdust, or leaf mold mixed with loamy soil, the results were quite satisfactory.

These raised beds give rise to some problems, of course. They dry out rather rapidly and water from sprinklers tends to run off. You may not care to have a mound of compost in your lawn with rhododendrons perched on top. However it is possible to grade up to such a raised bed, or place it in such a way on a rolling lawn that it will appear to be a part of the natural soil contour. Appropriate low-growing plants may be established around the edges of the raised bed, to tie it down and make it an attractive part of the landscape.

RHODODENDRONS IN PLANTERS

This leads naturally to the question of planters. Since one might wish to get plants above the surface of the ground, for better drainage, then why not build a planter of some sort to support or contain the above-ground planting? This is fine, provided the planter is large enough and has sufficient drainage to function satisfactorily. Many planters are too narrow, or too small, or located under the drip of the eaves, or for some other reason are unsatisfactory. Some are designed to conform with the architecture of the house rather than to provide ideal growing conditions for plants. I have seen planters or raised beds, perhaps 15 inches high, held in place by a brick wall, which worked very satisfactorily—one reason for their success being that they were 4 feet across.

Single plants may be raised very nicely in redwood boxes or other containers of sufficient size to hold the compost necessary. In some very alkaline regions this may be the only solution to growing rhododendrons, although it would seem that planters, filled with straight peat moss, or acid compost if available, should be equally satisfactory if sufficiently large. Certainly plants in tubs have great possibilities for decorative use in the patio, on the terrace, flanking an entrance, or to supply bloom at any suitable point in the garden, and they can be moved to "change the scene." When selecting varieties for tub culture, type of growth and leaf characters should be given as much thought as the flowers. The growing of ornamental plants for garden use in containers has been restricted pretty largely to tropical and semitropical climates. There is room for greater imagination in this field in the temperate zone.

Incidentally, some fine specimen rhododendrons have been observed, both in this country and in England, growing in fairly large boxes in public squares and other similar places. They were grown in these containers, partly because the soil conditions would not have been favorable, and partly because the entire area was paved. This seemed to be the logical way to locate a few striking plants in the ocean of concrete, to provide a little color and beauty to those who hurried by.

DEEP DIGGING NOT THE ANSWER

Some may be wondering why we suggest the raised bed over the more common practice of digging out two or even three feet of soil and filling in with compost, organic matter, and whatever it takes to make a good rhododendron soil in the particular location. If such a bed is prepared, to overcome the bad effects of a heavy soil and poor drainage, the result is likely to be the formation of a catch basin, which simply permits more free water to accumulate around the plant roots, usually with serious results. Digging rather deeply and filling with acid compost might be more satisfactory in an area where the soil is heavy and alkaline, but where rains are not sufficient to make poor drainage a factor. I have known of some such beds' being prepared, and they were fairly satisfactory until the plant roots reached the edge of the hole, and then they were severely injured or died when they came in contact with the natural soil. This emphasizes the fact that if such a method is used, the amount of area and depth replaced with peat or a manufactured soil mix of some kind must be large enough to give plenty of room for the roots to run. The preparation of such a large area may be partially justified by growing smaller ericaceous plants in the prepared area around the rhododendrons. These plants, which otherwise might be difficult in some localities, should thrive where the soil conditions have been made ideal for rhododendrons.

SETTING THE PLANTS

Rhododendrons should not be set any deeper than they were in the nursery. This is especially true in heavy soils where the top of the root ball might well be left a very little above the surface of the ground. This will give a little better drainage, and aeration for the roots.

Balled plants are usually wrapped in burlap, which may be left on when the plant is set in the ground, or may be removed. My usual suggestion is that, if the ball seems to be quite firm and unbroken, it would be a little better to remove the burlap. If the plant has been tossed around or perhaps accidentally dropped, so that the ball of soil is broken, it would be better to leave on the burlap. In such a case, if the burlap is removed the whole mass of soil, or a great part of it, is likely to drop off, leaving almost a "bare root" plant. Rhododendron roots have no difficulty growing through the burlap. I have often seen balled and burlapped plants set temporarily in a sawdust bed, then pulled out a few weeks or months later with roots all over the ball and extending a couple of inches out into the sawdust.

In recent years some nurserymen have been using plastic bags instead of burlap to cover the ball and hold soil and roots in place. Where this is done the bag must definitely be removed before the plant is set, as the roots would not penetrate through it.

USE OF FERTILIZER AT PLANTING TIME

The question is often asked as to what fertilizer should be applied at planting time. The answer depends more on the nature of the soil and its composition than it does on the kind of plant to be set. If you feel that your soil needs fertilizer, apply a small amount of what seems to be most needed under your conditions around the plant after it has been set. Do not put fertilizer in the hole, unless you prepare a fairly large one and wish to mix a very little fertilizer with the compost to be filled in around the root ball. It is usually advisable to mulch rhododendrons as soon as they are planted, and the fertilizer should preferably be placed on the soil before the mulch is applied.

A dry commercial fertilizer is absolutely useless to the plants until it has been dissolved in water and washed down into contact with the roots. Hence if you set your plant in dry weather and then apply dry fertilizer, you should water thoroughly, partly to settle the plant into the hole, and partly to dissolve the fertilizer and start it percolating down through the soil toward the roots.

The amount of fertilizer to use at planting time varies so much with soil conditions that it is difficult to make any general recommendations. In poor, sandy soils, such as we have here, I usually suggest about half a teacupful of ammonium sulfate be scattered around a newly planted rhododendron in such a way that the material is kept away from direct contact with the stems. In fertile soils with a good supply of decaying organic matter, no fertilizer need be used at planting time.

USE WATER AT PLANTING

With bare-root plants, it is very important to work the soil in around the roots and to water in immediately, in order to get the soil into the closest possible contact with the roots. In the case of a balled plant, the roots are already in contact with the soil. If the ball of soil is reasonably moist, a minimum of water will be needed—just enough to settle the loose soil around the ball. If the ball has dried out, as very frequently happens during long shipment or where plants are poorly cared for in a retail yard, it may be desirable to dunk the ball, with the burlap in place, in a pail or tub of water. Soak for an hour, or several hours if extremely dry, in order that it may be thoroughly wet before planting. If the ball is planted dry, it is very difficult to soak it up after planting, even by almost continuous watering. The water tends to run down through the loose soil filled in around the ball, rather than to penetrate into it.

Heavy compaction of the soil at planting time is not so important as it would be with bare-root plants, where one has to go to some trouble to eliminate air spaces and get soil intimately in contact with all of the small, fibrous roots. I usually firm the soil fill around the root ball with my fingers, in the case of a small plant, and then step on it rather firmly.

Some may wonder whether or not the ball of soil should be crushed, as we sometimes read that certain potted plants should have the ball of roots torn apart, or broken up, when they are set out in the garden. This is not necessary or desirable with rhododendrons. In fact every effort should be made to keep the ball of soil from cracking or breaking off in any way.

CHAPTER 7

How to Care for the Plants

The fact that shade is essential for rhododendrons especially, and azaleas to a somewhat lesser degree, in climates where the summers are hot and humidity low has already been discussed. This does not mean that shade is always essential, as there are many places where these plants can be grown in full sun, and certain varieties are better adapted than others to growing without shade. Too dense shade will result in tall, spindly growth and relatively few flower buds. Too strong sun, on the other hand, is usually associated with a rather short, stubby growth, profuse formation of flower buds, and a tendency to have yellowish leaves.

In most cases rhododendrons are provided with shade by planting them where shade is already present. However, especially where summers are fairly cool, it is quite possible to add shade after the plants are set. The planting of shade trees in the proper place is frequently feasible, even though there will not be enough shade at the beginning to provide ideal conditions.

LATH-HOUSE CULTURE

There are many gardeners who might be called collectors or horticulturists, rather than landscape specialists. They enjoy plants for themselves, in addition to their contribution to the landscape picture, and like to see them growing under conditions where they are obviously happy. For such people a small lath house, or shade house of any type, will provide a great deal of enjoyment and permit the growing of certain varieties which would be unsatisfactory or impossible without it.

As I am writing this, I can see through the window a very useful and not unattractive lath house made of rough lumber, the shade being provided by 1×4 strips spaced about 5 inches apart. Other materials often used for shade include small plaster lath, aluminum lath or strips, and shade cloth of various types, including a plastic netting or screen material which is relatively long-lasting.

The care of plants under lath is not essentially different from that

required by plants outside. There will be slightly less watering because the shade will reduce evaporation. We have found it quite
satisfactory to have sprinklers on top of the lath house where it is
easier to get good coverage. The "throw" of sprinklers under lath
is somewhat limited unless the house is quite high. Under our conditions the lath give very considerable and much-needed protection
against strong winds. We also find about a 5° protection against
frosts of the type that occur during clear, quiet nights.

Plants may be set directly in the soil, or in raised beds, or in containers, just as for outdoor culture. Unless the lath house is to be
used strictly for propagation, there is no reason the plants should not
be arranged according to good landscape practice. Even if the primary interest is in building up and maintaining a "collection," it will
be more attractive, and the individual items can be seen to better
advantage, if each is located with some thought as to harmonious
relation to the other plants. A well-landscaped lath house can be a
very attractive place.

ALKALINE SOILS MAY NOT SUPPLY ENOUGH IRON

It has already been emphasized that soil for rhododendrons should
be acid. Just why these plants require an acid soil, whereas many
others will not grow in such a soil and may benefit by heavy applications of lime, is a somewhat difficult question to answer. Like all
problems dealing with living organisms, the answer is probably a
complex one. We do know that rhododendrons growing in a soil that
is not acid enough have difficulty obtaining enough iron, which is one
of the elements essential for plant growth. The amount needed by
plants is very minute, but in soils that are not acid enough, the iron
which may be relatively plentiful in the soil is simply not in a form
available to the plant. This results in iron chlorosis, which is a yellowing of the leaves, accompanied by stunted growth and possibly
eventual death of the plant.

In recent years it has been found possible to provide iron, in a
form in which plants like rhododendrons can use it, even under relatively alkaline conditions. Many ways to supply the necessary iron
have been studied, and at least two methods seem to have some
promise. One involves the use of a material known as fritted trace
elements. This, in common words, is a glasslike material which has

been impregnated with the minor elements necessary for plant growth, and then the entire mass has been shattered and ground. This substance is relatively insoluble in the soil, but plants seem to be able to extract from it the few molecules of the elements they need.

IRON CHELATES MAY BE USEFUL

The other comparatively recent advance in this field has been the development of chelates of certain materials, notably iron. These chelates are complex organic materials which hold the iron in a relatively insoluble form, so that it does not rapidly leach out of the soil but can still be taken in by the plant. Furthermore it is not turned into an iron compound unavailable to plants by the chemical action of the soil, as is the case where more soluble compounds, such as iron sulfate, are applied. Iron sulfate is a good source of iron for plants and is sometimes used as a spray to correct iron chlorosis. However, in soils which have the power of "fixing" or rendering iron insoluble at a rather rapid rate, the iron sulfate quickly disappears and the plants are unable to obtain the iron.

There are chelates for use in acid soils, and others for use in relatively alkaline soils. Whether or not your soil is one likely to need additional available iron is a problem which you may need to solve. The county agricultural agent in your neighborhood, usually located at the county seat, will have learned, in the course of his routine duties, whether the soil in your area is likely to be short of available iron, and if so will probably know something about the use of chelates for your particular soil condition. If your rhododendrons are yellowish and stunted, and the use of nitrogen fertilizers does not cause them to turn a normal green, then it would be well to look into the matter of iron chelates.

HOW TO MAKE THE SOIL ACID

Another way to solve the problem is to make the soil more acid, so that the iron in the soil remains in a more soluble and available condition. Unfortunately there is no material as cheap and as safe and easy to use for acidifying soil as lime is for causing it to become more alkaline. Ordinary sulfur can be used, but it has some disadvantages. On very alkaline soils it might be worth trying, perhaps 2½ pounds of agricultural sulfur per thousand square feet. This should be worked into the soil as thoroughly as possible, although it may be difficult to do this around established rhododendrons and azaleas because of their shallow root systems.

Aluminum sulfate has been recommended in the past for acidifying soil for blueberries, rhododendrons, azaleas, and other acid-loving plants. Although under certain conditions it does seem to have given fairly satisfactory results, I do not like it and have never recommended it. It leaves a residue of aluminum, which in any considerable quantity in the soil is likely to be toxic to the plants.

In soils which are not so alkaline as to require very extreme methods, I feel that ammonium sulfate is one of the best materials to use for acidification, much more desirable than aluminum sulfate. It does provide acidification, because the sulfate part of the ammonium sulfate molecule is left in the soil as the ammonium is absorbed by the plant. The ammonium provides nitrogen in the form in which rhododendrons and azaleas can most efficiently use it. In soils which are already very fertile, ammonium sulfate will have to be used very, very carefully, during winter or very early spring, or possibly not at all, because it may tend to overstimulate the plants and cause an excessively soft, vegetative growth. However, rhododendrons do best under a mulch of some type, usually an organic material which will eventually decay. As it decays, the microorganisms which are responsible tie up nitrogen in their own bodies, so that additional nitrogen must be applied for the use of the plants. This works out very well; the mulch increases the need for more nitrogen, which permits using more ammonium sulfate, which tends to increase the soil acidity.

DEGREE OF ACIDITY REQUIRED

There is a fairly wide pH range over which rhododendrons will grow. Growth should be satisfactory unless the acidity goes below pH 4.2 or even pH 4.0. At the other end of the scale, the reaction may go up to at least pH 5.5 without unfavorable results, and even at pH 6.0 fairly normal growth will usually be made if other factors are favorable.

For the fortunate gardener who can grow rhododendrons well just by setting them out in his garden, there is little need to worry about acidity. If the plants indicate by their dark-green leaves and good growth that they are "happy," then acidity is no problem at the moment and soil tests are superfluous. Where there is difficulty in growing the plants normally, soil acidity should certainly be checked.

In arid regions the pH is usually high, the soil being alkaline because of the accumulation of salts which, in a more rainy area, would be leached down into the soil or dissolved and carried away in surface runoff. Most gardeners in very rainy areas will not need to worry about pH, and in most dry areas it is generally known that the soil tends to be alkaline. It is the gardener in the intermediate area who most frequently does not know the degree of acidity of his soil. In some of the areas with moderate rainfall, the pH may vary over a wide range, depending primarily on the origin of the soil. Even in limestone country the surface soil is sometimes relatively acid, and so pH tests are almost a necessity.

CONTROL OF ACIDITY BY MEANS OF ORGANIC MATTER

We often hear of the use of various organic materials to increase soil acidity. I have recently been told about the use of rotten apples, coffee grounds, and other unlikely materials. Leaves—especially oak leaves—sawdust, and peat moss are other organic materials frequently recommended. Probably peat moss is the only one which will effectively make the soil more acid, although even this is not a very effective method unless it is used in large quantities. And some peat deposits are not very acid. Rhododendrons do like a great deal of organic matter, and peat moss is a more or less ideal material to incorporate into the soil. Its beneficial effect, in many cases at least, is due to other features than its acidifying properties, although that is of some value. Peat moss or other organic material, when added to a mineral soil, increases its moisture-holding capacity, makes a definite change in the soil flora (of microorganisms), provides increased aeration, and makes growing conditions generally better for the plants.

Sawdust was formerly condemned as a mulching material for other plants, because it was stated that it made the soil too acid. However in the few tests which have come to my attention, sawdust either tended to make the soil a little more alkaline or did not materially change the reaction. Sawdust is a good mulch and a good source of organic matter for rhododendrons, but any benefit will not be because of increasing the acidity of the soil.

Oak leaves are an old standby for making the soil more acid.

They do add to the organic matter and improve the general nature of the soil, but whether they provide very much in the way of acidification is a question. Some recent investigations in Ireland indicate that if the oak trees were growing on soil that was slightly alkaline, the leaves themselves were also alkaline, and would change the reaction of the soil rather quickly in the direction of greater alkalinity rather than greater acidity. We may conclude, therefore, that organic matter may be beneficial to rhododendrons, but not by making the soil more acid.

ACID FERTILIZERS

In many places one finds special brands sold as "acid" fertilizers, and particularly recommended for rhododendrons and azaleas. If such fertilizers are acid because the nitrogen contained in them is all in the form of ammonium, rather than nitrate, then they are desirable for these plants. This is true because ammonium sulfate, as previously stated, tends to make the soil more acid, and also because these plants prefer their nitrogen in the ammonium form. Some of these so-called acid fertilizers, at least in some states, are not accompanied by analyses which would enable one to know whether or not they really are acid-forming. In any event the amount of material put on in a normal mixed fertilizer application would probably not affect the acidity of the soil to any great extent.

There are many soils where increased acidification is not particularly important. In such soils a good garden fertilizer, suitable for the vegetable garden in your particular locality, would be quite satisfactory for rhododendrons, provided the nitrogen is in the form of ammonium, which usually means ammonium sulfate. Since ammonium sulfate is one of the cheapest sources of nitrogen, these commercial fertilizers are very likely to have their nitrogen in that form. In some states, at least, this can readily be determined by reading the analysis tag on the bag. I believe many rhododendron growers have been rather frightened into the use of these "acid fertilizers" because of the feeling that anything else would likely cause damage to their plants, a fear which is probably ungrounded. In other words they may be quite satisfactory but not essential. Where the soil really needs acidifying, it will usually require more strenuous treatment; where it does not, other garden fertilizers may be just as good.

Another fear, frequently expressed, is that the presence of lime in any form will seriously damage rhododendrons. This is undoubtedly true in soils which are already approaching the danger point in the direction of alkalinity. However, there are other soils which naturally are entirely too acid, such as our own, which has a pH range from pH 3.7 to about pH 4.0. We use a moderate amount of lime on our nursery areas, as rhododendrons, like all other plants, must have some calcium for normal growth. We use a slow-acting lime, such as ground oyster shell, and are careful not to apply it in too large quantities.

There is some evidence that alkaline soils may be harmful to rhododendrons because of the excessive calcium content rather than the high pH. By creating an alkaline condition with some salt other than one containing calcium, acid-loving plants have been grown under alkaline conditions. This is interesting but does not materially alter our practical problem of maintaining acidity or a low calcium content, whichever is more important.

FERTILIZERS FOR RHODODENDRONS AND AZALEAS

Aside from the fact that rhododendrons use their nitrogen in the form of ammonium, rather than nitrate, there is relatively little difference between their requirements for the various nutrients and that of other garden plants. For the most part, this should be considered from the standpoint of the special requirements of the soil in our garden, rather than from the standpoint of the specific type of plant. Some years ago it was the custom for fertilizer companies to put out special mixtures for potatoes, another mixture for tomatoes, another for corn, and others for different crops. At the present time the tendency is to reduce the number of different mixtures available and tailor them to fit the needs of soils in the local area, rather than the individual crop. If your soil is deficient in available potassium, for instance, then a high-potash fertilizer is obviously called for, whether you are growing rhododendrons or apple trees.

NITROGEN FERTILIZERS

In a great many soils nitrogen is the element most likely to be lacking in sufficient quantity, and the element which will give the greatest response on the part of the plants. Lack of nitrogen is indi-

Mollis azalea seedlings in flat at left, various rhododendron species at right. These are half-size flats, with polyethylene-covered frames to hold moisture until the seedlings have become well established.

A flat of seedling rhododendrons, spotted about an inch and a half apart.

The first thing in making a rhododendron cutting is to shorten the shoot to about 4 inches.

The leaves have been reduced to three, and now a wound to induce better rooting is being made. Some do this with a knife, but a sharp pair of shears is quite satisfactory.

The wounded cutting ready to dip in hormone powder and insert in the rooting medium.

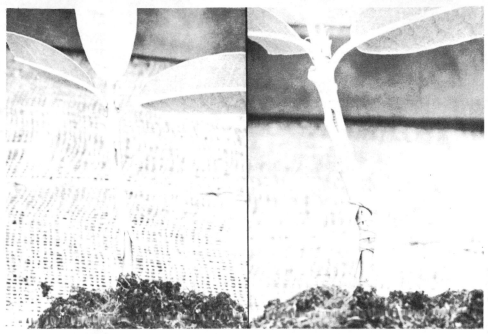

Stock and scion cut for a saddle graft.

Saddle graft wrapped with a rubber budding strip, which must be cut after union has taken place.

Most rhododendrons are trained to a bush form with several trunks. Here is one, variety 'Naomi', trained to a single trunk, an interesting treatment for occasional use.

Rooted cuttings, established in a box of peat and now ready to be planted in the ground, preferably in partial shade.

Plants of 'A. Bedford' two years from cuttings. This is a vigorous, rapid-growing variety.

Blossom bud on the right, vegetative bud at the left. Flower buds are not hard to distinguish after the early fall. This variety is 'The Honorable Jean Marie de Montagu,' one of the best in spite of its long name.

An 'Antoon van Welie' liner. The rooted cutting had its terminal bud broken out and several shoots then developed from lateral buds.

A plant of *R. oleifolium* in a gallon can.

A balled and burlapped plant of 'Sapphire,' a good blue-flowered dwarf rhododendron. There are certain advantages to canning and others to use of burlap. The plant will indicate by its appearance whether it is happy with the way it is being handled.

A comparison of leaf size. 'Unique,' with medium-sized leaves, on the left; 'Sapphire,' with very small leaves, on the right. Each type has its use.

Lath shade results in vigorous growth and relatively large leaves.

A picket fence 4 feet high gives good protection against wind, and supports a wandering clematis.

R. racemosum used in a "mixed bouquet" type of arrangement, with cherry blossoms and clematis.

Simplicity of arrangement is necessary when using flowers with heavy stems and large leaves.

Azaleas with driftwood.

Driftwood may add accent to an arrangement but it also helps hold up rhododendron flowers, sometimes inclined to be top-heavy.

cated by a generally pale leaf color and poor growth of plant. Occasionally these symptoms may be the result of girdling by some insect, death of the roots because of poor drainage and high water
table, or the presence of some root disease. It can usually be determined whether the yellow color of a rhododendron plant is due to
lack of nitrogen or to some pest by examining weeds or grass or other
ornamental plants in the immediate vicinity. If they are making a
green, vigorous growth, then the chances are that the rhododendron
is suffering from something other than simple nitrogen deficiency.
The presence of a high water table can be determined by digging a
hole about one foot deep. If free water accumulates to a depth of
two or three inches, it would be enough to indicate poor drainage. If
the water comes to within three or four inches of the top and remains
that way for any length of time, rhododendrons would be adversely
affected, and yellowish leaves, poor growth, and possible death of
the plants could be expected.

It must be remembered that the more nitrogen is applied to a soil
—provided the other elements are reasonably sufficient—the more
vigorously the plants will grow. This can easily be overdone, in which
case the resulting growth is extremely soft and generally undesirable. Most of the other nutrient elements can be applied in some excess
without actually causing injury. Any benefit from potassium or phosphorus, for instance, will be evident only if the soil is deficient in that
particular element. If it is not, then the application of that element in
a fertilizer mixture will usually cause no visible plant response. Nitrogen, on the other hand, will nearly always cause a response of some
kind, which may be undesirable if the amount is in excess of the
plant's needs.

Although ammonium sulfate is probably the most generally satisfactory nitrogenous fertilizer material for rhododendrons, another
form well suited to their peculiar requirements is urea. This is a
crystalline material, somewhat resembling sugar in appearance,
which dissolves readily. It contains about 46 per cent nitrogen,
whereas ammonium sulfate contains about 21 per cent. The urea
becomes available to the plant as such, and also in the form of ammonium, which is the form rhododendrons seem to require. If urea is
used, the amount to apply must be calculated on the basis of its
relatively high percentage content of nitrogen. For a rather infertile
soil where other crops normally require nitrogen fertilization, an ap-

plication of one pound of ammonium sulfate to 200 square feet is usually sufficient. For one plant, two or three feet in height, this would be about a heaping tablespoon. If there is a mulch of organic matter, such as sawdust, this amount should be at least doubled. Even more may be necessary the first year or two the mulch is used, if the plants tend to remain a light, yellowish green in color.

Since ammonium sulfate is a rather effective acidifying agent, there is some possibility of getting the soil too acid if it is used year after year. In areas where the soil is normally alkaline, or at least above pH 6.0, there is little likelihood of overacidification. For soils such as ours, where the normal reaction is about pH 4.0, continued use of ammonium sulfate may need to be offset by adding lime— very carefully, of course, and only if pH tests show the soil is definitely becoming more acid than pH 4.0.

There is some evidence that rhododendrons may be injured, or at least held back in their growth, by the presence of nitrogen in the form of nitrate, such as would be found in sodium nitrate or calcium nitrate. Actually some of the nitrate nitrogen will eventually be changed in the soil to the ammonium form, and so will be usable by the plants. This raises the question of ammonium nitrate, one of the newer fertilizing materials. My feeling is that it would not be as satisfactory for rhododendrons and azaleas as ammonium sulfate, although I do not have any data to back it up.

ORGANIC FERTILIZERS

The organic forms of nitrogen, such as cottonseed meal, dried blood, tankage, or barnyard manure are quite satisfactory if enough is applied to provide the amount of nitrogen that the plants need. These materials are usually much more expensive per pound of nutrients than the inorganic fertilizers. They have an advantage in that the nitrogen becomes available in the ammonium form over a rather long period. However, by applying an inorganic material once in very early spring and once during late spring, there is usually sufficient nitrogen available over as long a period as it is needed.

Organic commercial fertilizers are sometimes recommended because of the supposed direct benefit of the organic matter. It is true that organic matter is beneficial, and especially to rhododendrons. However there is so little actual organic matter in these fertilizers that any benefits from it, such as improving moisture-holding capacity of the soil, would be infinitesimal. If your soil lacks organic matter, apply it in the form of peat moss, sawdust, leaves, chopped straw, or other material which will provide enough to do some good.

The question is sometimes raised as to the suitability of barnyard manure for plants of this type. It is perfectly all right to use manure for rhododendrons and azaleas just as you might use it for other plants. You would not normally apply as much as is sometimes used on roses, where a very lush growth and long stems are desired.

One of the precautions which must be observed when using nitrogen fertilizer of any kind is to avoid applying it too late. If it becomes available to the plants during late summer, there is danger of stimulating late, soft, shoot growth, which is much more susceptible to frost or freezing injury than is well-matured or hardened growth. The danger of such injury by cold weather is much greater in some climatic zones than in others. I have a feeling, however, that gardeners sometimes become supercautious, and send their plants into the winter season partially starved and probably not quite as well able to withstand the cold as if they were more adequately nourished, but still well matured.

PHOSPHORUS FERTILIZATION

Phosphorus is deficient in some soils, in which case a material such as bone meal or superphosphate should be used. Complete fertilizer formulas, such as a 5-10-5, include phosphorus. In such a formula the first figure indicates the percentage of nitrogen, the second the percentage of phosphoric acid, and the third the percentage of potash.

Some soils have an ability to "fix" phosphorus in an insoluble form so that, although present in large quantities, it is not available to the plants, somewhat the same as iron in alkaline soils. Usually a rather heavy application to such soils will provide sufficient phosphorus for the actual needs of the plants, in spite of the fact that a large part of the phosphorus will be fixed in an insoluble form, unavailable to the plants. The amount of superphosphate to use might range from one to five pounds per 100 square feet, depending on the soil and the relative availability of its phosphorus. Phosphorus becomes available slowly, and may be released for the use of the plants for as much as two or three years after an application of superphosphate. It is useless, therefore, to make more than one application per season. Put on enough during early spring and let it go at that.

Phosphorus moves very slowly through the soil and, if applied on the surface, will be available only to the roots in the top inch or so of soil. For most crops grown on soils low in available phosphorus, the superphosphate, or whatever form is used, is placed at the bottom of a furrow, or otherwise worked into the soil so the roots can readily reach it. It is hardly practicable to cultivate fertilizer into soil filled with rhododendron roots, but a fairly heavy application can be worked in before the plants are set, to give them at least a good start. After that, if the soil is such as to need annual phosphorus applications, the material might be placed in crowbar holes around the plant, in the same way trees in lawns are sometimes fertilized. Where rhododendrons are mulched, the roots often grow up into the mulch, and those roots would be in a position to benefit from a surface application.

Lack of phosphorus in the soil may be indicated by rather weak, spindly growth, quite a bit of red pigment in the new shoots (more than is characteristic for the variety), and failure to blossom normally. These symptoms are based primarily on the results of nutrient-deficiency studies reported for other plants. If the plants are making a vigorous growth and the leaves are of normal size and dark green, there is not much likelihood of phosphorus deficiency.

POTASSIUM FERTILIZATION

Potassium deficiency may show up as brown spotting of the leaves and, particularly, burning along the margins. This would probably be fairly easy to confuse with the marginal burning caused by frost while the buds are just opening, or with damage caused by heat on a very dry day, or even with the spotting caused by certain fungi.

The usual carrier for potassium is either muriate of potash or sulfate of potash, with the latter probably safer and more satisfactory. Only rarely will a soil require potassium alone and not benefit from a complete fertilizer. Gardeners who use a complete mixture, such as a 5-10-5 or a 10-20-20, every year or every other year will very seldom find any evidence of potassium deficiency. In some soils, plants may be grown for years without any potassium's being added, the amount naturally present in the soil inducing good growth. Advice of the local agricultural agent as to probable phosphorus or potassium deficiency in your area should be a valuable guide in working out a fertilizer program.

MAGNESIUM DEFICIENCY

Magnesium is another element essential to all plant growth, and usually present in sufficient quantities. In some soils, however, there may be a deficiency sufficient to cause what is known as magnesium chlorosis. The over-all appearance of affected plants will be light-colored, sometimes almost yellow. Close examination will show that this yellow or ivory color is between the veins, and that the veins themselves and the tissues adjacent to them are green, resulting in something of a herringbone pattern.

The most frequently used method of correcting magnesium deficiency is application of dolomite limestone, a form of lime which is high in magnesium as well as in calcium. This is not a very good solution for magnesium deficient soil in which rhododendrons are to be grown, unless it is extremely acid to begin with. The use of magnesium sulfate, which is common Epsom salts, is much more satisfactory under such conditions. Usually an application of a pound to 200 square feet would be sufficient. Rhododendron varieties differ somewhat in their ability to get along with what magnesium is normally present in the soil. I have seen (Loderi G) 'King George' show rather distinct magnesium deficiency symptoms when some 20 other varieties in the same small lath house showed no symptoms. An application of a magnesium-carrying material soon made the leaves a uniform green again.

THE MINOR ELEMENTS

There are a number of other elements, such as iron, zinc, copper, and manganese, which are essential to plant life and normal growth. Iron has already been discussed in connection with soil acidity. In most cases the other minor elements are present in sufficient quantities for rhododendrons. This is particularly true if a generous supply of organic matter is used. These elements had to be present for the growth of the plants from which the organic matter was derived, and as this plant residue decays, the elements are again released for use by growing plants. There are proprietary mixtures available which carry almost all of the minor elements in available form. The fritted trace elements have already been mentioned. Other combinations are made up of soluble salts of the minor elements, and are satisfactory unless the soil has some peculiar ability to "fix" one or more of the elements and make them unavailable for plant use.

Agricultural authorities are learning that certain parts of the country are more likely than others to be deficient in specific minor elements. Fertilizer manufacturers, using this information, frequently include in their mix for a general area those minor elements which are most likely to be deficient there. This means that if you have purchased a mixed fertilizer designed for the needs of your own particular area, it will probably contain all the minor elements that are needed for your soil.

METHODS OF APPLYING FERTILIZERS

Some hints have already been given as to methods of application of certain fertilizer materials. The most frequently used method is to apply dry fertilizer on the surface of the ground, early in the spring. It may be spread broadcast over the whole border area or under the spread of the branches of an individual plant. By making an early spring application, one more or less assures that spring rains will dissolve the fertilizer materials and wash the needed nutrients down into the soil. If spring rains are not dependable, application should be made any time during the winter when rain can be expected.

For quick results, or if the spring application was missed, readily soluble materials such as sulfate of ammonia or urea can be dissolved in a pail of water and poured around the plants, or applied through a siphon hose attachment. Superphosphate, being rather insoluble—or perhaps I should say slowly soluble—does not lend itself to this type of application. Any of the materials may be applied dry and watered thoroughly enough to dissolve the soluble part and wash it a little way into the soil. There are some complete fertilizer mixes which are completely and readily soluble, but they are more expensive than the ordinary types, and are probably worth the extra price only for special uses.

CULTIVATION NOT DESIRABLE

The method of handling the soil for rhododendrons and azaleas is a little different from that for other plants which have deeper root systems. Since the rhododendron roots are close to the surface, any cultivation is likely to cause damage. In nurseries or other places where cultivation is almost essential, a hoe with a small knifelike blade may be used to scrape the surface and cut off the weeds, but without going deeply enough to disturb the roots.

There is a great interest in chemical weed killers to do the job without disturbing the soil at all. Some of the weed killers are very promising, but I am not going to make any specific recommendations for rhododendrons at this time. Often there are other ornamental plants growing close to rhododendrons, and there might be danger of the herbicide's drifting and causing damage, which would make it undesirable. Numerous materials are coming on the market, some of which will probably be very satisfactory and useful.

MULCH FOR WEED CONTROL AND MOISTURE RETENTION

One of the best methods to control weeds and to obtain other benefits is to use a fairly heavy mulch of some organic matter. It will tend to control weeds, although not entirely, of course, and provide a favorable growing environment for the root system. Mulches help to keep the surface soil moist, and the rhododendrons will often send some of their roots clear out of the soil into the moist mulching material.

One of the materials commonly mentioned for mulching is peat moss. This would be fairly satisfactory except for one characteristic: if it gets completely dry it is very difficult indeed to wet it. A sprinkler can run over the dry peat for a long time, and most of the water may just run off and not really soak through the mulch. This need not always be true, for if the peat is loosened up a little and kept from getting too dry, it may let the water through to the soil.

Another material which is being used more and more for mulching is sawdust. This usually permits water to run through more readily than it does through peat. However if the sawdust becomes very dry and has been undisturbed for a long time so that it is rather compact, water does have a tendency to run off the surface. Light raking will break the surface crust and, if necessary, small ridges may be formed to prevent runoff. Sawdust is rather effective in protecting the soil from drying out, and rhododendron roots like to grow up into it. It is more effective than most mulches in discouraging weed growth, and when weeds do grow up through it, even some of the bad perennials, they are relatively easy to pull. They become very shallow-rooted under the mulch, producing most of their roots just beneath the soil–sawdust interface. Of course if the sawdust is put on over well-established, deep-rooted weeds, they may give trouble.

EXTRA NITROGEN NEEDED

Sawdust has the same drawback as most other dry organic mulches: namely, that more nitrogen will have to be used than if the plants were unmulched. In order to take care of the needs of the decay-inducing microorganisms, there should usually be two or three times as much nitrogen for the first year or two after the mulch is applied, and perhaps 50 per cent more than would otherwise be needed in future years. This will depend a lot on specific soil conditions, and each gardener will have to watch his plants and be guided somewhat by their appearance.

It is often suggested that certain types of sawdust are superior to others. So far as I know, most experiments have shown that one kind of sawdust is about as good as another. Well-rotted sawdust is recommended by certain garden writers. This was worth considering before it was known that extra nitrogen had to be used on mulched plants. I like to use fresh sawdust as a mulch, because it lasts longer as a soil cover. Sawdust is sometimes incorporated into the soil to improve its texture and make it more generally suitable for rhododendrons. For such a use, well-rotted sawdust, or that from a quick-rotting species such as alder, might get the soil into the desired condition somewhat more quickly, but by the same token its effects will more quickly disappear.

Any other dry organic matter that will shade the soil and keep it moist will probably prove quite satisfactory. Straw, especially if chopped, makes a good mulch, but is something of a fire hazard during very dry weather. If it is sprinkled frequently, it will remain damp enough under the surface so that fire of any consequence is unlikely. In the East, salt hay or pine needles raked up in the woods would be very good. In the Middle West there are areas where chopped corncobs can be obtained at a reasonable price, and these would be quite satisfactory. In the South, peanut hulls, and in certain areas of the northern states, buckwheat hulls may be obtained. These materials vary in price according to the supply, but all of them will make a good mulch. In some places wood chips are available from the machines used by road maintenance or public utility crews to chop up tree and brush prunings along the power line or the highway. These chips work out very well because they are long-lasting and tend to suppress weed growth more than some of the other materials.

Leaves are often used, although I would prefer something more porous, as some kinds tend to mat down tightly and to smother anything that is covered. There is usually some difficulty in keeping leaves in place during windy winter periods. Evergreen boughs, slat frames, or sections of wire fencing may be laid over the leaves during the winter to hold them in place. Ground up leaves would be fine. In some municipalities the leaves raked up by the street department are discarded, and may be obtained by simply requesting that a load be dumped where specified. Lawn clippings are satisfactory, but soon disintegrate and disappear. Even so, the plant nutrients that are present in the grass will be washed down into the soil and add something to its fertility.

MULCH HAS SOME DRAWBACKS

The use of a permanent mulch around woody ornamental plants is often recommended unreservedly. However it does have certain faults, at least under certain conditions, and these should be considered by the gardener.

I have heard comment by one or two people that they thought certain root diseases were more prevalent on rhododendrons under a sawdust mulch than on unmulched plants. It is possible that this is so, as some of the fungi prefer a moist environment to one with less moisture. I do know that we have used a great deal of sawdust as a mulch, and find it in general quite satisfactory.

Recent research work by the U.S.D.A. in the East indicated that mulched Glenn Dale azaleas may be more subject to winter injury than those not mulched, presumably because of two things. The mulch is favorable to late plant growth, which does not mature sufficiently before cold weather. Mulch acts as an insulating layer to prevent radiation of heat from the soil; hence the temperature at critical periods is lower above the mulch than above bare soil. The research indicated that injury could be lessened by removing the mulch in early fall to hasten plant maturity and eliminate any insulating effect. Such removal would undoubledly result in the death of some of the roots which have grown close to the surface or even into the mulch. Where mulch has been used and given satisfaction, with no apparent trouble from increased winter injury, there would seem to be little reason to discontinue its use. On the other hand, if evergreen azaleas—or any other plants, for that matter—seem to be especially susceptible to winter injury, the gardener might well try removing the mulch from a few plants along in August. It would be of interest to leave a few mulched as a check. Under our own conditions, sawdust mulch is likely to be pretty well saturated with water by the time fall frosts occur, and hence not so effective as an insulating layer.

VERY LITTLE PRUNING NEEDED

The pruning of rhododendrons is usually not a very serious problem. Most varieties, and especially azaleas, grow into a bush that is attractive in general outline, and with a density which is quite satisfactory. However, a few varieties do tend to grow into rather leggy, awkward shapes. The best way to shape these to a more desirable form is by pinching out the growing buds of young plants as they start to push in the spring. The terminal bud of any twig or branch, when it has grown about half to three quarters of an inch, can be very easily broken out by a slight push to one side. This seems like a heartless thing to do to a favorite shrub, but at that stage it will retard growth only for a week or so. Then two or three or four dormant lateral buds, already present in the axils of the leaves around the terminal bud, will start to push. Consequently, instead of having one unbranched stalk, extending straight out from last year's growth, there will be two, three, or four shoots. In this way the plant can be made much more dense and somewhat more spreading.

It is always well to look over rhododendrons in the spring, especially young plants, and decide whether you would like to have the terminal buds grow out in a straight, pole-like manner, or whether you would prefer to have several branches coming out at an angle from the original axis. If the latter type of growth is preferred, then simply pinch out the terminal bud, and in nine cases out of ten that type of growth will result. This does not mean flower buds should be broken out. The presence of a flower bud, because of its terminal location, automatically stops straight shoot growth, just as pinching would do, and stimulates the lateral buds to start growth.

Nurserymen begin pinching at the time the cuttings are first rooted. A good rhododendron plant, at least in the opinion of most people, consists of some three or four trunks arising very close to the ground, rather than one single trunk extending up several inches before side branches are formed. These several trunks, arising from near ground level, are the result of pinching in the nursery right after the cuttings are rooted.

VARIETIES DIFFER AS TO PRUNING NEEDS

Some varieties are naturally very dense and bushy, and any pinching to make the bush more dense is entirely unnecessary. In some cases it may even be advisable to do a little pruning to thin out such bushes, although that is seldom necessary.

Actual cutting with pruning shears of growth already made and matured is seldom needed except to correct faults, which probably could have been corrected much more easily by pinching when the plant was small. A plant may grow out over a walk or in front of a door or window in such a way that it needs to be cut back. Occasionally some varieties may become rather tall and leggy, and the gardener would like to reduce them to a lower height. Pruning back to a side branch, just as would be done in pruning any other ornamental shrub, is the usual method. When reducing a plant in height, it is best not to attempt a very drastic pruning at one time. If there are a number of tall branches which should be eliminated, remove two or three of the tallest, cutting back to a side branch going in the direction desired. The next year, two or three more of the tall branches may be removed in a similar fashion. If about a third of the offending branches are removed each year, the bush will usually send out good growth near the bottom, and the final result will be a well-shaped plant.

With a good many species and varieties, plants can be cut back drastically, even to stumps, and they will push out new growth and eventually make nice-looking plants. Some kinds, and it is said that these are the smooth-barked types, do not readily make new growth from stumps. This fact and the rather unattractive appearance of such dehorned specimens leads me to favor the gradual cutting back as described. Most of the dwarfs may safely be cut back rather drastically, if necessary to keep them within size limits.

It is a mistake to cut off a limb of a rhododendron—or any other plant, for that matter—leaving a stub, rather than cutting back close to a side branch. Such stubs usually die back to the side branch anyway, and in so doing provide good conditions for certain diseases and insects, some of which may later work back into living wood. If the cut is made close to a side branch, the wound will heal over much more rapidly.

The time of pruning is not extremely important. If the plant needing pruning is in bloom, it seems quite reasonable to prune off some of the flowering branches for use in the house, taking those which should be removed anyway. However, the usual and probably preferred time to prune, in mild climates, is during the winter. I would not recommend fall pruning in areas where there is any likelihood of winter injury, as it seems that such injury is often more severe around pruning wounds. Some prefer to prune immediately after blossoming so the plants will not have their appearance hurt by the cutting.

WATERING IS VERY IMPORTANT

Because of their shallow root systems, and because rhododendrons and azaleas are rather sensitive to drought, provisions should be made for summer watering when necessary. Rhododendrons seem to like to have their foliage wet, and may ordinarily be watered in full sun without harm. It has often been said in the past that watering of any garden plants should be done at rather long intervals, with a real soaking being given, rather than more frequent waterings with less water applied. There seems to be some evidence that this recommendation is not always correct, and it is being changed by some garden authorities. I am sure rhododendrons appreciate the frequent sprinklings. The real danger is that the soil, three or four inches under the surface, may become extremely dry because the frequent surface waterings give one the impression that the soil is wet enough. Where frequent light waterings are given, it would be advisable to dig down occasionally, to be sure that the soil is adequately moist in the zone where the roots are most numerous.

Rhododendrons are quite sensitive to temperature on terrifically hot, dry days. The water loss by transpiration may be more rapid than can be replaced by the roots, even though the soil may be moist, and so the tender young leaves wilt, and may develop large brown patches, or "scorched" margins. During such days the sprinklers should be kept on, so the foliage will be wet as long as the terrific heat continues. In very dry country this may be a problem, as it might involve sprinkling every day for a long period, to a point where the soil becomes waterlogged. That is something one would have to consider and provide for. In such country it will probably help to build up the soil with organic matter to provide better moisture-holding capacity, and, at the same time, better aeration. Where sprinkling for prevention of heat damage is anticipated, very fine nozzles may be installed to use a minimum of water, but at the same time keep the foliage wet.

REMOVAL OF DEAD FLOWERS

An operation performed systematically by many rhododendron fanciers is the removal of the wilted flowers after blooming. There are good reasons for this, of which the best, I suspect, is improved appearance. This operation, often called deadheading, also prevents the formation of seed, which in some climates and with some varieties may be a somewhat devitalizing process. In our climate most of the hybrids do not normally set seed, so this reason would be of little importance here. However, we do sometimes have a misty rain, during or soon after bloom, which seems to encourage the development of Botrytis, or gray mold, on the dead petals. This makes a slimy, unattractive mess, and more important, the fungus may grow into the living twigs and cause some to die back. So deadheading may be considered a desirable cultural practice, but don't worry too much if you have to be away from home at the critical time and it doesn't get done.

CARE OF GIFT PLANTS

A few words about the care of potted azaleas received as gifts on some important occasion are included, as questions are so often asked. These greenhouse azaleas usually belong to the group known as Belgian Indicas, which are relatively tender to cold. They are considered by the florists as expendable, to be enjoyed, as one would enjoy an orchid or a bunch of roses, and then discarded. They are so beautiful, however, and the plants look so vigorous and sturdy that many people try to save them. If one has a greenhouse it is easy—just treat them like a tender greenhouse subject. If the recipient of such an azalea lives along the Gulf Coast or in some other very mild area, the plant may be set in the garden with some hope of success. For the colder parts of the country the best way is to keep the plant relatively cool while it is blooming. Don't set it directly above a radiator. Then, after the blossoms have faded, remove it to a sun porch or a cellar window or other place where it will not be very warm, nor yet freeze, and where it will have light. After danger of frost is past, plunge the pot in a semishaded spot, give it a feeding or two with liquid fertilizer, and see that it does not dry out during the summer. Before freezing weather in the fall, it must be lifted and brought into the sun room or cellar window again, and kept rather cool until it is ready to bloom. This treatment may give you some blossoms, but don't expect quite the show the plant put on when it came direct from the grower, where it had been given ideal conditions for several months.

HOW TO MOVE LARGE PLANTS

The moving of very large plants is usually a job for the specialist, one who has the necessary equipment and some experience in using it. But rhododendrons or azaleas are relatively easy to move before they get really large, and most gardeners, sooner or later, are confronted with the problem of destroying a plant, leaving it where it is not wanted, or moving it. If the plant is only 4 or 5 feet high or less, moving it should not be an impossible task.

The best time for the moving job would be late winter or early spring. Dig a trench around what is to be the root ball, possibly 2 feet in diameter for a plant that is 4 feet high, unless it is very broad and dense, in which case it might need to be larger. Then with a sharp shovel or spade undercut the root ball. It may not need to be so very deep, depending somewhat upon the variety and the nature of the soil—just deep enough to get under the main mass of roots, possibly 9 to 12 inches. When the root ball is cut free, a piece of canvas or burlap is worked under by tilting the plant first one way, then the other. With enough manpower the plant can be carried a short distance on the canvas, or dragged, to the new planting site, where the hole should be already prepared. The real problem comes when it is desired to move the plant a considerable distance. Loading it on a truck may require more equipment, a ramp, or possibly a crane, if it is extremely heavy. Somewhat smaller plants are quite easy to move, as the root systems are rather shallow and compact, and the ball of soil usually holds together quite well.

If an old plant is being moved, it will be a good time to give it any pruning it needs. Reducing the size of the top will make it lighter, it is not so likely to be blown about after being replanted, and transpiration from the reduced leaf surface will be less so that it will not suffer so much from dry weather. Plants of quite large size can be moved, but of course the larger they are the more difficult is the operation. Unless an old plant has some special value, it would be well to consider carefully the possibility of setting a plant of a new and perhaps superior variety, and simply discard the old plant.

CHAPTER 8

How Rhododendrons and Azaleas Are Propagated

In spite of the fact that most gardeners find it best to purchase plants of rhododendrons or azaleas, many like to propagate their own. It is certainly not recommended that the beginner make a start in that way, but there is widespread interest in propagation, among gardeners in general, and so it is felt that a rather extended discussion will not be out of place.

There is a challenge to rooting a difficult subject, and many people get a real kick out of it. There are no trade secrets of any importance in this field, and no reason anyone should not do his own propagating if he wishes. The belief that it is best to purchase the plants is based on the fact that rhododendrons are somewhat difficult to propagate, although some azaleas are relatively easy. There would be a considerable amount of time involved, and some space and equipment. So far as that is concerned, it is like any other hobby, and the gardener may feel that the time and the money would be well spent. There is sometimes a problem of getting cuttings to start with. It may be necessary to purchase a plant from which to take the cuttings, and in that case one already has the plant, and so there is no need to make the cuttings, unless additional plants of the same variety are desired.

Sometimes it is hard to find a plant of a variety that is desired, and if a neighbor or acquaintance has one, the rooting of a few cuttings may be the simplest way to get it in your own garden. A neighbor may have a variety that is very desirable under local conditions, but the name has been lost, or it might conceivably be an unnamed seedling. It would be impossible to purchase a plant, and the only way to get a start of it would be to propagate it yourself or get some nurseryman to do it for you. Many gardeners are interested in propagation as a hobby, and it can be a really interesting one. It involves some care and skill, but the rewards may be considerable in satisfaction as well as in plants to be used in your own garden or to give to your friends.

METHODS OF PROPAGATION

In any discussion of plant propagation it seems best to start by distinguishing between the two major types, namely sexual and asexual. By sexual propagation is meant growing the plants from seed, which must have been pollinated, or fertilized, in order to be viable; hence the term "sexual" as used here. Asexual propagation is the increasing of plants by layers, cuttings, grafting, or any method other than by seed. Seedlings may be necessary as understocks for grafting, but the actual grafting is an asexual method. Since propagation by seed is the usual method in nature, that will be discussed first.

GROWING PLANTS FROM SEEDS

Before going into methods of growing seedlings, it should be brought out that rhododendrons in the wild normally grow from seed and, as most gardeners know, the seedlings of a particular species will in general reproduce that species. However the individual seedlings will not be exactly identical.

Whether a particular species comes nearly true from seed or not presumably depends on its ancestry. If it is a type which is normally self-pollinated, because of some peculiarity of the flower or time of flowering, or because no other species is in the vicinity to cross with it, then the species becomes more or less homozygous. That is a way of saying that the genetic makeup of the species is such that it comes practically true from seed. On the other hand if two or more species which will intercross and some which will not are growing in the same general locality, there is almost inevitably going to be a certain amount of cross-pollination, and so, in the wild, one would find the true species and also intermediate types or hybrids.

In some wild rhododendron areas there are so many hybrids that there is difficulty in separating out distinct species. Variants may be found that represent all sorts of intermediate types, and the botanist has more or less arbitrarily to pick out type specimens to represent what he considers to be the original species. Seedlings from such a plant population, exhibiting a great deal of variation in the wild, naturally produce the same amount of variation if grown under cultivation.

WHAT MAY BE EXPECTED FROM SEEDLINGS

The ordinary garden hybrids have been produced by intercrossing species, and sometimes several species are involved in the ancestry of one particular hybrid. Plants such as this are said to be heterozygous; that is, their genetic make-up has been derived from several different types of plants, either in the wild or as a result of actual crossing of different species by plant breeders. The point is that seed of hybrid varieties—that is, named varieties such as are found in the nursery trade—will produce offspring the nature of which is more or less unpredictable. If one plants open-pollinated seed of a variety like 'Pink Pearl,' for instance, the male parent of any seedlings raised is unknown. Beyond that there is the heterozygous condition of the 'Pink Pearl' parent and of the male parent, whatever it may be. The net result usually is extreme variation in the seedlings, none of which, in this particular example, is likely to be identical with 'Pink Pearl.'

This variation of seedlings would be very undesirable from the standpoint of a gardener who is trying to reproduce a 'Pink Pearl' rhododendron. That would be very difficult, if not impossible, although some of the seedlings would undoubtedly resemble 'Pink Pearl.' From the standpoint of the breeder, however, who is looking for new types, this variation in seedlings is what makes possible the creation of new varieties worthy of taking their place in the garden. Many varieties, used as parents, will not produce any seedlings which have very much promise, whereas others tend to produce a fairly large proportion of good seedlings.

The breeder will probably have to raise several hundred, or possibly thousands, of seedlings in order to find any which are better than the ones he has available to start with. In other words, most of the seedlings would be inferior to the parents, and a large proportion not worth keeping. Thus it is evident that the average home gardener, who might have room to grow only a few dozen individual seedlings, would be unlikely to find any that are really superior, although he would probably find some which under his particular conditions would be good ornamental shrubs.

Actually I feel that for many people, the growing of seedling rhododendrons or azaleas might be an interesting hobby, and an eventual asset to their garden. This may be a little hard to reconcile with my previous comments on the seedlings one may purchase from some of the advertising nurseries. The difference is mostly in the objects the gardener seeks to attain. The usual reason for the purchase of seedlings from an advertisement in a newspaper or a garden magazine is to secure rhododendron plants for the garden at a very low price, with results that are seldom really satisfactory. On the other hand a gardener may raise rhododendrons from seed to test his ingenuity and ability as a plant propagator, or as a plant breeder, in an attempt to make a new combination of plant characters. Perhaps he may want to plant a fairly large group of seedlings of a type that is a bit unusual, and that no one else would have. At any rate he will expect to raise more seedlings than he will eventually set in his garden, permitting the discarding of the poorer ones. Such a gardener is showing a spirit of adventure, and doing it usually with the realization that he is taking a long chance. Of course if he is growing seedlings from species seeds, the results can be forecast more closely.

SOURCES OF SEED

There are a few dealers who handle shrub and tree seeds, including some of the common rhododendron species. However only a few specialists have a very large list. There are seedsmen in some foreign countries who make a specialty of this sort of thing, and the earnest amateur may be able to find sources of at least a few of the better species.

In some localities seed-bearing plants may be available. If a neighbor has a particularly good species he can usually be induced to permit a few seed pods to ripen, and the seed may be sown with reasonable assurance that it will germinate. Seed from the named hybrids may be more easily obtainable in many localities, but here we are dealing with very heterozygous material, which will produce seedlings exhibiting great variation. Seed from some hybrids will produce mostly weak-growing plants, and from others plants which have a relatively high average of vigor and quality. Whether seedlings will average good or worthless is something no one can tell for sure until the cross has been made and the plants grown.

The dead blossoms are quite frequently picked off immediately after blooming. If the corolla only is removed, and the pistil permitted to remain, and if the particular plant will produce seed in the climate in which it is growing, a seed capsule or pod may develop. In our own climate, few varieties will set seed without hand pollination. The seed pod will be very green and hard until sometime in late fall, or perhaps even during the winter, at which time it will open up and the seed will be scattered to the winds, unless you get there first. The ideal time to harvest the seed is when the pods have reached full size and are beginning to be hard and brown. If you open them up at this time they may seem rather immature, and the seed may be soft. However if the entire pod is removed and permitted to dry out thoroughly, it will split open at the tip and the seeds may be tapped out, somewhat like pepper from a pepper shaker. A considerable portion of the seed may get stuck in the pod, and it may be necessary to break it open or pry it apart in some way in order to get all the seed.

A great deal could be written about rhododendron seed. It varies with each species as to size, shape, and the presence or absence of various appendages or wings. Most of it is very small, and some so minute that it is very difficult to tell, without a hand lens, whether it is good plump seed or simply chaff which shattered out of the pod. One pod may produce as many as several hundred seeds.

It is probably best to plant the seed soon after it is harvested, although any time during the following spring should be satisfactory from the standpoint of germination. Actually most of the seed would germinate a year later, and some of it perhaps two or even three years later, but it does not maintain its viability much longer than that.

PLANTING THE SEED

January or February is a good time to plant, as the seed will be fresh, and if there are greenhouse facilities or a satisfactory place in a window, planting near the beginning of the year will give time for the seedlings to reach a fair size by the following winter. The seeds will germinate within two to six weeks, and will grow quite slowly for a couple of months. By the time late spring has arrived, with its higher temperatures and longer days, the seedlings should be making a fairly rapid growth. Some of the more vigorous types should be two to three or even six inches high by the end of the summer. If the seeds are planted later in the spring, they will be quite small by fall, and the most critical time in the life of young seedlings is the first winter after germination.

Various directions have been given for the sowing of rhododendron seeds, mostly somewhat similar to the following: We use ordinary granulated peat moss as a growing medium, filling a flat level full of the dampened peat, and firming with a piece of 2×4, so that the level of the moss will be about a half inch below the edge of the flat.

The seeds may be sown directly on the peat moss. However, we like to cover the peat with about ⅛ to ¼ inch of granulated sphagnum moss and place the seeds on that. This is the type of moss used by many nurseries to pack around the roots of plants to keep them moist. It has a very high water-absorbing capacity, and holds the moisture for a long time. More important than the moisture-holding power, which possibly does not exceed that of ordinary peat moss, is the fact that the sphagnum seems to have certain antibiotic qualities. Experiments have shown that seeds planted in or on sphagnum moss are less likely to "damp off" than if planted on most other media. There is even a story, probably true, that sphagnum was used by certain Asiatic armies for the binding up of wounds, because of the absorptive power of the moss and the lack of other absorbent materials. Apparently the sphagnum had enough antiseptic qualities to be noted by the military personnel.

We take dry sphagnum, remove any sticks or foreign material, and then rub it through a ¼-inch mesh screen so that it falls in a uniform layer over the moist peat moss. We then wet down the moss-covered flat, and prefer to leave it at least twenty-four hours, so the sphagnum will absorb enough moisture to be thoroughly soaked. It may look to be soaked, but if any of it is dry inside, that part of the flat will dry out before the rest, resulting in uneven germination.

The rhododendron seed is scattered very thinly over the surface. We find no need to cover the seed, although some of the finer types will filter down between the particles of moss, but the larger seed will remain on top. We have made little frames, about ¾ inches high and covered with polyethylene, which just fit on the rim of a flat. A loose sheet of polyethylene will work, but it is likely to stick to the sides of the flat or to blow off, or to be otherwise unmanageable.

HANDLING THE FLATS

The flats are placed on a greenhouse bench in semishade. A north window would undoubtedly be just as satisfactory, provided the temperature does not fluctuate too widely. Rhododendron seedlings are not very susceptible to damage by periods of low temperature, as long as it does not actually reach the freezing point. If the flat was properly moistened before the seed was planted, it will not be necessary to add any water for a good many days, possibly not until after the seeds have germinated. We add moisture whenever the surface of the sphagnum shows, by its lighter color, that it is beginning to dry out.

A sheet of glass may be used to cover the flat, but it is more likely to be broken, and a little less convenient to handle, than the poly-ethylene-covered frame. If glass is used, it will be advisable to put a sheet of newspaper over it and wet it down so it will stick to the glass, in order to cut down on light. The polyethylene we use is only translucent, and after it gets a little dirty it transmits just about enough light. Young rhododendron seedlings are very sensitive to light, and if they were germinating in a glass-covered flat in full sunlight, they would undoubtedly be injured. I have seen flats of seedlings, covered with a lath screen, injured in distinct stripes where the sun reached them between the laths. We leave the plastic covers on until the seed-lings are about ¼ inch in height, at which time they will begin to stretch out because of the shade. We like to remove the polyethylene cover in stages, giving a little ventilation first, then more, and then remove the cover but leave the flats shaded by lath, or by the usual summer shading on the greenhouse glass. If one were growing them in a north window, no additional shading would be needed after the plastic is removed.

NOVEL GROWING CONTAINERS

A method of handling seedlings in small quantities has been reported both in this country and in England. It consists of using plastic icebox dishes as the growing containers. The lower half of the dish may be filled with peat and covered with sphagnum, as previously described, and then the lid put in place to insure against loss of moisture. The young plants would not require any extra supply of oxygen when they are small, and it should not be necessary to raise the lid until the seedlings are about ready to be pricked out. However, it would be well to keep a sharp watch, and at the first sign of any fungus growth or damping off, ventilation should be given.

We usually apply a dust of the fungicide captan to the surface of the flat as soon as the seeds have been scattered over it. This is an added precaution, as the antibiotic qualities of the sphagnum are not always sufficient to prevent Botrytis mold or other organisms from getting started.

SEEDLINGS MAY NEED NITROGEN

At the time of planting the seed, no fertilizers should be applied.

However, soon after the seed has germinated, the young seedlings will benefit from an application of a little nitrogen, or even complete fertilizer. One of the readily soluble, complete fertilizers now found on the market or, perhaps, just a little ammonium sulfate or urea may be used. The application at this time, of course, should be extremely dilute. If one were to dissolve a teaspoonful of ammonium sulfate in a sprinkling can holding about 2½ gallons, and the flat were sprinkled fairly lightly with this solution, the amount of nitrogen applied should be about right. If the seedlings seem to remain a little yellow, another application could be made in three or four weeks.

It has been our experience that different lots of peat moss may vary a great deal in their nitrogen content. On some lots young rhododendron seedlings will grow along for several weeks in apparently normal condition, without any fertilizer's being added. Other lots are apparently deficient in nitrogen, and the seedlings will turn yellow very soon unless additional nitrogen is given. A good rule might be to refrain from applying nitrogen as long as the growing seedlings remain a good dark green in color and make normal growth.

During the period before the covers are removed from the flat a careful watch should be kept for gray mold and other fungi. If any should appear, a good application of 10 per cent captan dust should be made immediately. At this stage it is important to prevent the flats from drying out, but it is also important to refrain from watering so frequently that the peat will get soggy. It should never get so wet that one could take a handful and squeeze free water out of it. One very good method of checking, which develops after long experience, is to lift the flat, or one edge of it, and judge by its weight whether or not it is dry. With the very young seedlings which are rooted just at the surface, it is important that the surface not dry out either, but that will not happen as long as there is plenty of moisture in the mass of peat or sphagnum.

GIVE THE SEEDLINGS MORE ROOM

After the seedlings have developed about one true leaf beyond the cotyledon stage, they should be spotted into flats of peat moss to give them more space to develop. The seedlings, although very small, will stand quite a bit of handling. To remove them from the flats, use a knife blade or a wooden stick to lift out gently a clump perhaps as thick as your finger. This might contain anywhere from a very few to 50 or more seedlings—preferably the former, as too thick seeding is conducive to slender, weak seedlings. By grasping the top, a leaf, or perhaps just one of the cotyledons, the individual seedling can fairly easily be pulled free from the sphagnum or peat moss.

A flat should have been filled to the rim with loose, damp peat, then pressed down with a flat board, so that there is about ½ inch of space above the peat. Use a pointed stick about the size of a lead pencil, or use a lead pencil if you wish, to make a little hole into which the tiny seedling's root system will drop without its having to be pushed in. The peat may then be pressed in gently from the side with the stick or with the fingers, and the seedling is set. If there are very many flats, a marking board will be needed, so the seedlings will be in straight rows and there will be a uniform number per flat. This may be done by inserting pegs in rows in a board to cover the flat, or a peg strip may be made to mark one row across the flat. As soon as the seedlings have been set, water the flat gently with a fine-mist spray to settle the peat around the roots. At this time no fertilizer is needed, but a little nitrogen in the form of a very dilute solution of urea or ammonium sulfate might be added a few days later, after the seedlings have become established.

THE SEEDLINGS GO INTO POTS

The next step would normally be to put the seedlings in pots, of a size to fit the particular plant you are transplanting. Some of the very small, plastic pots, about 2×2 inches, are very convenient. If the seed was sown during January or February, the seedlings should be in pots by fall, and may be wintered over in a protected frame or in a greenhouse, depending on local weather conditions.

By the following spring the seedlings will have filled the pots with roots. They may be set directly into the lath house at that time, or they may be permitted to make one flush of growth and go into the lath house during early summer.

The term "lath house" refers to conditions rather than the actual structure. Nurserymen, in order to have a large area with uniform semishade and good growing conditions, construct shelters out of wooden or aluminum lath or other material which provide some protection against high summer and low winter temperatures. The same protection might be given in the home garden by planting in a bed on the shady side of a building, or in a protected place under low-growing trees. If such a place is not available, an ordinary cold frame with a lath-screen cover will provide very similar conditions. After the young plants are large enough to survive in an open bed, they may be set out the same as any rhododendron from a nursery.

One of the facts of rhododendron life is that usually seedlings all die, because of damping off, or drying out, or some other environmental factor; or else the fortunate gardener finds that he has a terrifyingly large number of the seedlings of a particular species or variety or cross. Then comes the problem of what to do with the plants.

WHAT TO DO WITH SO MANY PLANTS

If you have a large garden area still to be planted, it is only logical to fill certain borders or beds with seedlings of a particular species or cross. Some of these will be weak plants and eventually die off. Others will be undesirable from the standpoint of foliage or type of growth and may likewise be eliminated. As soon as the plants begin to bloom, there will be many which are expendable. They could be moved into some other area if a hedge, or service planting, of that type is needed. However if you have had success in growing this many rhododendron seedlings, you will probably have a few hundred or thousand more coming along, and will find it most satisfactory to pull out and destroy all plants that are inferior.

You will want to wind up, of course, with a few superior plants to show the results of your efforts. There will be many others a little too good to throw away, but not good enough to keep. These might be donated to a park planting, or to some neighbor who wants a mass of foliage and is not particularly concerned about the superiority of the bloom. However they will always be known as your seedlings, and if you do not want people making sarcastic remarks about your rhododendron-breeding ability, it would be desirable to destroy any which you do not want known as your product.

PROPAGATION BY LAYERING

One of the oldest methods of growing plants asexually is by layering, as plants often layer themselves in nature. Low-lying branches become covered with leaves and, if in contact with the soil, may eventually form roots. This depends on the kind of plant, as some root relatively easily and others are difficult to root, although rooting may be accomplished eventually with almost any kind of plant, branches of which can be bent down and actually covered with soil.

Rhododendrons root fairly easily, and layering has long been a commercial method of propagation, especially in England. The usual method there is to set stock plants a a distinct angle so that branches can easily be bent to the ground. Sometimes they are layered all the way around in cartwheel fashion. Each branch is inserted into the soil, so that it is actually covered 2 or 3 inches deep at the lowest point, with the tip leaves and bud projecting above the surface. It is usually necessary to peg down the branch or put a brick or stone over the buried portion, to prevent its working loose during windy weather. The time of insertion does not make a great deal of difference, if one is prepared to wait for a reasonably long period of time. However, late summer is the time preferred by some nurseries.

Roots should be formed within a year or eighteen months at the longest. Rooting will usually be hastened if a cut is made about half-way through the branch to be layered, at the point which will be most deeply covered. Cut away from the root of the plant, on the underside of the branch, so that when it is bent down and then upward, a tongue will point toward the base of the plant. Some go to the trouble of inserting a small splinter, such as a toothpick, in this cut to keep the tongue separated from the branch. Dusting the tongue with a root-inducing hormone may also help with certain varieties.

After a fair number of roots have been formed, in perhaps eighteen months, the layer may be separated from the parent plant and transplanted into a nursery row. Because of the inevitable bending upward of the end of the branch, layered plants are usually poorly shaped and awkward, until after they have been grown for a couple of years in the nursery row.

If the soil is rather heavy clay, or very light and sandy, it would be advisable to work in enough peat moss so that the soil around the layer will be about half peat. The length of stem covered is not too important, but will usually be about 12 inches.

AIR LAYERING

A method known as Chinese layering, or air layering, may be used if desired, although it has not proven especially adapted to rhododendron propagation. It might possibly be useful for varieties too stiff or brittle to bend over for ordinary layering. This method was used in ancient times when there were no greenhouse facilities to root plants which were otherwise quite difficult to root. The bark was removed from a ring around a twig or small branch, and this wounded area was then covered with a rather large ball of sphagnum moss, which had to be kept moist. If it dried out, the process was ineffective. At best it was relatively slow and involved a considerable amount of effort.

When polyethylene plastic sheeting became available, experiments were conducted to see if it could be used to improve this ancient propagation method. It was found that a relatively small ball of sphagnum could be placed around the branch where the bark was removed and be held in place with polyethylene sheeting. A root-inducing hormone could be dusted over the area where the ring of bark was removed, but no fertilizer needed to be included in the sphagnum. The plastic was tied rather tightly around the twig, to enclose the mass of sphagnum completely and make the whole thing as airtight as possible. If the sphagnum was well soaked before being applied, the moisture usually remained sufficient over a period of several weeks or even months, to encourage the formation of roots.

As the roots would be growing in pure sphagnum without any direct application of nutrients, it is important to use great care when the air layer is severed from the parent plant and set in the soil. The roots may take a little time to get adjusted to growing in soil, and so one should be careful to keep the plant shaded and well watered until it becomes established in its new location.

It has been indicated by some that air layering makes possible the production of very large plants in a very short time. It is my feeling that any air layering of rhododendrons should be done on relatively small twigs. It might be possible to induce roots to form from an air layer made on a rather large limb, as some advertisements indicate, but there would be great difficulty in getting such a plant established in the soil after it was removed from the parent plant.

It is my own feeling that air layering of rhododendrons is just a novelty, and not a very practical method of increasing plants, except possibly in the case of a variety or species which is very difficult to root, where no understocks are available for grafting, and where, for some reason, ordinary layering is impractical.

GRAFTING VERSUS CUTTINGS

By far the most satisfactory and most generally used method for propagating named horticultural varieties of rhododendrons and azaleas is by cuttings. Most varieties can be rooted, with a little care, and the plants are usually easy to train into a desirable shape; they grow along rather fast, and there is no graft union to give trouble, or understock shoots to puzzle and plague the gardener. However, grafting has long been used by amateurs and as a commercial method of propagation. There are a few varieties which are very difficult to root from cuttings, and with these, grafting or layering is necessary.

PROPAGATION BY GRAFTING

Grafting is the joining of a scion, or shoot, of the variety desired to a seedling plant or rooted cutting of another rhododendron, or azalea, known as the stock or understock. Stocks for rhododendrons are most commonly seedlings of *R. ponticum.* Many other species, such as *R. catawbiense,* could be used. Some growers have used rooted cuttings of varieties, such as 'Cunningham's White,' which are fairly easy to root, and which make a good root system and vigorous growth. In any event the seedling or cutting should be grown until it is about the diameter of a pencil, or a little less. If seedlings of *R. ponticum* are to be used, they will probably be about two years old, and in pots or a nursery bed. If they are growing in pots, then they may easily be brought into the greenhouse at the proper time for grafting, usually early spring. In this locality we would bring the understock into the greenhouse during late February, and be ready to graft by the middle of March. The usual system is to plunge the pots, or transplant seedlings from the lath house, into a peat-filled bench. A little bottom heat will start the seedlings pushing, and as soon as some growth is evident, it is time to make the grafts. The scions should be as dormant as it is possible to find.

Various methods of grafting have been used, but there are two which have been favored. One is the side graft, in which a slanting cut is made downward into the stock plant about an inch and a half from the surface of the soil. This slanting cut, in a pencil-size stock plant, might go down ¾ of an inch and cut halfway or a little more through the trunk. The scion, which is a 4- or 5-inch length of the previous year's growth, including the tip bud, is cut to a wedge shape at the base, the length of the wedge depending on the size of the scion. For a pencil-size scion, the length might be around ¾ of an inch. The wedge is then pushed down into the cut in the stock in such a way that the cambium layer of one is in contact with the cambium layer of the other, at least on one side.

The union is tied by wrapping with rubber strips, known as budding strips, available from nursery supply houses. The person who is grafting only a very few plants could get by by using rubber bands cut to make a straight strip. Wrapping is from the bottom up. The first lap goes over the end of the strip to hold it, and then the free end is taken around and around the graft, until it has covered the length of the cut, and is then put under one of the loops so that it will not unwind.

Waxed string was formerly used to do the wrapping, and it is still satisfactory but will require watching, for if one forgets to remove the string, it will girdle the plant and kill it. The rubber strip will stretch, to a certain extent, and may rot off, but it too should be checked, and cut if necessary, before the graft union begins to increase in diameter.

THE SADDLE GRAFT PREFERRED

The side graft was for many years the standard method, but I have found that such grafts are easily broken out if the growing scion is pushed or blown in a direction away from the original stock trunk. It does not break out so easily if pushed in the other direction.

Our preference is for the saddle graft, which seems to give a stronger union, less likely to blow out. For a saddle graft, a slanting cut upward is made on one side of the understock as close to the ground as one can work, usually less than 2 inches, and then a similar cut is made directly opposite, so that the top of the understock is completely severed, and the stump has a wedge-shaped end pointing upward. This is a little more difficult to do than making the single cut for the side graft. It will require a very sharp knife and careful operating in order to get a good clean cut and avoid damage to the fingers. The cut in the scion has to be the reverse of the one on the stock—that is, a wedge-shaped cut pointing in toward the tip of the scion. This should be approximately the length and the same angle as the one on the stock, so that when the cut scion, with the deep notch in the end, is settled over the wedge of the stock, the sides of the notch in the scion will coincide as nearly as possible with the sides of the wedge on the stock.

Tying is done in much the same manner as for a side graft, the wrapping beginning at the bottom of the union and proceeding upward until the union is covered. It is not essential that the wraps be so close together that one cannot see between them, although some propagators do make a complete cover. Others seem to prefer to space the string or rubber strip a little, in order to provide some aeration to the cut surfaces.

TREATMENT OF NEWLY MADE GRAFTS

Whichever type of graft is made, the treatment following is essentially the same. The newly grafted plant is put immediately into a place where it will be kept warm and moist. In commercial nurseries this usually means plunging the completed graft—at an angle, if a side graft—in a fairly deep bench where it may be covered with damp peat moss, completely over the pot or root ball, and usually over the graft union. A hotbed sash or a polyethylene sheet is then placed over the bench to form what is known as a sweatbox. Bottom heat is used to maintain a temperature of about 70°.

The beginner, who may wish to try just two or three grafts, can provide essentially the same conditions in a box partially filled with peat moss and covered with a sheet of polyethylene plastic. The box can be placed in a warm room and given a little light, but no direct sunlight. The danger at this point is that gray mold, or Botrytis, may get started and cause a dying back of the scion. A dust of captan, as soon as the graft is put in the box, will be helpful. No watering need be done for several days if the peat is moist and the polyethylene cover is fairly tight.

Usually the graft will unite at once, or it will not unite at all. Within a couple of weeks one should be able to see some white callus growth where the union is taking place. When this is evident, it would be wise to begin giving a little ventilation by opening the plastic occasionally, then leaving a small opening, and a little later taking it off altogether. If the work is being done in the house, where the atmosphere is quite dry, it might be advisable to keep the polyethylene over the grafting case, with occasional ventilation.

The seedling stump will usually put out a number of shoots, which have to be rubbed off, as it is essential to force all the growth into the scion. With the side graft, the understock above the graft will start to grow. This can be reduced materially as soon as it is evident that the graft is taking, and within a month or so all of the understock above the union should be removed. One advantage of the saddle graft is that there is no understock top to be reckoned with and removed after the graft has taken.

ROOT GRAFTING

One of the objections to grafted plants is that shoots frequently develop from the understock, usually from just below the graft—that is, from stem, not root, tissue. By using a fairly long scion, perhaps 4 to 6 inches, and grafting in a piece of root at the bottom, it is possible to get a grafted plant which will not produce suckers from the understock. Some propagators use this method to encourage "own rooting" of hard to root variotioo, by providing a "nurse root."

The roots may be secured from an old plant, or seedlings may be grown, dug, and the root system cut up. The size of piece to use will depend on whether the object is to obtain large roots from the understock or just to keep the scion alive until it can develop its own roots. For the latter purpose a piece of root ¾ inch long and the diameter of a match, or smaller, should be sufficient. The graft is made like a veneer graft in reverse: a slanting cut upward from the base of the scion, into which a wedge-shaped bit of root can be slipped and tied. It is important that the root be properly oriented, with the tip pointing down.

TOP GRAFTING

It is possible to top-graft several varieties on one plant, although few gardeners will find much need for such an operation. Where top grafting is done, it may be by the ordinary cleft-graft method, such as is used for apple trees, or it may be by saddle graft, previously mentioned. A method of cutting which permits fitting and holding the cambium layer of the scion tightly against the similar layer of the stock is essential. Tying must be carefully done, as the wind will exert considerable pressure against the scion. It would probably be advisable to reduce the length of the scion leaves, particularly of large-leafed varieties, by cutting straight across the blade, leaving perhaps a third or a half of the original length. This will reduce wind pressure, and also the leaf area through which moisture is lost. The best time would be just before growth starts in the spring.

An important part of top-working is to cover the union with wax of some kind to prevent drying out. Any type of grafting wax may be used, or even parowax, although it is usually rather brittle and not particularly well suited. The placing of a polyethylene bag over the completed graft to cover both scion and union might be considered. It would prevent drying out and might hasten union of the graft, although conditions within the bag would be favorable for development of fungi. The fungi might be discouraged by use of captan dust.

PROPAGATING BY BUDDING

Another method of propagation, similar to grafting, is known as budding, in which case the scion is just one bud, on a little shield of bark, rather than an entire shoot. Budding is used very generally in the propagation of roses and many types of fruit trees. It is possible to propagate rhododendrons by this method, but not especially easy. The bark of the stock has to be in proper condition so that when cut, it will readily split from the woody cylinder. This is to permit the bud shield to be slipped in, and thus place the cambium layers in contact. Budding is usually done during the middle or latter part of the summer, during the active growing period. One advantage of this method is that the seedling stock, if the bud does not grow, may be used later for another try at budding, or for grafting, or may itself be permitted to grow into a flowering plant. A grafted seedling stock is usually lost if the graft does not take.

There are various ways of cutting buds and inserting them, but no extensive experimenting has been done to determine which method is superior for rhododendrons. I would suggest, if you wish to try this method, that you bud into young seedlings or cutting-grown plants with trunks not over half an inch in diameter, and preferably about pencil size. Make a crosscut close to the ground, just through the bark and not into the woody cylinder. Make a vertical cut about ¾ inch long below the crosscut. Use the knife blade or a thin piece of metal to lift up the two flaps resulting from this "T" cut. If conditions are right, the bark will separate from the wood rather cleanly, leaving a moist, slick appearance.

Find a plump, mature bud, of the variety desired, in the axil of a leaf on a current season's shoot. Cut from about half an inch below the bud, under it, and to about half an inch above it—deeply enough so that a thin sliver of wood is present on the underside of the shield. The shield may then be slipped down between the two flaps of the "T" so that it is completely within the "T." If it sticks out above, it can be cut off at the crossbar of the "T." Tie with rubber strips, beginning below the bud and wrapping upward, leaving the bud itself uncovered, but being sure to have it firmly wrapped both above and below the bud. No wax is needed.

If the bud is going to unite, it will usually do so within three or four weeks. If at the end of that time the bud looks plump, and the bark on which it is borne still seems to be green and alive, the operation is probably a success. At this time it will be necessary to cut the band so that the plant will not be girdled at this point. Simply pass a sharp knife up the back of the stock, cutting through the rubber strip, and it will fall off, exposing the bud. If the bud has "taken," it would be advisable at this time to cut back about half of the top of the stock seedling, and somewhat later it should be cut off just above the bud. If the budding was done in early summer, this removal of the entire top of the stock plant might be done within five or six weeks, in which case a shoot should develop the current season. Usually the budding is done during the latter part of the summer, and the top is not cut back to the bud until the following spring.

GROWING RHODODENDRONS FROM CUTTINGS

Most of the rhododendrons being grown commercially in this country are propagated by cuttings. This is also true in Holland, where there is a large rhododendron nursery industry. In English nurseries, layering is still being used, but in the United States layering is considered too slow for commercial production. In most cases the methods used by commercial nurseries are best for the beginner as well, because they are based on simplicity, economy, and successful production of plants. Certainly the growing of rhododendrons or azaleas from cuttings is the best method for increasing plants quickly and efficiently.

Cuttings taken during the dormant season can be rooted, but with some difficulty. The most satisfactory time to take them is during the summer, usually early summer for azaleas and mid- or late summer for rhododendrons. The shoots will be somewhat pliant and flexible, and the leaves at the tip not quite fully grown. Cuttings can be taken a little earlier than this, but there will be more likelihood of their drying out or rotting. They may be taken later with some success, although the harder and more mature they get, the more difficult they are to root. In our locality the best time for most rhododendron varieties extends from August through September and into the first part of October. Some varieties will root quite readily throughout this period, or even later into November. Others are rather tricky and have to be taken at just about optimum condition.

AVOID FLOWER BUDS

By the time the shoot is mature enough for use as a cutting, it will likely be evident from the size of the bud at the tip whether it is developing a flower bud. Flower buds should be broken out when the cuttings are made, but it is usually possible and better to select shoots which have not formed flower buds. Heel cuttings, made from short shoots broken out instead of being cut, are sometimes recommended. I see no advantage, and there are several disadvantages to this method.

It must be remembered that cuttings are living material, and that they should be handled in a way to prevent drying out as much as possible. If the weather is warm and dry, the cuttings should be taken early in the morning and kept in a polyethylene bag or covered with a damp cloth or damp burlap until they are inserted in the cutting medium. As a general rule, shoots from young plants are more satisfactory, as there will be fewer flower buds to deal with, and rooting will probably be better. Where cuttings are to be taken from older plants, it will help to break out the terminal bud just as it starts growth in the spring. This will result in the formation of three or four or five small lateral shoots, which will be good cutting material and which will, in most cases, have no flower buds. Such cuttings are easier to root than the very thick, heavy shoots made at the ends of the larger branches.

The length of the cutting will depend somewhat on the variety, sometimes as short as half an inch on the very dwarf types. On the large-growing rhododendrons, the current shoots may be as much as 8 or 10 inches long, in which case they should be shortened to about 4 inches. I prefer the cuttings to be rather short, as they will make sturdier plants. The roots will be formed almost entirely at the base of the cutting anyway. If the cutting is too long, it either sticks out of the cutting medium too far, or has to be put too deeply into the medium, or has to be put in on a slant, which takes more space.

Research has shown that it may help in the rooting of the cuttings if a wound is made at the base. We usually slice, just through the bark, for about a half to three quarters of an inch, cutting toward the base. This can be done very quickly with a sharp knife. When doing large quantities, we cut the shoot to proper length in one movement and then, holding the shears exactly the same, use the sharp blade to slice the bark from the base of the cutting to make the wound. The wound seems to expose more cambium layer, and that is where the callus will develop.

ROOT-INDUCING HORMONES

Most propagators use a rooting hormone for rhododendrons to increase the likelihood of roots' being formed. It is true that many varieties, and especially evergreen azaleas, root fairly easily without such hormones, and presumably all can be rooted, at least to some degree, without their use.

There are various proprietary mixtures on the market, most of which presumably will work. We make up our own hormone powder from indole butyric acid and talc, and add 10 per cent of a good fungicide, such as Tersan. For general use, our hormone contains 0.8 per cent by weight of the indole butyric acid. For very difficult varieties, 2 per cent may be used. By far the simplest and most satisfactory thing for most gardeners is to purchase the hormone powder. The proportions are given for those few who like to experiment and to do everything possible themselves. Hormones may be used in the liquid form, in which case the cuttings are allowed to stand in the solution for a given period of time. The powdered material seems easier to use, as one can collect half a dozen cuttings in a handful, and at one operation dip the bases of all in a container of the powder. The handful is then given a light tap to remove the excess, and the cuttings are ready to be inserted in the propagating medium.

MEDIA FOR ROOTING CUTTINGS

Various combinations of peat moss, sand, vermiculite, perlite, ground sphagnum, and other materials have been recommended by various people as the best medium into which the cuttings are to be inserted. We have tried several, and now use straight horticultural peat moss. Whether the addition of other materials might improve it slightly is a question. Certainly it is easier to use straight peat than it is to mix it with anything else, and cuttings root very readily in it.

The propagating medium, in greenhouse bench or in a flat or box, should be at least 3 or 4 inches in depth. It should be well moistened, and firmed to some extent before the cuttings are inserted.

With the larger rhododendrons, after having removed all but 3 or 4 leaves at the tip, it might be well to remove a portion of the remaining leaf blades—especially if they are large—perhaps a half to two thirds, in order to reduce transpiration as well as the amount of space needed. Some propagators say that such cutting of the leaves will prevent rooting, but I have not found that it makes any particular difference in the rooting percentage.

KEEP THE CUTTINGS MOIST

After the cuttings have been inserted in the propagating medium, it is very important that they not dry out. The old method was to place a glass frame over the greenhouse bench. This was called the double-glass method, the greenhouse itself with the smaller, glass-enclosed structure inside. Later it was found that the glass enclosure on the bench could be eliminated if a fine mist were discharged frequently enough to maintain the humidity in the greenhouse at practically full saturation. This has many advantages, because the cuttings can be examined without lifting heavy glass covers, ventilation is better, and disease control is easier.

Various methods have been worked out for turning the mist on and off automatically, based on the rate of evaporation of the moisture. Our own method has been to let it run almost continuously during the daylight hours for several days after the cuttings are inserted, after which the hours of misting are reduced until the cuttings are actually rooted.

A few amateurs have greenhouses where they may use mist, but most do not. A good substitute for the old glass-enclosed bench is simply a box of convenient size, covered with sheet polyethylene. If the outside of the box is fairly smooth, and wet, the polyethylene can be plastered against the wood in such a way that it will be very tight. It may be held on with strips of wood or a frame, or even by tying a string around the box to hold the plastic in place. With this method the cuttings should be examined from time to time, and it may be necessary to add a little water if the peat seems to be drying, but it should not be soggy. Each time the plastic is removed, it should be replaced wet, and care taken to insure its remaining tight.

BOTTOM HEAT

It is well known that bottom heat is helpful in the rooting of cuttings. It stimulates the growth of roots while shoot growth is held back by the lower air temperature. In the small greenhouse or outdoor frame, an electric heating cable may be used very satisfactorily. These cables have thermostatic controls so that the heat remains relatively uniform. Bottom heat of 70° is about right for the starting of cuttings. After they have begun to form roots it may be reduced to about 60°, and soon cut off altogether. The providing of bottom heat in a small box kept in the house or sun porch is a little difficult. If the general air temperature is around 70°, however, the cuttings would probably root fairly well. Bottom heat by electric cable in an outdoor frame is not hard to arrange.

After roots have formed on cuttings in an enclosed case, a little ventilation should be given, and progressively more until the cuttings are completely uncovered. If they are in the dry atmosphere of a house, it would probably be best to keep a polyethylene cover over the box, with some ventilation, in order to prevent drying out of the leaves. Watering at all times should be done with great care, keeping the peat moist but not soaking wet. It is true that the use of a mist nozzle over the cuttings may keep the peat very wet. It has been our experience that if there is proper drainage, so that the water can drip through, it apparently carries oxygen with it, and the plants do not seem to react as they would ordinarily do in a waterlogged soil.

The time required for rooting varies with different varieties, and may range from about three or four weeks for evergreen azaleas and easy rhododendrons to possibly several months for very tough varieties. The average rhododendron varieties will usually root within a couple of months.

THE NEARING FRAME

Some years ago Mr. Guy Nearing developed a method of propagating rhododendrons which has been used extensively in the East. It is described in detail in Bulletin 666 of the New Jersey Agricultural

Experiment Station, "Rhododendrons from Cuttings," December 1939, by Nearing and Connors. I understand some modifications have been made during recent years. Although I have not used the Nearing method, and hence am not personally familiar with it, I do know that many have used it successfully.

Since the method stresses adherence to details, no special effort will be made to give directions for using it. This brief description is simply to give an idea of what the method is. If a reader wants to try the method he should obtain the New Jersey Bulletin 666 or some other set of detailed directions, or visit someone who already has a frame in operation.

The method depends upon two essential factors: a stratified rooting medium and a specially designed outdoor, unheated frame. The medium, as given in the above publication, consists of three layers—the top of sand, the middle, sedge peat and sand, the bottom of German peat moss and spent mushroom manure. The frame itself consists of a wooden box with very little, if any, drainage, of a size to be covered with a standard hotbed sash. This box is buried in the soil, as deeply as possible without making it so low that surface water would flow over the edge. An integral part of the method is a wide hood over the frame, opening directly to the north, so that practically all direct sunlight is excluded, but northern light is reflected by the hood down onto the cuttings.

Cuttings are taken in the usual way, but are left in the stratified medium for approximately a year, mostly rooting in the summer, after having been put in the previous fall.

Whether this method or the one previously described is superior would depend on many factors, including local conditions. Most commercial growers use the greenhouse bench, although some in the East use the Nearing frame. Most amateurs in the Northwest use the greenhouse, or an ordinary cutting frame. Many amateurs in the East, possibly most of them, use the Nearing method. The beginner would probably do well to imitate a neighbor or acquaintance who is successful, or choose the method which most appeals to him after careful study of the various factors involved.

AFTERTREATMENT OF CUTTINGS

After the cuttings have developed a good ball of roots, the usual procedure is to transplant them into a bench, box, or flat filled with straight peat moss. They could be left in the propagating box for a while, if there is room and other conditions are satisfactory, but if they are pretty close together, spacing them out about 6×6 inches will be better. They should remain growing in the peat until they are well established and the leaves are fairly mature. We like to leave them until they have made one flush of growth, and that growth has hardened up considerably.

Tip cuttings usually push the terminal bud, which would normally grow into a straight shoot perhaps 2 or 3 to 8 or 9 inches high, depending on the variety. When this growing bud is about ½ to ¾ inch extended, a light pressure on one side will snap it off cleanly and easily. If it is broken out at this stage, growth will be made from two, three, or four lateral buds. This gives a plant branched almost at ground level, generally a better-shaped and sturdier plant than one which starts off with a single stem. It may seem somewhat rash to break out a growing bud just as it is getting started, but a better plant will result.

We make our cuttings during September or October, move them out of the cutting bench into beds of peat from December to February, and by the first of June they are ready to go into the lath house. Most gardeners may not have a lath house, but they can usually find similar conditions where it is moderately shaded and protected against strong winds. The plants will remain in the lath house or protected nursery bed at least one year, and possibly two or three. In some areas where conditions are not very favorable for rhododendrons, those fortunate enough to have lath houses or other shade structures may want to keep their plants growing there permanently. Most gardeners will want to move the plants out of the lath house or nursery bed into the landscape planting as soon as they are big enough to take their places, usually within three years from the time the cuttings were taken.

CHAPTER 9

Pests and Their Control

Many rhododendrons and azaleas are grown with no special pest-control measures. In general, these plants are not especially subject to pests, and in areas where other gardeners grow either rhododendrons or azaleas satisfactorily, without particular attention to pest control, the logical thing would be to start with that procedure in mind, but be prepared to start control measures if some particularly obnoxious pest shows up. There are such pests, and control methods for most of them have been developed.

As rhododendrons and azaleas are so closely related, it would be expected that essentially the same pests would attack both groups. In general this is true. The term plant pests is understood to include insects, diseases, and certain animals, such as rabbits and moles. It might seem that weeds should be included, but they are customarily discussed under culture, probably because cultivation was for so long the principal means of control. As we develop new herbicides, and spray to eliminate weeds as well as insects and diseases, we may eventually come to think of weeds as pests, which of course they are. But here we shall stick to the three groups, and begin with the insects.

INSECT PESTS

A discussion of insects may well begin with their mouth parts, as these are used in classification, and determine the type of material to be used in their control. Some are sucking insects, with mouth parts which consist essentially of a hollow needle, which can be pushed into the leaf tissue, and through which the liquid and semiliquid cell contents may be sucked to nourish the insect. They must be controlled by contact sprays or dusts which kill when they touch, for sucking insects do not chew portions of the leaf, and so would not take in any stomach poisons with which it might be coated. Fortunately these insects are mostly soft-bodied, and fairly susceptible to good contact insecticides.

The chewing insects chew up and swallow portions of leaf or twig or bark, and so may be controlled by stomach poisons, although many are actually controlled in practice by contact sprays. Some insecticides work as both stomach and contact poisons. Leaf-eating caterpillars are examples of chewing insects, although the adult form, if a moth, may have sucking mouth parts for feeding on nectar.

A third type of insect has rasping mouth parts, exemplified by the various species of thrips. Contact sprays are most often used for this group.

APHIDS AND THEIR CONTROL

One of the common insects, and yet a type which seldom does much damage to rhododendrons, is the plant louse, or aphid. Aphids occasionally appear on the young leaves as they are beginning to expand in the spring. They may cause some twisting and curling of the leaves, yet seldom do any great amount of actual damage. The aphids may not be observed while they are feeding, but after the leaves have expanded they may be mottled or crinkled or otherwise distorted, and, the aphids having disappeared, the gardener may be baffled as to the cause. A further complicating factor is that this early-season aphid injury somewhat resembles that caused by spring frosts occurring as the buds begin to expand. Obviously there is nothing to be done when the misshapen leaves are seen, as the injury occurred long before.

As aphids normally feed on the underside of the leaf, and do not bite out a portion but simply suck the liquids out of the plant cells, they may easily be overlooked. When young leaves appear a little dull in color, and the blade tends to pucker and curve down more than usual, aphids should be suspected and examination made. Perhaps only a very few may be present, but they apparently inject a poisonous material when they feed, so the amount of damage may be out of proportion to the number of insects present.

Occasionally aphids may become fairly numerous on young seedlings or recently rooted cuttings in frames or greenhouse. When this is observed it would be advisable to apply an insecticide.

Nicotine and soap was the standard remedy for aphids for many years. However nicotine is not satisfactory unless the temperature at the time of application is fairly high, 70° or above. In many areas where rhododendrons grow well, such temperatures in early spring are not usually found. Malathion, one of the best contact insecticides, will give effective control at lower temperatures. Follow the manufacturer's directions as to proportions.

We have not observed any injury to the plants from the use of malathion, but some growers have reported that it caused damage to young seedlings in the greenhouse. When we have used it on such seedlings, hoping to profit by their experience, we have applied it as a dust, left it on for perhaps an hour, and then washed it off with an ordinary sprinkling nozzle on the hose. Since malathion is rather quick-acting, it apparently killed the insects with which it came in contact before it was washed off, and no damage was done to the plants. On larger plants no washing off would be needed.

THE LACE BUG

One of the most commonly observed insects on rhododendrons is the lace bug, or lace-winged fly. This is a small insect, the adult of which has lacy wings, which makes its identification easy. The young lace bugs, or nymphs, are rather spiny in appearance. They work on the undersides of the leaves, and cause injury by sucking the plant juices. The chlorophyll is destroyed where feeding punctures are made, resulting in a mottled, grayish or yellowish-gray discoloration. Where the insects are sufficiently numerous, the entire leaves may turn brown and die.

There is a separate but closely related species known as the azalea lace bug, which resembles the one attacking rhododendrons and causes damage in the same general way. These lace bugs are more numerous in the warmer parts of the country, and do the greatest damage during hot weather. In the Pacific Northwest, the azalea lace bug is apparently not established, and the rhododendron form is considerably less important as a pest than it is in the East and Southeast.

Lace bugs are controlled by contact sprays, which have to hit the insect to kill it. New spray materials are coming on the market all the time but, at the present writing, malathion seems to be one of the most effective. Nicotine sulfate is satisfactory where temperatures are high, although it is not too pleasant to apply. Lindane and DDT may be used. The latter may encourage the development of spider mites, and should be avoided as the killing agent in a regular schedule.

The spray should be applied in time to kill the nymphs before they have developed into adults. Two sprays, about ten days apart, should be sufficient to get a good cleanup.

RHODODENDRONS AND AZALEA WHITE FLY

Another insect which feeds on the underside of the leaves is the white fly. Here also there are separate species which work on rhododendrons and azaleas, but they are similar enough so that the same control measures are suitable for each. The white fly might be confused with the lacewing fly by those who are not familiar with both. The white fly, with its dull-white wings, appearing as if coated with flour, is about 1/10 of an inch across the expanded wings. The lace bug is considerably larger, and the lacy nature of the wings is quite evident.

The white fly also sucks plant juice from the underside of the leaves, and may cause a yellowing and mottling, which in some cases might be serious enough to cause appreciable injury. Control of white fly is also by contact sprays, such as those mentioned above.

SPIDER MITES

Another type of pest is the red spider, or spider mite, which also feeds on the underside of the leaves. This pest, not technically an insect, actually belongs to the closely related group of spiders. The mites cause small white dots to appear on the upper surface of the leaves, where they have sucked the plant juices from the underside. As the damage becomes more severe, it may cause the entire leaf to become whitish in color, and later brown and dry. With some susceptible plants, under hot, dry conditions, the plant may be killed.

There are different species of spider mites, but their type of feeding and the injury they cause, are somewhat similar, so I will not try to differentiate between them. They are very small, and almost always the damage to the plant is evident before the mites themselves are seen, unless one is looking for them with a hand lens. It takes a sharp-eyed person to spot the adult mites without a lens.

These mites are important greenhouse pests, where they attack many different kinds of plants. In the open they are likely to be serious only in regions where the climate is rather warm, and then particularly during spells of hot, dry weather.

Malathion, recommended for sucking insects, will give some control of spider mites, but it would be preferable to use one of the materials developed especially for mite control, such as Aramite or Ovotran.

Because the mites develop so rapidly and are so small, the infestation may become quite heavy before the gardener realizes it. These mites do some webbing, and may eventually be protected by these webs to an extent that makes good spray or dust contact rather difficult. In any case it is important to do a very thorough job, and to cover both sides of the leaves.

SCALE INSECTS

Scale insects comprise another group which suck the juices from the leaf, usually from the underside, but occasionally from either side. There are several species which attack rhododendrons and azaleas. They are very inconspicuous, and because they are covered with a grayish or brownish scale, it is difficult to tell without a hand lens whether what you see is a normal excrescence on the bark of the twig, or actually a scale insect. If a plant is growing vigorously and there is no stunting of leaf or shoot, scale insects are probably not present, at least in any serious quantity. However, if the plants are failing to grow as vigorously as they should, and certain branches seem to be stunted, it would be well to look for scale. In some areas these insects are frequently present on other woody plants, and that should give one a clue to inspect his rhododendrons and azaleas occasionally for evidence of these pests. In the Northwest a soft scale, rather large and brown, is occasionally found. They are not hard to see, as they are often on the top of the leaf, and so fairly conspicuous.

A type of insecticide which has been used effectively against scale insects is summer oil emulsion, applied at the manufacturer's recommendations. To effect control, of course, each insect has to be hit, and wet, with this material. Oil sprays will usually penetrate the protective covering, and actually kill the insect under the scale. Most other materials have to hit the young nymphs, or crawlers, when they are relatively unprotected. After the adult scales have developed a protective covering, they do not move about, and so would not pick up any contact material by crawling over it. When the eggs hatch, the nymphs do move about considerably, as that is the way the insect spreads from one part of the plant to another. The nymphs are fairly easy to kill by a contact material such as malathion. Different species of scale insects have slightly different life histories, so it is difficult to say just when a particular spray should be applied to hit the nymphs, in which case the oil emulsion might be most satisfactory.

It would be feasible to add a small amount of one of the other contact materials, such as malathion or lindane, to the oil emulsion, in order to increase the likelihood of good control.

If your rhododendrons are infested with scale insects, your county agricultural agent may be able to identify the species and tell you about its life history, so that an effective control program may be devised.

INSECTS IN THE GREENHOUSE

Insects not commonly found on plants grown outdoors may be a problem in the greenhouse. Among these are the cyclamen mite, which is sometimes a pest on greenhouse azaleas being forced for the florists' trade. These mites are practically invisible to the naked eye. They do, however, feed on the very tender tips, and cause the growth to stop and be somewhat distorted and stunted. The flowers will also be distorted and off-color.

The cyclamen mite is extremely difficult to control, partly because it feeds down in the unfolding buds, where it is almost impossible to make contact with a spray or dust. Fumigation may be effective, but should only be attempted after thorough study.

Thrips are also found occasionally on plants in greenhouses or cold frames. The adult thrips are tiny, cigar-shaped, black-bodied insects, about 1/20 of an inch in length. They are quite active, and will be seen running around on the leaves and new shoots if present in any quantity. Thrips feed by rasping the surface cells and eating the plant juices. The type of injury somewhat resembles that caused by spider mites. Greenhouse thrips can be controlled by a spray or dust of DDT, used according to the recommendations of the manufacturer. Malathion and lindane are also effective.

THE ROOT WEEVILS, CHEWING INSECTS

One of the most annoying pests of rhododendrons and azaleas, at least in the Northwest, is the larval stage of the root weevil or strawberry weevil, or black-vine weevil. There are three species of weevils which may cause damage, but as they are all somewhat similar in habit, and control measures are the same, they will be discussed together. These insects normally pass the winter as larvae, although some may winter over as adults. Usually the larvae are about half grown during the winter, and feed a little while in the spring, after which they pupate, and emerge from below the soil as adult weevils. The most common one, the black-vine weevil, is fairly typical, the adults being glistening black in color, and about ⅖ of an inch in length.

Injury by the vine weevil is of two types. The adults feed on the leaves, cutting little rounded notches into the leaf margins. This is usually not very serious, but it may disfigure the plants. The more serious damage is caused by the larvae's feeding on the bark just below the surface of the ground. Young rhododendrons or azaleas may easily be girdled, with all of the bark eaten off for a space of about an inch extending downward from just below the surface of the ground. This damage will not be visible for some time, as the plant can still take in water through the roots and transport it upward through the woody cylinder. However, complete girdling will cause death, usually within a year. When the plants begin to wilt and look very sick, it is too late to do anything about it.

CONTROL METHODS FOR WEEVILS

There are various control methods. Poison baits have been used for many years, and are fairly effective if placed around the plants early in April to kill overwintering adults, and along in May and June to kill the newly emerged adults. The baits, to be effective, must be in good, fresh condition when the weevils appear, but they tend to dry up soon or to be dispersed by rain, leaving the plants relatively unprotected.

A better control procedure is to use one of the newer insecticides such as aldrin or chlordane. If one of these is applied in the form of a dust, 2½ per cent for aldrin, or 5 per cent for chlordane, at the rate of about 1 pound to each 200 square feet, it will rather effectively protect against the weevil. Wettable or emulsifiable forms of these chemicals may be obtained, to be sprayed on the ground.

Where there are only a few plants, it is usually practical to make some kind of a "salt shaker," or secure a duster which will put out a fairly heavy volume of dust, and make a good application immediately around the base of each rhododendron or azalea plant. The newly hatched larvae crawl down into the soil at the crown of the plant, and will be killed when they come in contact with the insecticide.

Where the weevil larvae are already feeding on the roots, it would be possible to kill them with a good drench of one of these materials, but usually it is not very practical. By the time the damage is observed, it is usually too late to protect the plant showing the damage. The main thing is to keep a protective zone of treated soil around the stems of the undamaged plants.

OTHER INSECT PESTS

Asiatic beetles, including the Japanese beetle and the brown garden beetle, where they are prevalent, may feed on rhododendrons. They can be controlled by keeping the foliage covered with a stomach poison, such as DDT, during the latter part of the summer. Chlordane, aldrin, or lindane, used at the strength recommended by the manufacturer, should also give control.

There is a borer which may girdle the tips of azaleas or rhododendrons, and place an egg below the girdle. When the larva hatches from the egg, it bores downward through the pith, cutting holes to the outside at intervals. Usually the stem tips wilt and are quite evident. These weakened stems should be broken off, whenever seen, and destroyed.

APPLICATION OF INSECTICIDES

It should be remembered that while most sprays for the control of plant diseases are preventive in nature, and should be applied before the infection occurs, most of the insecticides, the contact sprays at least, are designed to actually kill the insect when it is present. This means, for instance, that putting on a spray of malathion early in the spring as a general treatment to ward off insect damage would not be successful. True, certain overwintering specimens might be killed, and thus prevented from starting an infestation. It is usually advisable to wait until the insects are visible, or perhaps some damage seen, and then go in and clean up the infestation. Sometimes no insect trouble may develop, and you may not need to spray at all. The danger is that the gardener may delay too long, and not notice the infestation until serious damage has been done.

In the Northwest, for instance, application of insecticides for many of the insects discussed is usually not necessary. In areas where lace-winged flies or white flies or aphids are prevalent, the gardener will come to learn about when to expect them and should be prepared, with the insecticide material on hand, to make the application at the proper time. A notable exception is the vine weevil, for which a preventive application is needed to kill the larvae, if and when they appear.

Many of the insecticides, such as malathion, may be applied as either a spray or a dust. They are about equally effective if properly applied. If the material is to be applied as a dust, it should be done early in the morning, or when there is very little wind. It may be difficult to direct the dust so that it comes up under the leaves in sufficient amounts. One of the usual hazards in dusting is a very small or inefficient duster, which does not put out enough material really to cloud up throughout the bushes to cover all parts, including both tops and bottoms of the leaves. With a spray it is possible to use an angle nozzle, so that the material may be forced up from the underside. It is fairly easy to tell whether the foliage has been wet or not, but it is sometimes difficult, after putting on a few puffs of dust, to tell whether the material has given thorough coverage.

DISEASES OF RHODODENDRONS AND AZALEAS

Just as insect pests often have to be identified by the type of injury that they produce, so diseases cause certain spots, discoloration, or abnormalities which provide circumstantial evidence that the disease organism is present. Most insects, when found, are large enough to be readily identified, whereas diseases are caused by microscopic organisms which usually operate inside the cell tissues. Positive identification in a laboratory involves not only microscopic examination, but often the growing of the fungus on some artificial medium, until it has produced fruiting bodies, or spores, which are important identifying characters. This being the case, it is understandable that gardeners may tend to suspect every spot and twisted leaf as being the result of a definite plant disease, and frequently that is true. However there are so many types of defects and injuries that resemble diseases that it is worth while to devote a section to them. As a matter of fact, of supposedly diseased leaves brought to me for identification, I am sure that at least half have been due to what I interpreted as physiological, or non-pathogenic troubles. It is hardly correct to call them diseases, although sometimes that term is used. The more accurate method is to use the term "disease" only when some living organism, as a fungus or bacterium, is definitely responsible.

PHYSIOLOGICAL TROUBLES

A common cause of rhododendrons' making poor or abnormal

growth, or even dying, is girdling. By this is meant the death or removal of the bark entirely around the base of the trunk. Since the nutrients elaborated in the leaves are translocated to the roots through the bark tissues, anything which interferes with their movement will result in eventual starvation and death of the roots. If the stem is only partially girdled, then only one side of the plant may die, or there may be just a slightly abnormal growth and eventual recovery. The first evidence of girdling is usually a pale color which resembles ordinary nitrogen deficiency. Actually it is a deficiency, because the roots, having been starved, are no longer able to take in nitrogen and other elements, and start them on their way throughout the plant. Later the leaves will droop and possibly curl, and eventually turn brown or drop off. By that time the damage is too severe to be remedied.

Fruit growers often rescue girdled apple trees by planting seedlings around the base of the trunk, and grafting them into the trunk above the girdle. This could possibly be done with rhododendrons, although I have never seen it tried. One would have to have seedlings available and do a careful job. It might be worth considering on a very large and valuable specimen if the damage is observed before the plant shows too much evidence of injury.

The causes of girdling are several. One fairly common cause is failure to remove plant labels attached by means of a wire. As the plant grows larger, the wire cannot stretch, so the plant grows around it but the conducting tissues of the bark do not join outside the wire. They turn in toward the center of the trunk, under the wire and out again. Eventually they are so restricted by the growth of the woody cylinder against the wire that they cease to function, and the plant is girdled. Plants affected in this way not only have their nutrients reduced or eliminated, but are very likely to break off, because the top is no longer adequately supported by the small amount of woody tissue enclosed within the wire girdle. This type of injury is less common than it used to be, due to the trend toward the use of paper labels rather than wired wooden labels. If you get any kind of a plant with a wired label on it, remove it from the main trunk and attach it very loosely to one of the side branches.

GIRDLING OFTEN CAUSED BY LOW TEMPERATURE

Another common cause of girdling is freezing injury. It seems that the most susceptible tissue of a rhododendron or azalea, at the time of late fall or early spring freezes, is just at the surface of the ground and two or three inches above. Very often the bark will be killed in this area, with no apparent damage to other parts of the plant. Consequently the injury is not observed at all until a few weeks later, when it will be found that the bark has cracked or split and the woody cylinder is exposed. If this damage extends entirely around the trunk, it is completely girdled and will usually die.

It is not advisable to discard such a plant as soon as the cracking of the bark is observed unless you consider it to be expendable anyway. Sometimes a few strands of cambium tissue will remain uninjured, sufficient eventually to regenerate good bark. I have seen badly injured plants which apparently had some undamaged cambium cells remaining attached to the split-off bark. These cells eventually produced some woody tissue inside the strands of bark. The old woody cylinder, completely exposed, died out, and the strands of bark developed enough wood to maintain the plant and eventually to close over the damaged area, thus hiding the no longer useful old woody cylinder. Such plants may be weak for two or three years but eventually recover. On the other hand they sometimes linger along for three or four years and then die.

There is so little anyone can do when an unseasonable freeze has occurred, except to hope that the injury has not been too severe. In some cases it might possibly help to bind the damaged bark tightly to the woody cylinder to prevent its splitting away entirely. This, if it has any value, simply gives a little better protection against drying out to possible undamaged strands of tissue. If the plant is completely girdled, and the bark and cambium are actually dead, then binding or other treatment would have no value. Later treatment of a plant injured but not killed is largely a matter of pruning out dead or severely injured wood, and shaping what is left by pinching or pruning to form as attractive a plant as possible.

Another very common cause of girdling which has already been discussed is that caused by feeding of the larvae of the black-vine weevil. It is mentioned here because the reaction of the plant to the girdling is the same, whether it is caused by insect feeding, by freezing, or by a root-rot disease organism.

NUTRIENT DEFICIENCIES AFFECT LEAF COLOR

Poor color of the leaves is sometimes thought to indicate a disease, when it is, in fact, caused by a deficiency of some essential nutrient element in the soil. Where nitrogen is deficient, the leaves will be yellowish in color, rather than a good, deep green. Certain varieties, such as 'Britannia,' normally have a light, yellowish-green color, whereas other varieties normally have a deep-green color. Where nitrogen is extremely deficient, the color becomes almost a bright yellow. It is sometimes a little difficult to tell whether a plant is deficient in nitrogen, or whether it has been girdled. However, nitrogen-deficient leaves usually remain erect and seem to be perfectly normal, aside from color, whereas the leaves of girdled plants are inclined to droop and curl. Obviously the cure for plants which are of poor color because of nutrient deficiency is to correct that deficiency, as discussed in Chapter 7.

Another cause of abnormal color is alkaline soil, which sometimes prevents the absorption or utilization of certain nutrient elements, depending on the degree of alkalinity, and the natural supply of those elements. Obviously the leaf color, pattern, or abnormality would vary somewhat, depending on how the various nutrient elements are affected.

As already stated, rhododendron leaves quite frequently are found to be dwarfed, crinkled, and abnormal in shape, the deformations' being caused by the feeding of aphids or other insects, or by slight frost injury when the leaves were very young. Whatever the cause, it may have occurred just as the buds were opening. Frost at this time may not have been noticed, or at least not in connection with the rhododendrons, which at the time showed no signs of injury. However, as the young leaves develop, the cells which were killed by frost or insects fail to grow, and the other cells expanding around them cause a crinkling and mottling of the leaves, and possibly serious deformation. A second flush of growth may produce perfectly normal foliage, so that there will appear to be a collar of deformed leaves. Obviously the only thing to do is to do nothing, as they will drop within a year or two, depending on the variety.

NORMAL LEAF DROP

Although most rhododendrons are evergreen, that does not mean that the leaves will remain attached to the plant indefinitely. Usually they will hang on for two, three, or even four years. Some varieties hold their leaves for a relatively long period, and so appear to be quite dense bushes, full of leaves well down on the branches. Others tend to drop their leaves after a year or two, and the general appearance is of rather open bushes with a tuft of leaves at the tips of the branches. The leaves that are normally getting ready to drop usually turn brown around the edges, or sometimes over the entire leaf, just before they fall. Such leaves may seem abnormal to the eye of the gardener, who may expect to see only broad, smooth, green leaves, especially if he does not realize that these leaves are on old wood, and have been subject to pests and the weather for three or four years. If the gardener becomes alarmed at the browning, and suspects a disease, it is easy to tell from the rings of foliage, indicating years of growth or, at least, cycles of growth, whether the brown leaves are recently developed or are at least two years old or older. If the latter is the case, and if the younger leaves are green and healthy-looking, there is nothing to be concerned about.

SUN AND DROUGHT INJURY

Certain varieties are rather susceptible to sun scald. If they are growing where they can be hit by the direct rays of the sun during midday or early afternoon, and if there is a period of very low humidity, possibly drying winds, and a fairly low soil-moisture content, the leaf tissues may be killed in large areas or splotches. This is called sun scald, although actually it is due to the drying out of certain areas of leaf tissue. After such tissues are killed, fungi sometimes start growing in the dead area, and may even produce fruiting bodies, which tend to confuse the correct identification of the trouble. However, it is usually obvious that such scald develops after extremely hot, dry weather, and mostly on plants that are exposed to full sun.

Another phase of such injury is that caused primarily by drought. Although there may be no actual death of leaves, plants suffering from lack of moisture, whether because of general drought or because of competition of trees or for other reasons, may make very poor growth and have very small leaves that tend to be rather pale and dull-looking. They may show some burning around the edges. Rhododendrons and azaleas, being relatively shallow-rooted, may show such damage when other shrubs, with deeper root systems, do not seem to suffer.

WIND DAMAGE

Most rhododendrons do not have a great deal of resistance to high winds. The usual way of saying this would be, "They do not like windy places, or do not like high winds." Plants with rather large leaves are more likely to suffer, because the wind exerts considerable pressure on the large surface, and thrashes the leaves around more or less violently. Such leaves may be blown from the plant, or the petiole may be broken so the leaf will hang downward.

Even where the leaf is not blown off, it may be banged against other leaves or twigs with the result that the tissue will be damaged around the edge or in certain spots, resulting in dead, brown areas. Such leaves may look rather bad. If one sees them at a later date, when the browning has become obvious and when no winds are blowing, a disease may be suspected. However, careful examination and consideration will usually enable one to identify such damage. Again one must think of prevention rather than treatment. The planting of rhododendrons where they will have some protection from winds, or the erection of a windbreak of some sort are the obvious procedures.

SYMPTOMS ASSOCIATED WITH POOR DRAINAGE

Rhododendrons and azaleas, although they require a plentiful supply of moisture in the summer, are easily damaged by too high a water table, or by the effect of heavy, poorly drained soil during the winter months. The damage may resemble that caused by girdling, or nitrogen deficiency. The leaves may be a little pale and dull, and even tend to droop. Gardeners are sometimes inclined to think that such plants are suffering from a disease, because other plants that may be well adapted to the poorly drained conditions make normal growth. Methods of avoiding this situation have been discussed in the chapter on soils.

THE ROOT ROTS

It is fitting that the discussion of diseases caused by actual pathogenic organisms begin with the root rots, as the symptoms are so similar to those caused by girdling or a high water table. The leaves will be rather yellowish and dull, and will droop rather distinctly.

There are several different organisms which cause root rots on rhododendrons or azaleas, some of which may occur in almost any locality. Probably the most serious one is a fungus called *Phytophthora cinnamomi*. The identification of the specific organism would be of no great value in many cases, as the treatment would be essentially the same whatever the organism.

If one suspects a root-rot disease he should examine the plant at the collar, just above and just below the surface of the soil. If the wilting or off-color is due to girdling by weevil or frost damage, that should be obvious after examination. If the bark appears to be undamaged, use a knife to cut into it at ground level. If a root-rot disease is present, the bark will be dead and brown, and the central woody cylinder will be brown, at least at its outer surface. This will mean that the root system is entirely dead, and the dying, from the tips of the roots upward, has reached the ground level. Obviously the plant is doomed.

The Phytophthora organism thrives primarily in poorly drained, heavy soils, and in lighter soils which are wet most of the time. The obvious thing is to provide good drainage. The old *R. ponticum,* so long used as an understock, was rather susceptible. Some varieties are undoubtedly resistant to a degree, but there is not enough data available at the present time to be able definitely to recommend varieties which would grow satisfactorily in Phytophthora-infested soil.

Phytophthora cinnamomi apparently grows throughout the soil mass, and has been reported at depths of 2 or 3 feet. It is obviously very difficult, if not impossible, therefore, to eradicate it by attempted soil sterilization. If conditions are such as to favor it, once it gets started in a rhododendron planting additional losses may be expected. This does not mean that all of the plants will die, but that occasional losses will probably occur.

REPLANTING WHERE PLANTS HAVE DIED
It is obviously taking a chance to replant a rhododendron in a spot where one has died because of root rot, but it is sometimes done without the new plant's becoming infected. There would seem to be very little more danger of infection of the roots of a newly set plant if it is located exactly where a previous one died than if it were placed 2 or 3 feet to one side, in view of the general distribution of

the organism in infested soil. Success will depend somewhat on the natural resistance of the variety, and whether or not the soil may be better drained than it was previously. There is a chance that the plant might grow indefinitely without becoming infected. Whether one replants in the same spot where plants have died, therefore, will depend on how much space he has and how anxious he is to have rhododendrons growing in that particular area. Certainly there is more likelihood of such a plant's succumbing to root rot than if it were planted quite a distance from where such damage had been observed. It is extremely difficult to determine whether the organism is present in the soil except by the death of susceptible plants. It may be present in soils where its presence is unsuspected, because soil drainage and aeration are good, providing good conditions for plant growth and poor conditions for the fungus.

BRANCH BLIGHT

A related disease, sometimes called branch blight, is caused by *Phytophthora cactorum*. Where this is prevalent, individual twigs may wilt and die. The disease may be confined to a small twig or it may move downward into a larger branch and eventually kill a large part of the plant or, in some cases, an entire plant.

It would probably be possible to prevent infection by the branch-blight organism by keeping the leaf and twig surface covered with a protective fungicide. However, the disease is usually not serious enough to warrant such heroic measures, as applications would have to be frequent and thorough. Many rhododendron plantings are never attacked by this disease, and most of those which do show some damage lose only a few twigs or branches. The usual procedure is to prune out and burn diseased branches whenever they are seen.

GRAY MOLD

In the humid part of the Northwest, gray mold, or *Botrytis cinerea*, occasionally attacks faded flowers. This is more likely to occur if there is a long rainy period during and immediately following blossoming. Such diseased flowers turn brown, and there is usually gray mold visible over the diseased surface. This would be of little importance except that the disease may extend down into the twig. Occasionally there may be enough of this to cause the loss of a number of twigs and branches. The removal of flowers as soon as they have faded is usually sufficient to prevent Botrytis infection of the twigs.

Botrytis has already been mentioned as a possible hazard in the seedling flat and the cutting bench. It may also attack seedlings and young, cutting-grown plants in the lath house or in the open, under conditions of lush growth and high humidity. Where such conditions exist, keeping the foliage covered with a protective fungicide such as captan will keep damage to a minimum.

LEAF SPOTS

There are various leaf spots affecting rhododendrons and azaleas. The causes of some are known, but others are caused by organisms not well known, or not identified. It may be rather difficult to tell whether spotting is due to an actual organism or to some weakness accentuated by poor drainage, drought, or other climatic factor. Most rhododendron growers do not become particularly concerned about a few spots on the leaves, especially if they occur on the older leaves, which may be partly hidden by the newer and uninjured leaves.

If the leaves of a particular variety, under your conditions, are usually covered with spots, it might be best to move the plant to a site where it would have better growing conditions, or to eliminate it and plant some other variety less prone to leaf spotting, which would probably remain undamaged. The standard treatment for leaf spots on all kinds of plants is to keep the leaf surface covered with a protective fungicide. Where damage is only occasional, or only on one or two plants, it may hardly be worth the effort to maintain this protective covering. However if the damage threatens to be severe enough so that it seems desirable to do something about it, then a protective fungicidal coating should be applied, following the directions of the manufacturer.

FUNGICIDES ARE PREVENTIVE ONLY

In using fungicides, it must be remembered that they are primarily preventive, rather than curative, and that applying them will not eliminate any spots that are already present on the leaf. The spots will not go away, and the disease organism inside the leaf, which caused them, will usually not be killed. In order to prevent such spots' forming in the future, the leaf surface would have to be covered with the fungicide at the time when the spores of the disease alight on the leaf. This is sometimes difficult to determine, unless extensive life-history studies of the disease organism have been made. If the time of spore formation is not known, to be sure of effective control, spraying would have to begin early in the spring and continue at least through the early summer, while the new leaves are developing.

Some gardeners seem to feel that they are morally bound to apply corrective measures when spots or disease injury of any type occurs. I have had friends describe a disease situation or bring in a specimen and want to know what to do about it. When I have said that I would just forget about it, and that the treatment is more troublesome than the amount of disease present would warrant, they feel much relieved and somewhat surprised at that philosophy. However, I think it is justified in many cases because of the fact that the treatment usually would not be effective if applied when the injury is evident, and it would require several applications of spray some months in the future to prevent possible damage which might not even occur the next year. There are some diseases, such as petal blight, which warrant serious attempts at control, especially in certain localities. I am simply pointing out that the gardener might well give serious thought to the effort and expense involved, as related to the probable benefits of attempting control of relatively unimportant diseases.

Although "typical" leaf spots are usually rather small and somewhat circular in shape, there are other foliage diseases which cause the death of larger areas of the leaf. Some may cover a rather large area, the injury's somewhat resembling sun scald. This may occur during the winter, and obviously is caused by an organism and not by heat or drought. It has been my experience that such injury may appear during certain winters and not others, and it is also more serious on some varieties than others. It could, in all probability, be controlled by a spraying program, but again the cost of prevention would probably outweigh the benefits, unless this leaf-scorch type of disease is very abundant.

AZALEA LEAF GALL

Evergreen azaleas are occasionally attacked by a fungus which causes leaves to swell and become thick and fleshy. The prevalence of this disease, known as azalea leaf gall, will depend somewhat on weather conditions. Picking off the galled leaves whenever they are seen and burning them is a good means of reducing the likelihood of infection the following year. Where the disease is very prevalent and causes enough disfiguration of the plants to be important, spraying with bordeaux, or other fungicides during spring and early summer will usually control it.

RUSTS ON RHODODENDRONS AND AZALEAS

There are several rust diseases affecting rhododendrons and azaleas, all characterized by masses of yellow or orange-colored spores. These spore masses erupt from the surface of a leaf, usually the undersurface, and of course provide the means of spreading the disease. In most cases the rust is probably not worth trying to control, partly because these organisms are notoriously difficult to control by the usual fungicides. In the second place, they usually cause very little actual damage to the plant. Sometimes the spots do not show up at all on the upper surface of the leaf, and so the presence of the disease may be entirely overlooked, unless one happens to turn the leaf over and see the fruiting bodies. One of the so-called antibiotic sprays, known as actidione, has shown evidence of giving rather satisfactory control of certain types of rust. Its use should be considered where the rust is particularly destructive, which is usually not the case.

At least some of the rusts tend to build up to a considerable degree during certain years, and then practically disappear during others. This behavior of the disease should be considered in planning any long-time control program. Furthermore many varieties exhibit what seems to be complete immunity, and others are highly resistant, to certain rusts.

DISEASES WHICH KILL THE FLOWER BUDS

The presence of dead flower buds in the spring is always a shock and an aggravation. This situation may be due to more than one cause. In some localities, and with certain varieties, the dead buds may be caused by low winter temperatures, sufficient to kill the buds but not otherwise seriously injure the plant. Obviously nothing can be done about this except to give protection the following winter, or to grow hardier varieties, or hope for milder winters.

In other cases the dead buds are due to the presence of certain disease organisms. In the humid areas, Botrytis occasionally affects the buds during the winter, so that by spring they are brown and lifeless. The obvious treatment is to spray with a fungicide during fall and early winter, which is a rather heroic treatment, as frequent applications would have to be made because of the frequent rainfall. Before doing much winter spraying, a rhododendron fan will put up with the loss of a few buds, or may even eliminate certain varieties which are especially susceptible to this type of injury.

Another disease resulting in the death of buds has caused some damage in other countries as well as in the United States. It is known as bud blast. Diseased buds turn brown, and the dead buds are covered with short, black bristles, each ending in a tiny knob, in which are borne the spores of the disease organism. The diseased buds should be removed and burned, as should all dead buds, whether or not the damage was caused by a disease. Spraying with a fungicide in the fall would probably check the bud-blast disease, but it has caused so little damage in this country that it is questionable whether such sprays are justified.

AZALEA PETAL BLIGHT

The most serious disease of this group of plants in the southeastern and southern states is undoubtedly flower blight or, as it is sometimes called, petal blight. It is especially serious on azaleas, but may also attack rhododendrons. The fungus causes small white spots to appear, which a little later turn brown. If the weather is warm and moist, the spots will rapidly enlarge and run together, so that the whole corolla becomes a slimy mass. These wilted flowers will remain on the plant longer than is normal, causing not only the loss of the flower, but the presence of an unsightly reminder of that fact. The organism overwinters on diseased petals which have dropped to the ground.

Control of petal blight is extremely difficult, and so prevention is much more satisfactory, if at all possible. If you live in an area where petal blight is not present, it would be well to be very careful about bringing in plants from areas where it does occur. If there is any doubt, when a new plant is received, remove and bury deeply the one inch of topsoil in which the disease might possibly be overwintering. Spraying with nabam or zineb has given effective control of the organism, but it is necessary to spray two or three times a week in order to keep the expanding petal surface covered with the protective fungicide. There is some evidence that actidione also may be effective against this organism. Since such frequent applications are costly and somewhat discouraging, it is suggested that, in areas where petal blight is prevalent, rhododendron or azalea growers should check with their local county agent or state experiment station to obtain the latest information on methods of control.

USEFUL FUNGICIDES

In discussing possible control of diseases, it has been suggested that fungicides be applied, sometimes without specifying which ones should be used. This was because there are several which would be about equally effective, and it seemed best to discuss them with respect to disease control in general, rather than in connection with specific diseases.

One of the oldest fungus-killing materials is copper, which has been used for so many years in the form of bordeaux mixture. That is still a very good fungicide, but is somewhat troublesome to mix, and it will leave a whitish residue on the foliage. Some of the newer formulations of copper, available in most garden stores, are easier to use than bordeaux, leave less residue, and will be just about as effective. The copper sprays are more or less general fungicides, whereas some of the newer materials will be very effective against one disease and much less so against another.

New and effective fungicides are appearing on the market quite frequently. In some cases the same fungicide may appear under more than one trade name, but usually the effective chemical will be specified on the package. Among the newer and more useful chemicals are captan, fermate, nabam, zineb, and others. They are somewhat simpler to use, and seem to be more specific in their fungicidal action than bordeaux.

Captan has proven effective as a fungicide for a number of diseases, and especially for the widely prevalent gray mold, *Botrytis cinerea.*

Fermate is a good fungicide for a wide range of diseases attacking horticultural crops. It is black in color and leaves a sooty deposit on the plants. Nabam and zineb are somewhat more specific in their actions, being used, as far as rhododendrons and azaleas are concerned, especially for petal blight.

Fortunately rhododendrons and azaleas, in most places, will require very little if any spraying, hence further discussion of fungicidal materials is hardly warranted. Certainly the beginner may assume that he can grow these plants satisfactorily without spraying, except in areas where petal blight or some other very destructive disease is prevalent.

MOLES AND THEIR CONTROL

Moles are frequently listed as pests causing damage to rhododendrons and azaleas. I doubt that they are any more harmful to these than they are to other plants, but they may make their burrows under rhododendrons and azaleas, resulting in the drying out of the soil which, for these plants, may be very harmful. At any rate, they are a nuisance and should be controlled, not only from the standpoint of the shrubs, but especially to protect the lawns. Various methods of controlling moles have been developed, some more fanciful than effective. Our own experience has been that a systematic trapping program is probably the best method of control.

RABBITS AND OTHER ANIMALS

Under our conditions, rabbits have not been serious pests. However in areas where the rabbits are numerous and where other food may be scarce, especially when there is heavy snow on the ground, there may be some likelihood of damage. The surest way to avoid damage is to fence out the rabbits. Obviously this is not always feasible or desirable. Repellent materials, if really effective, would be very helpful, and there are some on the market which are said to be useful. Where rabbit damage is seen or feared, it would be advisable to contact the county agent and see what is being recommended in your own locality. In many cases the family cat or dog, with a little help and encouragement, may prove to be useful repellents and may even succeed in catching a few of the marauders.

Deer, mountain beaver, and other animals occasionally cause damage to rhododendrons and azaleas. Physical exclusion, by means of fences, or trapping or otherwise destroying the offending animals, seems to be the only feasible solution. Repellents so far have not seemed to be particularly promising except, possibly, for rabbits.

Part Three

SPECIES AND VARIETIES FOR
GARDEN USE

CHAPTER 10

Rhododendron Species and Their Place in the Garden

The terms species and variety have been used rather freely in the preceding chapters. Most gardeners are probably familiar with these words and understand exactly what they mean, but we are writing primarily for beginners, and so it might be useful to define them at this point. The term "species" is used by botanists to designate groups of plants in the wild, groups of which all the plants are essentially alike. Of course the plants within a species are all individuals, and they do exhibit some variation, but they more nearly resemble other individuals within the species than plants in other species. Species may differ from one another in such characters as number of petals, or type of calyx, or in the number of stamens, or the presence of glands or scales on the pistil or on the underside of the leaf. In other words the distinguishing characters may be rather minute, but for botanical purposes they are sufficient. Some of the characters of greatest interest to gardeners, such as size of plant or of flower, or even color of flower, are less likely to be used to distinguish species because they tend to vary with the environment.

HOW NEW SPECIES ARE DETERMINED

The determination of species, especially in a large and varied group such as the genus *Rhododendron,* is a very difficult task. Collectors in the field may thrill to the sight of a new species, at least they feel sure it has never been named, but they do not forthwith name it after their youngest child or their home town. Instead specimens of leaf, twig, flower, seed pods, anything available, are collected and sent back to a botanic garden or other institution where specialists painstakingly compare the dried specimens with hundreds of others previously collected. With many plants, as is often true with rhododendrons, there may be a great range of types growing together, with ample opportunity for hybridization. A large number of specimens may have been collected, and when they are all examined and laid out for comparison, there may be an almost continuous series, with only very small differences between individual plants; and yet the extremes, at either end of the series, may be quite different, much too unlike to be placed in one species. And so the problem is to find the dividing point, where one species leaves off and another begins, and which specimens represent hybrids between two rather similar species.

The classification of rhododendrons has been a terrific job, and we can appreciate the problems of the botanists as they restudy the herbarium material and occasionally conclude that two previously named species should have been considered as one and the same, or that some other species includes such varied forms that it ought really to be two, or even three. Or perhaps the same type of plant had been collected by two fieldmen, and one deposited specimens in Germany, the other in Japan, where they were studied by different botanists and were, inevitably, given different names. Eventually herbarium sheets would have been exchanged, or perhaps seed, and it would finally be evident that there were two names for what should be one species. Then it must be determined which has priority— which was first published, not first discovered. There is little wonder we occasionally find names listed as synonyms. We sometimes feel rather unhappy when the botanists change a name with which we have been long familiar to one that may seem strange and somewhat outlandish. But there is a reason, and if scientists did not live up to the rules of classification they have established, confusion would reign supreme.

THE HORTICULTURAL VARIETY

The word variety has a slightly different meaning as used by botanists and by horticulturists. As used by the former, it is a term to designate a group, within a species, which exhibits some rather slight difference from the other individuals of the species. As used by horticulturists, and usually specified or implied as horticultural variety, the term, when used for woody plants, ordinarily refers to shrubs or trees which have been propagated from one single, original, individual plant. Such a group, which goes back to one individual plant, and which has been propagated asexually—that is, by cuttings, layers, or grafting—constitutes a clone. Clonal varieties, therefore, are always increased by some asexual means of propagation.

Species plants are usually propagated by seed, but when superior forms are selected for increase, they must be propagated asexually, and so become clonal forms of the species. Most of the rhododendron species were collected originally as seed. When a plant explorer is "far enough out" to find previously undiscovered species, the bringing back of living plants is usually impossible. This is especially true of those species from the foothills of the Himalayas, a number of which were discovered at elevations of 10,000 to 14,000 feet, in remote valleys where it was extremely difficult just to get in and out, to say nothing of taking out plants or living propagating material other than seed.

HOW SPECIES PLANTS ARE PROPAGATED

Many of the species, as would be expected, come very nearly true from seed. Most of the species plants now being sold have been grown from seed obtained from plants grown from the original seed introduction. These plants have been in botanic gardens or in private collections, frequently in large collections where there is a great opportunity for cross-pollination with other species. Under these conditions some species still come very true to type, indicating that practically all the seedlings are the result of self-pollination, or crossing between two plants of the same species. In other cases there is such wide variation that apparently intercrossing between species must occur about as readily as self-pollination, or crossing within the species. To be really certain that one has a particular species, therefore, it is almost essential to go back to the botanical description and see whether or not the plant fits.

Where the seed from a particular species ordinarily produces a rather varied lot of seedlings, it is obviously taking a chance to purchase such a seedling if what is wanted is a plant that is definitely representative of a given species. For the average gardener interested in the landscape worth of the plant rather than its ancestry, this is not too important, provided the plant one gets is desirable from the standpoint of its flowers and plant characters. Where there is a great deal of variation in seedlings, there is a good chance that some will be inferior. It is not always feasible for the nurseryman to grow the seedlings until they blossom in order to determine their horticultural value. This is particularly true of some of the larger-growing species, where several years may be required before flowers are produced.

SELECTED FORMS

The obvious way to insure desirable plants of the species you want is to purchase individuals which have been propagated asexually from superior, selected plants of the species. Such selections have actually been made in a number of species. As an example, *R. augustinii* at its best is a rather satisfactory, free-growing type with flowers that are as blue in color as will be found in the genus *Rhododendron*. When seedlings of *R. augustinii* are grown, however, many of them will produce flowers inferior in color, somewhat muddy and purplish or pinkish, rather than a good blue. Various people have noted this, and have selected out especially fine forms with good blue flowers, some of which have been named. When these are grown from cuttings, of course the resulting plants are all genetically alike and, except for environmental differences, are identical.

These clonal forms of certain species have sometimes received names, sometimes not. From comparatively few of the 800 to 900 rhododendron species have superior clones been selected and named, or otherwise identified. This may be because the general run of seedlings of a particular species is good, or no especially outstanding individuals have appeared, or the species is easy to grow from seed, or it is difficult to root from cuttings, or a combination of any or all of these factors. Many rhododendron species are still quite rare. It might be said that there has not yet been time enough for selections of superior forms to have been made. Undoubtedly there will be many more selections in the future.

A nurseryman may have a good clonal form of a species and use it in propagating, but never bother to name it. He probably advertises the plants as grown from cuttings of "a good form." Sometimes these become known by the man's name, and so we might speak of Smith's form of *R. racemosum*. In other cases a particular plant may have received an award from the American Rhododendron Society, the Royal Horticultural Society, or possibly some other group. The plants propagated asexually from that original award plant would then be known as the award form, or the P.A. form, or the A.M. form, as the case might be. Still other selections may have a horticultural name given to them just as is done for a superior selection from a group of hybrid seedlings. This name may be descriptive or may simply be the name of a person, or a place, or anything else that the person who names it decides to use to distinguish this form from all others. There are rules of nomenclature to be followed in order to avoid duplication or confusion. One of these is that horticultural varieties are to receive names in English or the language of the country of the breeder, and not Latin. Latin is reserved for botanical names. Most horticultural varieties are the result of hybridization between two species, or between a hybrid and a species, or between two hybrids. Most of the presently cultivated rhododendrons and azaleas fall in this category, and they will be discussed in Chapter 11.

WHY GROW THE SPECIES?

The question might well be asked as to why species rhododendrons should be discussed at all in a book for beginners. Nearly all of the rhododendrons and azaleas on sale in the nurseries are hybrids, and it is somewhat difficult to secure species except from various specialists. Many known species cannot be purchased anywhere in this country. Why bother with species at all?

Most other ornamental plants are grown as hybrids. We do not usually think of trying to find for our gardens the original species from which our dahlias or gladiolus or other garden flowers were produced. Presumably what we have now is superior to the original species, which were collected in the wild. That is true for most plants, but not all. It is not entirely true for rhododendrons.

It has been said that a rhododendron fan who eventually becomes a real "bug" begins with the larger, gaudier hybrids. Next he may grow some of the more subdued types of hybrids, then dwarf hybrids, and finally, after some years, most fans become interested in the species. There is enough truth in that to indicate that the species have something to attract the gardener. A few might be attracted by the historical or scientific aspect and want the original species, whether they are decorative or not, but that is not why most rhododendron fanciers plant the species. It is because there are types and colors and forms available in the species which are not available in the hybrids. Many of the species are probably a little more refined, a little better "balanced" as to plant and flower.

THERE IS A PLACE FOR BOTH SPECIES AND HYBRIDS

In the case of many of the dwarf species, and some of the large-leaved ones as well, no hybrids have been made which are superior to the species themselves. Many of the species provide excellent and unusual landscape plants. It is my opinion that it will be many, many years before the growing of species rhododendrons is eliminated, or reduced to any great degree, by the availability of hybrids that are superior to the species as garden plants. Better hybrids are being produced, but more species are becoming available for American gardens, and better selections of species already well known are being made. The practical way to look at it would be that both the species and varieties will continue to be important landscape material for the average gardener, as well as for the hobbyist, for a long time in the future.

The first rhododendron species were introduced to cultivation about 150 years ago. Most of the important and some of the most decorative species, however, were not introduced until about 100 years ago and later. As indicated in Chapter 2, these were mostly established in private collections and botanic gardens in England, and were introduced into this country at a much later date. As a matter of fact, there are many species described in botanical literature which are not yet being grown any place in the United States. In many cases the plants raised from the first seed which was introduced into England are still alive and growing there.

When some of the early-introduced species were crossed with each other, the offspring were particularly impressive so far as size and color were concerned. At that time the emphasis was on plants for large estates, where a rhododendron plant 15 to 20 feet in height and spread, with very large, brightly colored flowers could be grown with many other plants on a similar scale to make a magnificent picture. As with most other plants, the emphasis for some time was on improvement, by breeding, of size of flower and brightness of color. These characters are impressive and have value, especially for use in large gardens. For the impulse buyer in the nursery or garden center, they probably may be the deciding factor.

Many of the species, especially the dwarfs, produce very fine plants when grown from seed. The plant characters—that is the bush, its

general shape and compactness, the foliage, and the harmony between flower and plant character—are especially good. One can be
amazed and attracted to a large plant of 'Pink Pearl,' for instance,
with its very large blooms and attractive show. However when the
flowers have fallen, the plant looks rather open—perhaps a bit leggy
—and one is tempted to plant some other shrub in front of it to hide
the lower half of the rhododendron. A great many of the species
plants are better balanced and better filled out, and bear close inspection very well whether in bloom or out of bloom.

There is further reward in the growing of species seedlings. As
previously indicated, they may come relatively true to type, but not
identically so. Even those which come very nearly true will have
enough variation so that one can pick out individuals which are a
little better than the average. With some of the others, where variation is considerable, or where cross-pollination may have occurred,
there is always the incentive of possibly finding a superior plant or a
new hybrid which may be outstanding and worth while.

HOW TO OBTAIN SPECIES RHODODENDRONS

Since most nurserymen handle only the hybrids, finding a source
of species plants may be something of a problem. However there
are a few nurserymen who do specialize in the growing of species
plants, and if one really looks for them, they can be found. Perhaps
as many as 300, or even more, species of rhododendrons and azaleas
are available in nurseries in this country. The beginner who becomes
a real rhododendron fan may soon become interested in raising his
own species plants from seed. This will give him plants at a reasonable price, if he is lucky, and will present him with an opportunity to
look for superior seedlings of his own raising. The growing of rhododendrons from seed was discussed in the chapter on propagation.

HOW THE SPECIES ARE CLASSIFIED

Although possibly less than half that many are available in this
country, there have been close to 1000 bona fide species described
by the botanists. The problem of classification is very difficult in a
group as large as this. The botanists, therefore, have devised a
method of grouping the large number of species so they will be easier
to study and easier to keep in mind. This has been done by placing
each species in one of a number of so-called series, forty-three series

in all, as presently constituted. Each series is named after a type species. For instance, the Fortunei series is typified by the species *R. fortunei,* and includes others which are somewhat similar. The true rhododendron fan soon becomes interested in the series and speaks glibly of them, and the beginner should know at least that there is such a thing as groups of species, which are known as series.

Where as many as several hundred species of a particular plant group are available, it is obviously impossible for the beginner to go into the field very deeply. On the other hand, this very large number of species and the extreme variation from small prostrate, ground-cover types to large trees does provide a wonderful opportunity for a garden enthusiast to make a thorough study, and possibly a large collection, of species. It is true that many people who have been growing rhododendrons for years and have become really interested in them have become collectors, although their collection may be used strictly as a landscape planting around their home.

In a book of this type it would seem that the discussion of species should be limited to those which are good garden subjects, and which have some reason for being preferred to hybrid varieties. On that basis a few of the many rhododendron species worthy of considera-tion by the beginner are listed, with some comments based largely on personal experience and, perhaps, personal likes and dislikes. A few azalea species are extremely fine things, and several are listed in Chapter 12, but probably there will be a greater preponderance of hybrid azaleas grown than may be true of the other rhododendron groups.

SPECIES WHICH ARE GOOD GARDEN PLANTS

The following species might be considered by any beginner to be good garden plants—as good as, or better than, named horticultural varieties. Whether a gardener can grow them depends on his climatic and soil conditions. Ratings as to hardiness have already been dis-cussed in Chapter 6, and should help considerably in enabling you to determine whether you should try a particular species. To be doubly sure, it might be well to check with some experienced rhodo-dendron growers in your community, if any are available. It will be noted that some are greenhouse subjects under any but semitropical conditions. The quality ratings, x to xxxx, are based on the better forms of the species and not on the average.

Above: (Loderi G.) 'King George,' one of the largest and finest of white rhododendrons.

Right: A prize-winning truss of (Loderi G.) 'Pink Diamond,' as exhibited in an American Rhododendron Society show.

Below: A very full, tight truss of 'Lake Labish,' which won a gold cup as best American seedling in the show.

Right: A grand-champion truss of 'Mars.'

Rounded trusses of 'Dr. O. Blok.

R. *calophytum* is grown almost as much for its large, attractive foliage as for its beautiful flowers.

A free-blooming plant of 'Countess of Derby.'

'Mrs. Charles Pearson' has fine foliage as well as attractive flowers.

Rhododendron flowers are always at their best with trees as a background. This is 'Mrs. Charles Pearson.'

The golden-yellow azalea 'Altaclarense.'

Light-pink, 'Mrs. E. C. Stirling' has tall, well-shaped trusses.

Heavy bloom for a small plant of 'Aunt Martha.'

The blue dwarf 'Sapphire' rhododendron has small, neat foliage, attractive all the year.

One of the more reliable large-leafed species is *R. fictolacteum*.

R. makinoi is a hardy and decorative species.

A very early, large-leafed species is *R. calophytum*.

'Countess of Athlone' is of that mauve color not favored by most rhododendron fanciers, but it is early-blooming and reliable.

'China,' pale ocher in color, is a beautiful sight, contrasted against an evergreen background.

The choice of these particular species to be listed in a book for the beginner may raise a lot of questions and some objections. However it is not suggested that any beginner, or even any advanced amateur, try to plant all of the species here listed, any more than he should attempt to plant all the hybrid varieties to be discussed later. When making up the list, I attempted to put down only those which had something special to recommend them, in addition to being relatively easy to grow.

Those who know rhododendrons better than I may not agree entirely with this list. Certainly there are many species with which I am not familiar that may eventually become common garden subjects.

R. augustinii—xxxx, H–3. This is one of a number of species belonging to a group known as the Triflorum series, all of which are rather slender-twigged, upright-growing, with fairly small leaves and small to medium-sized flowers. This one grows to 12 feet or more in height, reaching 4 to 6 feet in ten years. The color, in seedlings, ranges from a lavender blue to violet blue—some rather muddy, but a few with a very good blue color. There are some selected forms, such as the Exbury and Tower Court forms, better in color than the average of seedlings, although some seedlings may be as good or even better. Plants of this species are particularly good to use in the background of a shrub planting, especially among or in front of coniferous evergreens. The flowers always look better at a little distance than they do close up.

R. auriculatum—xxx, H–3. Plants will reach 6 feet in ten years. The flowers are attractive, white and sweet-scented. This is one of the latest-flowering species, blossoming into July and August. Such late flowering brings out the blossoms at a time of high temperature and low humidity, therefore the plants should have a little shade and careful attention to adequate watering.

R. burmanicum—xx, H–5. This plant, with greenish-yellow flowers, will reach a height of about 3 feet in ten years. It is rather tender, but has done well in the San Francisco area. It is sweet-scented.

R. caeruleum—xxxx, H–3. This particular species, of the Triflorum series, has flowers from practically pure white to deep rose-lavender. The charm of this species, and others closely related to it, is in its airy beauty as a flowering shrub in the landscape, rather than in the size and brilliant color of individual flowers. The white form in particular has been very attractive in the Northwest. The leaves have a glaucous or whitish appearance which makes them attractive throughout the year.

R. calophytum—xxxx, H–3. This rhododendron will make a small tree eventually, but will reach a height of about 5 feet, and somewhat greater spread in ten years. The leaves are large and striking the year round. A particular merit of this species is its extremely early blooming habit, during March or April in the Northwest. It has fairly large white or pinkish flowers with a deep blotch.

R. calostrotum—xxx, H–3. A dwarf type reaching about 2 feet in ten years. The bright, rosy purple flowers stand up above the foliage in clusters of one to three. The slightly grayish, small leaves stand up pertly and are attractive the year round.

R. campylocarpum—xxxx, H–3. Yellow color in a number of well-known hybrids is derived from this species, which usually produces canary-yellow flowers. The species plants are very attractive, and frequently have better foliage characters than some of the hybrid offspring of campylocarpum crosses. It will make a small-sized bush, some 3 or 4 feet tall, in ten years.

R. campylogynum—xx, H–2. A dwarf, spreading shrub, eventually reaching 1 to 1½ feet in height. The leaves are small and an attractive shade of green. The flowers are also small, bell-shaped, and rosy purple in color.

R. camtschaticum—x, H–2. This is a novelty for the rock garden, seldom reaching more than 1 foot in height. It is deciduous, and the reddish-purple flowers stand erect above the foliage. It is quite hardy, as the name would indicate.

R. carolinianum—xx, H–2. This native of our own Southeast is one which should be grown much more extensively. It will reach a height of about 3 feet in ten years, at which time it will have spread to a width of at least 5 or 6 feet. The rather small flowers are borne in profusion. The type is rosy purple or pink, but there is a white form which produces flowers that are white to very light pink in color. As with most species, some seedlings are much more attractive than others, and more selecting of good forms should be done. Its relative hardiness—although not quite as hardy as the following—and other good characters recommend it to gardeners almost anywhere rhododendrons can be grown.

R. catawbiense—x, H–1. This is another native species, covering square miles of hillside in the Blue Ridge Mountains. The rhododendron fancier may not think too much of it, because of its lilac-purple flowers, and as a specimen plant it is not very useful. However for planting in the background or in the edge of a woods, where it may be viewed at a little distance, it has a real place. Its extreme hardiness permits it to be grown where most other rhododendrons will fail. It is one of the parents of most of the old, hardy hybrids, and is responsible for their ability to resist low temperatures. Many thousands of plants have been collected from the wild and sold throughout the East. Selected nursery-grown forms would undoubtedly give better satisfaction, as many of the collected plants have had poor root systems, and either died or were slow in becoming established.

R. chapmanii—x, H–3. This is still another native to the United States, especially noteworthy because it grows naturally in the sandy soils of northern Florida. It is probably more tolerant of hot, dry weather than most any other species. It is reported to make a shrub up to 6 feet in height, although the ones I have seen have been rather reclining in growth, with ascending tips, reaching up to perhaps 3 feet above the ground. This species is suggested as a landscape item only in the South, where it is native. It should eventually be thoroughly tested in breeding experiments to see if it might provide more drought-resistant hybrids.

R. chryseum—xx, H–2. Yellow is rather rare in the dwarfs, and this is one of the best, although the color is usually a rather light yellow. It will reach little more than 1 foot in height in ten years. I have seen it used very effectively with some of the blue-flowered dwarf hybrids and species.

R. ciliatum—xxx, H–4. This very early-blooming, white-flowered, small shrub is a relatively hardy species in that group known as the Maddenii series, which includes many of the very spectacular but very tender species, usually seen only in conservatories.

R. cinnabarinum—xxx, H–3. This is supposed to make a fairly large shrub eventually, but the ones I have seen have been rather small, reaching perhaps 3 or 4 feet in ten years. The flowers are cinnabar red, and rather long and tubular.

R. davidsonianum—xxx, H–4. This is another of the Triflorum group, forming slender-twigged shrubs to a height of 4 or 5 feet in ten years, and eventually to 8 or 10 feet. The flowers, mostly light pink or purplish pink with red spots, are fairly small, but borne in such profusion that from some little distance the plants in bloom have a very appealing, pink, cloudlike appearance.

R. degronianum—xx, H–3. The plants of this species that I have seen have made a fairly open, spreading growth, which would reach about 2 feet in ten years. The flowers have been a clear, soft pink, quite decorative, and worthy of being better known.

R. desquamatum—xx, H–3. Good background shrubs are not too numerous in the rhododendron genus, and this is a good one, growing quite rapidly when it is young and reaching a height of 5 or 6 feet, or even more, in ten years. The flowers are mauve, or pinkish purple, and not especially beautiful from close up. This, like many species of the Triflorum series, should be grown as a border shrub or in the background, where its rich green, shiny foliage makes it useful throughout the year.

R. falconeri—xxxx, H–4. This is one of the so-called large-leafed species that, in its native Himalayan region, reaches a height up to 50 feet. The creamy white to yellow, purple-blotched flowers are attractive, but the main attraction is the large shiny leaves. It is a bit tender for any but the mildest sections of the Northwest, but in parts of the South and some of the California coastal areas a few gardeners may grow it very successfully. Not for the average gardener, perhaps, but it becomes a conversation piece in any garden where it will thrive.

R. fictolacteum—xxx, H–3. Another of the large-leafed species, grown more for foliage than flower, this has a distinct appeal and is probably the hardiest of the group. It grows rather tall, reaching some 6 feet in ten years. The creamy white flowers are fairly large and attractive. Anyone who wishes to experiment with the large-leafed types might well begin with this.

R. hippophaeoides—xxx, H–3. This upright-growing little shrub, with pale-lilac to rose flowers, is grown fairly widely in the Northwest. It will reach a height of 2 feet or a little more in ten years. It is rather upright in growth, and perhaps is best used behind other, lower-growing plants, rather than at the very front of the border.

R. impeditum—xxx, H–2. An attractive rock garden plant with purplish-blue to mauve flowers, this little rhododendron at ten years will be not much over 1 foot in height. It is good not only for the rock garden but as a border plant in front of larger shrubs. Its hardiness and general desirability have made it one of the most familiar of the dwarf species.

R. keiskei—xxx, H–2. There are two distinct types of this species being grown in American gardens at the present time. At least it is presumed that they are the same species, although one is a very distinct dwarf and the other is a more upright type that will reach around 3 feet in ten years. Both have a rather attractive, light-yellow flower, appearing early in the spring. The dwarf *R. keiskei,* in my opinion, is a very valuable plant. It makes a little rounded mound, which probably will not get much taller than 1 foot. The foliage is good, and the plant is hardy in the vicinity of New York City. This species comes as nearly true from seed as any I have seen. We will undoubtedly hear more of this dwarf form.

R. keleticum—xxx, H–2. The name means "charming," which well describes this spreading, dense-growing little rhododendron. It will reach a height of about 1 foot or less in ten years. The flowers are wide open, resembling in size and shape the flowers of a pansy. The color is purplish crimson with crimson spots. The flowers stand up singly above the foliage, flower and stem on young plants often reaching to double the height of the foliage. Very desirable for the rock garden.

R. leucaspis—xxxx, H–4. This is another dwarf, with small, rather fuzzy leaves. The buds develop to an immense size, compared to the size of the plant, during the fall, and burst into bloom in February or March in the Northwest. Unfortunately this early blooming frequently results in flowers' being caught by an early frost with disastrous results to the open flowers, although the plant itself seems to be quite hardy. It would seem to me that in milder areas—in California or the South —this little dwarf might be very satisfactory, and would probably bloom in midwinter. The flowers are relatively large, milky white.

R. lutescens—xxx, H–4. There is an F.C.C. form of this, which I shall describe because it seems to be quite superior to the average run of seedlings. This form has slender, upright twigs, which seem to grow continuously, rather than form large terminal flower buds, as do most rhododendrons. The spring foliage is bright, bronzy red, a color which may fade somewhat during the summer and deepen again in the fall, one of the brightest foliage colors in the genus. The flowers are primrose yellow, and appear quite early in the spring. For an unusual rhododendron, which has a most striking and unusual plant and foliage appearance, this is worth considering in areas suitable for plants with an H–4 hardiness.

R. macabeanum—xxxx, H–4. This is one of the large-leafed species, which is reasonably hardy and which has a very beautiful yellow or yellowish-white flower, blotched with purple at the base. As it becomes more generally available, it should increase in popularity wherever it can be grown.

R. macrophyllum—x, H–2. This is the native rhododendron along the West Coast and on some of the foothills of the mountains in the Pacific Northwest. The color is pale rose to purplish rose, and only moderately attractive. Most rhododendron fanciers would not include it in their collection for its flowers. However in the coastal areas of the Northwest, many plants transplanted from the wild have developed into rather striking, large, late-blooming shrubs. Frequently seen as specimen plants, it would seem that they are best fitted for background or light woodland use. Although rated rather hardy, it is quite possible that some of the seaside strains may be moderately tender.

R. makinoi—xx, H–3. This makes a low, rounded bush, up to about 3 feet in ten years. The foliage is particularly good—rather narrow, but dark, lustrous, green leaves. The flowers are a good, soft pink, and the plants should be very useful in the landscape.

R. maximum—x, H–1. Shade-tolerant and hardy, this species, native to the eastern United States, makes an attractive shrub, up to 5 or 6 feet in height in ten years. The flowers are pale pink to deep pink, and the leaves tend to develop before the late-opening flowers appear, which detracts from its value as a flowering shrub. For woodland planting in very cold areas, it is quite useful.

R. micranthum—x, H–1. The tiny white, spirea-like flowers may cause some rhododendron fanciers to treat this as a "poor relation." However for border planting or mass planting in relatively cold climates, it is worth consideration. Size will run up to 4 feet in ten years.

R. moupinense—xxxx, H–4. This is one of the very early-blooming dwarfs, or semidwarfs, which will grow to perhaps 2 feet in ten years. The pink or rose-purple, spotted flowers are quite attractive, and particularly so because of their early appearance. This is a very desirable rhododendron species.

R. mucronulatum—xx, H–2. There are relatively few deciduous rhododendrons, and none more commonly grown than this. Its hardiness and very early blooming have made it a popular subject over most of the rhododendron-growing part of the United States. The bright, rosy purple flowers appear in very early spring, or in midwinter in mild climates, and make a very attractive sight, as they appear well before the leaves. A selected form has been given the clonal name 'Cornell Pink.'

R. neriiflorum—xxxx, H–4. This is a free-flowering, rather small-growing species, reaching perhaps 3 feet in ten years. The flowers are scarlet or crimson, and borne in great profusion.

R. nuttallii—xxxx, H–6. It is unfortunate that this, one of the most striking of the rhododendron species, is so tender that it is a conservatory subject in most parts of the country. It grows outside only in areas that are practically frost-free. The flowers are light yellow, or white-flushed yellow, very large, fragrant, and long funnel-shaped. The individual flower is as impressive as anything in the genus.

R. oleifolium—xx, H–3. This is a semidwarf species, with rather small leaves, and flowers of medium size, usually rose or light pink. It is a very pretty thing.

R. orbiculare—xxx, H–3. This is a rather spreading, slow-growing shrub, eventually reaching moderate size, but only 2 or 3 feet in ten years. The leaves are almost round, which gives it its name. The rose-pink flowers are freely borne, and the result is a very attractive landscape shrub, usually well rounded and symmetrical.

R. oreotrephes—xxx, H–3. Another of the very useful Triflorum series, this species has attractive leaves, rather small and glaucous, or whitish, over the green. Like others in this series, it is especially good for the background, or for planting in front of evergreen trees.

R. pemakoense—xxx, H–3. As a rock garden subject, this little shrub is very useful and attractive. It is very free-blooming, producing small pinkish-purple flowers, which appear rather large on the tiny plant. After ten years a plant of this species will probably be less than 1 foot high, but will have spread to a diameter considerably greater than that.

R. ponticum—0, H–3. This species is usually looked down upon by the rhododendron fan—partly, I suppose, because of its wide use as an understock for grafting purposes, and because it has naturalized so freely in parts of England. However the rosy, purplish flowers look quite attractive, if seen at a distance, especially if grown in an open woodland or against evergreen trees. This species, which has escaped from cultivation in England, makes dense thickets and is occasionally used for sheared hedges, much as English laurel is used in the Northwest. As a general rule, plants of this species are not sold as such, but gardeners frequently find them in their own rhododendron plantings where a more tender scion variety has succumbed, and the root stock has sent up shoots which bear the tell-tale purplish flowers. The reason for including this species, with an "0" rating, in a book of this kind is to suggest that if you have such an understock plant, don't dig it up and throw it away without consideration. If you have a place for it in the background, it will make quick and attractive growth, and the flowers, if considered as just part of the border and not as specimen flowers, will add to the garden picture.

R. prostratum—xx, H–3. This is one of the very low-growing, rock garden types. It might eventually reach a height of 1 foot after many years. The flowers, large for the very small plants, are open-faced and crimson, or deep purple-rose.

R. racemosum—xxxx, H–2. Of all the species rhododendrons, this is probably grown as widely and has proven as satisfactory as any. It starts out as a rather dwarf shrub, but might reach a height of 3 feet in ten years. However it may keep on stretching up and reach 4 or 5 feet eventually, unlike some other dwarfs which make a fairly rapid growth when young, but increase in stature hardly at all after they reach blooming age. This little species starts to bloom almost the first year, and never lets up, and apparently does not let its blooming interfere with a reasonably vigorous growth. The flowers are rather small, mostly deep pink to a fairly light pink or almost white. They are produced very profusely, and the over-all effect is of a very attractive, dainty little shrub. It is very easily grown, and resistant to unfavorable growing conditions. Some strains have been selected for hardiness, and so it can be grown over a rather wide climatic range. Other strains have been selected for dwarfness, but even the more rapidly growing plants stand pruning well and may be kept quite small.

R. radicans—xxx, H–3. This is one of the lowest of the rhododendron species, reaching 6 inches to 1 foot only after many years' growth. The flowers are purplish and the leaves small. Quite attractive in the rock garden.

R. rubiginosum—xx, H–2. Somewhat similar to *R. desquamatum,* but this species has slightly narrower leaves. The rosy lilac flowers and dark-green foliage make it an attractive plant for the back part of the shrub border.

R. russatum—xxxx, H–2. This is a rather upright-growing, small shrub with deep rosy-purple to blue-purple flowers, usually with a white throat. It may reach 3 feet in ten years.

R. sargentianum—xxxx, H–3. Of the very dwarf yellows, this is one of the daintiest and best. The color ranges from a medium light yellow to almost white, and I believe there is a pure white form. At any rate the small leaves and flowers make a very attractive and compact little rock garden shrub, seldom reaching more than 1 foot in height.

R. sinogrande—xxxx, H–4. One of the finest, if not the finest, of the large-leafed rhododendrons, this species, where conditions are to its liking, will produce leaves up to 18 inches, or occasionally more, in length. Like many of the large-leafed species, it takes some time to reach blooming age, but is worth growing for the foliage in areas where the winters are sufficiently mild. The flowers are dull, creamy white with a crimson blotch. The individual flowers are not very large, but there are a great many of them in a truss, so that the general effect is quite attractive, although not in a class with some of the smaller-growing and larger-flowered species. This very fine plant is not one for the beginner, unless he is sure that his conditions are satisfactory.

R. smirnowii—x, H–2. This is a very hardy species, which has been used to some extent in breeding for hardiness. It is, however, an attractive shrub in its own right. The leaves are densely covered below with a woolly, whitish to pale-brown indumentum. The flowers, on good forms, are pinkish to purplish rose, rather dainty and attractive in general appearance. For the colder gardens this is a species to consider.

R. sperabile—xx, H–4. This is a rather low-growing shrub, reaching to about 2 feet in ten years. The flowers are bright scarlet or deep crimson, and very showy.

R. spinuliferum—xx, H–4. Distinctly in the novelty class, this would likely not be recognized as a rhododendron by the uninitiated. The flowers are small and tubular, rather than open and flaring, as are most rhododendrons. They are bright crimson to brick red, with the anthers and stamens protruding from the corolla. This is a conversation piece in any garden. The growth is rather thin and upright, reaching perhaps 3 feet in ten years.

R. sutchuenense—xxx, H–3. This is a very early-blooming, large-leafed shrub, which will grow to 5 or 6 feet in ten years and eventually reach a much larger size. The flowers are light, rosy lilac. The botanical variety, geraldii, has a conspicuous blotch in the center of the flower. This is an excellent species where a rather large, coarse-textured but attractive plant can be used. It is not one for the small garden where plants have to be set very close together.

R. tephropeplum—xxx, H–4. This is a dwarf, reaching up to 2 feet or a little more in ten years. The foliage is very attractive, and the fairly small flowers are usually an attractive pink to carmine rose. It is a little slower in starting to bloom than some of the other dwarf species, but should bloom freely when three or four years old.

R. wardii—xxxx, H–4. Yellow-flowered rhododendrons are not as easy to find as those with white, pink, or red flowers. This species produces flowers that are light yellow to a rather good bright yellow, open, saucer-shaped, and very attractive. The leaf growth is rather neat and the bush character is usually good. It is one of the parents of a number of good yellow or near yellow varieties, but I think some seedlings of *R. wardii* itself are as beautiful as any hybrid yet developed.

R. yakusimanum—xxx, H–3. More recently introduced than most of the others listed here, this species seems to be very promising, and if one can find plants it is certainly worth trying in the garden. It is rather dwarfish, reaching about 2 feet in ten years, but the leaves are fairly large for such a small plant. They are covered on the underside with a thick, woolly, whitish indumentum. The flowers range from almost white to pink. It seems promising for breeding purposes, and many crosses have been made, but the species itself should become a good garden subject.

R. yunnanense—xxxx, H–3. This is another of the free-flowering Triflorum series. It makes an upright, spreading shrub to about 5 feet in ten years. The flowers are nearly white to pinkish, spotted with red. They are not very large, but produced so freely that the plant in full flower makes an extremely beautiful picture. This is one which may be used either in the background or in the foreground, as the flowers will stand close inspection. There is no named hybrid with which I am familiar that resembles this species very closely, and so here is a case where a species may be recommended with little competition from any hybrid variety.

SPECIES RHODODENDRONS FOR THE BEGINNER

Perhaps it seems unreasonable to describe so many species for the beginner who may be thinking of purchasing only one or two rhododendrons. However it is my feeling that even a beginner should not purchase "just a rhododendron." There should be some thought given as to how the plant will fit into the landscape plan although, of course, some may just want a plant they can enjoy as a specimen by itself, without much thought as to how it fits into the garden plan. However, the natural beauty of rhododendrons is enhanced when they are fitted harmoniously into the garden picture, where they supplement the beauty of other plants and, in turn, are made more beautiful by the supporting plants. Therefore the prospective rhododendron purchaser should, if possible, decide what color of flower he would prefer, the approximate size of the plant, whether the foliage is large or small, whether the bloom is relatively early or late, and in general what kind of a plant would give the greatest pleasure in the garden. It may be that one of the named hybrids will fit these requirements perfectly. On the other hand none of the hybrids available may fit as well as one of the species, and so the foregoing brief descriptions were designed to give a little help in the use of a few of those which are generally considered to be well adapted for garden use.

Many gardeners are interested in the unusual things—not sacrificing beauty and harmony for novelty, but if a plant does fit, the fact that it is not commonly grown in the neighborhood adds to its value in the garden. Some of the species described are well known to many gardeners, but others are completely unknown, except in a few localities. A species rhododendron, therefore, from far-off western China, or Sikkim, or Japan may have an element of romance and scarcity which gives it a certain appeal.

CHAPTER 11

Rhododendron Varieties for Many Purposes

The named varieties, for the most part, are those which have English or common names, and not Latin names. This is not a clear-cut situation, however, as years ago, before there was an accepted Code of Nomenclature, nurserymen were inclined to give Latin names to new varieties which they introduced. Presumably there was some appeal to such a name, although at the present time we would feel the opposite would be true. As an example, the old 'Catawbiense album' has a Latin name, but it refers to a clonal variety and not to a species or subspecies.

WHY HYBRID VARIETIES ARE NAMED
Most hybrids have resulted from crosses between two species or two varieties, in an attempt to combine in one individual plant some of the superior qualities of each of the parents. Unless plants superior in some ways to the parents are produced, the breeding is useless. Hybrid seedlings may be of value, even if not superior to the parents in every respect, if they have certain important characters that the parent plants do not have.

Seedlings which have received names were not always superior to existing varieties, although they may have appeared so to the breeder. Seedling plants may, at their first or second blooming, indicate a potential size, color, and vigor which they do not always maintain in later years. Consequently many varieties have been named which are not very outstanding, some of which should probably not have received names at all. Amateur breeders have given names to plants just to distinguish them in conversation, or have given plants to friends and designated them by a temporary name. Under certain conditions they appear to be rather good plants, and so they may be picked up by a nurseryman and propagated under the name originally given just for personal convenience, and not with the idea of launching a full-scale horticultural variety on the garden scene.

The above discussion is designed to emphasize that the mere fact that a variety has been named is not always insurance that it is really a superior plant. This is indicated by the ratings given by the American Rhododendron Society, which may vary from 0, unworthy of being grown, to xxxx, which indicates a really fine variety or species.

Just what per cent of the total number of rhododendron plants sold represents species plants and what per cent hybrid varieties I have no way of knowing. Certainly the hybrids account for somewhere in the high nineties. That being the case, one might ask, as was hinted in the previous chapter, "Why bother with species at all?" Another pertinent question is, "What do hybrids have that species plants do not have?"

WHAT MAKES A HYBRID SUPERIOR

There are a lot of things to be considered about a rhododendron plant besides its worth as a specimen plant from a score-card standpoint. Many varieties were introduced because they were better than anything available in certain particular characteristics. For instance, they may have been earlier or later in blooming, more resistant to cold, heat, or drought, a different color for the blooming season, and so on. Actually I am afraid some were introduced just because they were different enough from previously named varieties that they could truthfully be given a new name which, if the plant is reasonably adequate, might result in increased sales.

HOW VARIETIES ARE EVALUATED

There are various ways of conveying to a beginner with rhododendrons the story of varieties and how to choose the most satisfactory for one's own garden. In Chapter 14, lists are given for various planting purposes which might suffice for those who want a recommendation, follow it without question, and let it go at that. Others may want the recommendation, but they also want to know something about the thing that is being recommended, and why it is being recommended. Therefore it seemed that a brief discussion of some of the more important varieties would be useful for those inquiring gardeners who take their variety problems seriously.

In the evaluation of varieties, the A.R.S. Quality Ratings are very helpful. They tell how the variety, as an individual plant, appeals to a rather large number of people. They do not, however, tell whether the variety is especially good for this or that purpose, or that it has certain little faults that one might overlook under certain circumstances. One could go deeply into the literature and compile the information to be found in discussions of varieties in many magazines, yearbooks, and other publications. However, each of those discussions is primarily the opinion of one person, the man who is doing the writing.

In this chapter I am not trying to review the literature and give a consensus of all that has been written about the varieties listed. I have done considerable reading, of course, and have made mental, although perhaps subconscious, note of other people's opinions, and have added to that my own viewpoint about the varieties. True, I have not grown all of those listed in this chapter, although almost all of them. Since my rhododendron experience has been primarily in the Northwest, I am a little better informed on varieties grown here than on the old hardy varieties that still have to be depended upon for the colder areas of the Northeast and North Central parts of our country.

Varieties that have a great many serious faults have been left out, and while I may have omitted some that should have been included, yet I do not feel that a beginner will go wrong with any of the varieties listed here, provided he has reasonably good conditions for growing rhododendrons, and always provided he gives due importance to the hardiness ratings.

Presumably it would be truthful to say that some of the coastal area of the Pacific Northwest is more nearly ideal rhododendron country than any other on the continent. For azaleas, the Gulf Coast area or some of the Middle Atlantic and southeastern states would be considered more or less ideal. It is perhaps logical, therefore, to mention and briefly describe more varieties adapted to those particular localities than are suitable for other areas. There just aren't a great many varieties that are especially adapted to the less favorable localities. The breeders have worked diligently, and in many cases successfully, to produce better sorts for cold regions. Similar breeding has not been done for those areas where limiting factors are high summer temperature, low humidity, or soil alkalinity. Eventually it will undoubtedly be done.

OLD VERSUS NEW VARIETIES
Nearly all of the varieties described might be considered standard

sorts, or ones which are at least readily available. Promising new varieties are being developed, and some are in the process of being propagated and introduced. However, rhododendrons are relatively slow to increase and it will be some time before those we now think of as new become widely enough grown so that they are known as standard varieties, and are generally available. By that time there will be a new crop of the breeders' output, holding greater promise than any we now have.

Gardeners who are well informed about certain other plants, such as roses, may think this emphasis on the standard sorts, with less attention to the new varieties, is rather strange. With some other plants, new varieties appear yearly and may be planted very heavily almost immediately, so that the complexion of gardens may change radically over a ten-year period. In the case of rhododendrons and, to a lesser extent, azaleas, some very good and still very popular varieties are fifty to one hundred years old. A list of any length to include the best rhododendrons and azaleas would undoubtedly include a number of these older varieties. Unless there are significant breakthroughs in breeding, I would look for some of these old timers still to be worthy of planting in the gardens of fifty years hence.

My aim is not to discourage anyone from trying new varieties, but until quite a bit is known about the behavior of a variety under different conditions, and especially its hardiness, it probably should not be included in lists recommended for beginners. If a new variety or, for that matter, any older variety which is not discussed here is being grown successfully in your neighborhood, by all means try it if it appeals to you.

SOME VARIETIES QUICKLY BECOME STANDARD

It is difficult to give a good definition of new variety as contrasted with standard variety. For instance, 'Elizabeth' is relatively new, and yet it is so widely grown and sold that we have come to think of it in the Northwest as a standard sort. It propagates rapidly, and in the course of ten years or less it rocketed from unknown to being one of our most popular and readily available dwarfs. On the other hand many of the larger-growing rhododendrons make heavy twig growth, with relatively few growing points per bush. Unless one uses heroic measures to increase a plant of this type, it will take a long while to work up enough stock from the one original seedling that it can be put on the market.

THE VARIETIES BY GROUPS

Varieties are listed in alphabetical order, with the larger-growing types first, followed by the dwarfs. The larger varieties are divided into two groups, with the old hardies, or so-called ironclads, listed separately. Frankly, I have not had a great deal of contact with these varieties, some quite old, which get their hardiness usually from *R. catawbiense*. Those described here are ones which have been recommended in various listings by those who know them better than I. They are the only hybrids reliably hardy in most of New York and all but the southern part of New England. They have been grown but little in the Northwest, as other varieties have flowers that are of more varied and purer colors. It is likely that eventually the better colors will be available in conjunction with the ironclad hardiness, as a number of breeders are working in that direction.

There is no hard and fast line separating the dwarfs from the larger-growing types. Those usually called dwarfs are rather slow-growing, and have small leaves, but some may eventually reach a height of 4 or 5 feet. Some of the so-called larger varieties are also slow-growing, but have large leaves, and eventually grow to more than 5 feet.

The group varieties, where the name was given to all the progeny of a certain cross, are indicated by the letter "G" immediately following the name. Other varieties are clones. Actually some of the group varieties are represented in the trade by only one clone, others by several, usually similar, clones.

THE LARGER HYBRID VARIETIES

A. Bedford—xxx, H–3. This is a remarkably vigorous, tall-growing plant, reaching up to 8 feet in ten years. It is bluish mauve in color with a dark eye. The leaves are large, dark-green, and glossy, and are an important consideration in recommending this variety.

Annie E. Endtz—xxx, H–3. One of the parents of this variety is 'Pink Pearl,' and the foliage indicates it. It is light pink in color, and certainly an improvement on its parent.

Antoon van Welie—xx, H–3. This is another 'Pink Pearl' seedling from the same Dutch breeder who produced the preceding. It is exceptionally vigorous and has large, luxuriant-looking leaves. The flowers are deep pink. Either of these varieties may be expected to reach 5 or 6 feet in ten years.

Azor G.—xxx, H–4. This is a group variety, and there are several clones being grown in this country, some of which may be somewhat more hardy than H–4. It is a rapid-growing, rather open plant, inclined to be leggy, and reaching 6 feet or better in ten years. The blooming season is late. Most of the forms being propagated are a soft salmon pink in color, even more attractive because they come when most varieties are past bloom.

Beauty of Littleworth—xxx, H–3. This is a rapid-growing, fairly large-leafed variety, reaching 5 or 6 feet in ten years. The flowers are large, and although they have a number of small dots scattered over the petals, the general effect is pure white. Many descriptions list it simply as white, without mentioning the dots. It should be planted where it has plenty of room to spread out.

Betty Wormald—xxx, H–3. This variety has a rather large rose-pink flower, paler at the center, with a pale-purple blotch. At its best it produces a magnificent truss of flowers. It should reach 5 feet in ten years where growing conditions are favorable.

Blue Peter—xxx, H–2. Although well liked in the Pacific Northwest, 'Blue Peter' is also hardy enough to be grown in many places in the East. It is pale lavender-blue, with a deep blotch. The flowers are slightly crinkled and very attractive. The leaves are very dark, lustrous green. The young plants are a bit open and spreading, but usually develop into a nicely shaped plant.

Britannia—xxxx, H–3. This is a magnificent, bright, crimson-red rhododendron, making a fairly slow, spreading growth reaching to perhaps 4 feet in height in ten years. The leaves are large and, at their best, a rather attractive light green. Unfortunately, unless conditions are just right the leaves tend to be so light in color that they lose some of their attractiveness. For a long time this was considered by many in the Northwest to be the best of the red varieties, but more recently 'The Honorable Jean Marie de Montagu' has, to a large extent, replaced it in public demand. The latter variety has dark-green foliage and is apparently a little hardier. It also roots readily from cuttings, whereas 'Britannia' roots with some difficulty, and usually has been grafted. That may not affect its garden value very much, although I would certainly prefer to have a rhododendron on its own roots. It does, however, affect the general availability of the variety which, now that most nurserymen are growing their plants from cuttings, is less frequently found in the nurseries.

Broughtonii Aureum—xxx, H–3. This is an azaleodendron produced many, many years ago. The foliage is a little weak, as if the variety could not quite make up its mind whether to be evergreen or deciduous. However it has a rather good yellow color, and yellows in rhododendrons are not too plentiful. Its growth in the Northwest is rather spreading and inclined to be floppy. I have seen it in southern California, where it made a much stockier and more desirable type of growth. Pinching the tips out of the willowy new shoots before they get too long should do much to produce a better bush.

Carita G.—xxxx, H–3. Good yellows are so hard to find that it seems advisable to include this and one or two others that have not been around long enough to be considered standard varieties. It is one of the newer primrose-yellow sorts, and not too readily available at this writing. The foliage is attractive, and the plant habit is good. It may be that some other variety will surpass it, so far as color is concerned, but it does promise to be a very desirable garden plant. Certain clones of the group have been given names, but information as to their relative desirability is not available.

Christmas Cheer—x, H–2. Here we have a plant which has only a fair-sized flower, of a light pink color, which certainly would attract little attention during the normal blooming season. However it is relatively hardy, and tends to bloom extremely early. In the Northwest it will frequently start blooming in late fall, and may show flowers any time during the winter when the temperature is relatively high. There is another very similar variety, 'Rosamundi,' and it is quite possible that these two are sometimes interchanged in the nursery. The plant of either of these varieties is rather slow-growing, and will reach only about 4 feet in ten years.

Cornubia G.—xx, H–5. In the Northwest, 'Cornubia' is grown by a few enthusiasts who like its early flowering and its fine color, although cold winters sooner or later eliminate it. In California, and possibly in some of the southern states, it has a very definite place. It is a very fine, rapid-growing, blood-red variety which will reach around 7 feet in ten years. It blossoms very early.

Corona—xxx, H–3. This is not generally considered a dwarf, but it does grow very slowly and may be no larger at the end of ten years than certain varieties such as 'Bow Bells,' usually listed as a dwarf. 'Corona,' one of the parents of 'Bow Bells,' has a beautiful, small, coral-pink flower which is borne on a very high, well-shaped truss, carrying a rather large number of flowers. The impact on the viewer is not made by the individual flower, but by the entire truss. It has been used a number of times as a parent to transmit that tall-truss character which is liked by so many people.

Corry Koster—x, H–4. This light-pink, ruffled variety is not rated very highly, but has a lot of good qualities and should be worthy of consideration in areas where it will be hardy. It is a good grower and should reach at least 5 or 6 feet in ten years.

Countess of Derby—xx, H–3. Sometimes sold under the name 'Eureka Maid,' this variety is rose pink in color and somewhat resembles 'Pink Pearl,' one of its parents. It does well in the Northwest and in certain parts of California.

Cynthia—xx, H–2. This variety, introduced about a hundred years ago, is still a favorite in many localities. Some nurseries state that it is their best seller. It is rosy crimson in color. The growth is rather open and spreading, although old specimens fill up a bit and make rather nice-looking plants. On young plants the branches tend to break off easily. In ten years 'Cynthia' should reach at least 6 feet in height, so it is obviously a plant for the extensive shrub border, or for background planting, and not one for foundation planting under a low window.

Damaris G.—xxx, H–3. As previously stated, yellows are somewhat scarce, and so this variety with its rather attractive, pale-yellow flowers is worthy of inclusion here, even though the plant characters leave something to be desired. Several of the yellows, including this one, are inclined to have rather poor foliage.

David—xxx, H–3. Some years ago, 'Earl of Athlone' was considered to be one of the finest of the red varieties, having a rather large truss of small to medium, very bright, blood-red flowers. Unfortunately it is very difficult to root from cuttings. 'David' has flowers which are almost identical, but it is easily propagated and somewhat hardier. It makes a rather rapid growth, although while young it tends to be quite stiff and upright.

Diane—xxx, H–3. This is another primrose-yellow rhododendron with flowers which can be very beautiful at their best, but with plant characters which are not always so desirable. It should be planted in such a place that its yellow flowers can be used most effectively, but where the possibly light-green or yellowish foliage will not be too conspicuous.

Doncaster—xx, H–3. Another old variety, after approximately one hundred years 'Doncaster' still has much to recommend it. The color is bright scarlet-crimson. The type of growth is low, rather spreading, and open. There are better red varieties for the Northwest, but I have heard this one reported as doing rather well in southern California.

Fabia G.—xx, H–4. This is a somewhat controversial group of varieties, some people liking them very much and others having no use for them. The flowers, which are rather tawny orange-salmon in color, tend to hang down so that one usually does not see the most attractive aspect of the flower. The trusses do not stand up with a high center, as they do with many other varieties. However, the unusual color and the profusion of flowers make this an acceptable variety for a good many people. If it could be planted high on a bank so that one could look up into the flowers, it would be more attractive. Several selections of this group have been named, including 'Tangerine,' 'Tower Court,' and 'Roman Pottery.'

Faggetter's Favourite—xxx, H–3. This is a rapidly growing, tall variety, which will reach about 8 feet in height in ten years if growing conditions are good. The flowers are silvery pink and the leaves are large and attractive. As is true with many tall-growing varieties, it is inclined to be leggy, and should be so located that lower-growing plants will be in front of it. This may not be necessary on the large estate, where ample room can be given for the plant to develop freely and entirely uncrowded. This would mean ultimately at least 10 or 15 feet from other rhododendrons or shrubs or trees of other types, and obviously there are not too many gardens where such space is available.

Fastuosum Flore Pleno—xx, H–2. Another very old variety, this was for many years the only double-flowering rhododendron, although more recently various breeders have produced a few varieties that are double. The color is mauve, but hardly that shade which many people feel to be undesirable in rhododendrons. The bush grows fairly rapidly, and should be placed toward the back of the shrub border. In my experience it has had good keeping qualities as a cut flower, the the extra petals probably tending to support the flowers as they start to wilt.

Fragrantissimum G.—xxx, H–5. This is relatively tender, with a white flower, tinged pink. It grows very well in the San Francisco Bay area, although it tends to be a little leggy, and is most effective in a mass of several plants. As the name indicates, it is fragrant. Where it can be grown, it can make a beautiful showing.

Fusilier G.—xx, H–4. Where it can be grown, this is a rather desirable, striking, scarlet-flowered group variety. It is a hybrid between two rather tender species. It should reach 5 feet in ten years.

Gill's Crimson—xxx, H–5. This blood-crimson variety can be grown in the Northwest, although it will suffer during especially cold winters. It is more at home in northern and central California, where it may often be seen in bloom during midwinter. By central California, of course, is meant that part of the state near enough to the coast to have satisfactory rainfall and humidity. 'Gill's Crimson' is a rather free grower, with good foliage, reaching about 6 feet in ten years.

Goldsworth Crimson—xx, H–3. This is a rather dependable, free-flowering, crimson variety of midseason. It reaches about 5 feet in ten years, and while perhaps not outstanding, is worthy of being planted more than it is at the present time.

Goldsworth Yellow—xx, H–2. This is the hardiest of the yellow varieties, at least of those now available. Unfortunately the flowers do not open up wide, and are inclined to look, to me at least, as if they were just past full bloom. Its hardiness makes it worthy of trial where a yellow variety is wanted in the colder states. It is listed as apricot yellow, but is slightly spotted with green and bronze, so that the over-all effect is not a good, clear yellow.

Gomer Waterer—xx, H–2. Although often sold as a white, this variety is somewhat blushed, and the buds are fairly deep pink before opening. The leaves are large and dark green, giving a rather lush appearance to the entire plant. It spreads at least as much as its height, which may reach about 5 feet in ten years.

Grenadier G.—xxx, H–3. A rather vigorous, upright-growing variety, with large attractive leaves, 'Grenadier' has flowers which are very deep, blood-red. Such color does not carry very far in the garden, and so it should be located where it can be viewed from fairly close up. It is a group variety, but whether more than one clone is in the nursery trade, I do not know.

Hyperion—x, H–3. Which is the better, as a conspicuously blotched variety, 'Hyperion' or 'Sappho,' which it closely resembles, I hardly know, although I am inclined to think 'Hyperion' may be slightly superior. Like 'Sappho,' it is inclined to be somewhat open and leggy. It has a very light, bluish flower, almost white, with a large dark, bluish-maroon-colored blotch.

Idealist G.—xxx, H–3. This fairly new, pale, cream-yellow variety is a candidate to be included in any list of new and worth-while yellow varieties. I have heard it called one of the best of the yellows, but my experience with it is very limited.

Jan Dekens—xxx, H–3. In type of growth as well as in its rich pink flower, this tends to resemble 'Antoon van Welie' and 'Annie E. Endtz,' two other Dutch varieties. Which of the three is superior it is hard to say. They are all good, although 'Antoon van Welie' is a more rapid grower.

Lady Alice Fitzwilliam—xxx, H–5. This is another of the tender varieties, with large white and fragrant flowers. Somewhat resembling 'Fragrantissimum,' it is strictly for the warmer areas.

Lady Chamberlain G.—xxxx, H–4. Rhododendrons of this type are yet unknown to most American gardeners. The leaves are rather small, glaucous, covered with a waxy material which gives a blue-green cast to the leaves. Growth is quite upright, and the plant should reach 7 to 8 feet in ten years. The flowers are orange to salmon pink, and hang down in masses of very beautiful, trumpet-shaped flowers. A plant of this type has to be located very carefully to find its real place in the garden. The best plants I have seen have been near a garden path, where one could walk under them and look up to see the light coming through the translucent corollas, and also see inside the flowers, which would be impossible if one were looking down on them. 'Lady Chamberlain' is a group variety and certain clones have been named, including 'Gleam' and 'Chelsea.'

Lady Rosebery G.—xxxx, H–4. Another group variety, this grows somewhat similar to 'Lady Chamberlain,' as it resulted from a very similar cross. The flowers tend to be rosy pink, whereas 'Lady Chamberlain' is more orange to salmon. It should be used in the same way in the garden.

(Loderi G.) King George—xxxx, H–4. More than a dozen clones of the Loderi group have been named. They are all rather free-growing, open plants, reaching 7 or 8 feet in ten years. The leaves are large, but the over-all foliage is rather sparse for the size of the bush. The flowers are very large, and range from pure white to a rather light pink. Most are quite pink in the bud, and fade to a white. The most commonly grown is the 'King George' clone. This variety is not very hardy, and may be a little fussy to grow. I would not recommend it to one who is just beginning with rhododendrons, unless it is being grown successfully by other gardeners in the neighborhood. If, judging from your neighbors' experiences, your garden is suitable, then it might be worth taking a chance. If it grows satisfactorily, it will be a magnificent sight, and likely one of the finest things in your garden. Because it does grow rather tall and broad, it should have ample room to develop freely.

Loder's White—xxxx, H–4. As will be noted, this is on the tender side, but where it can be grown it is one of the finest of the white varieties. It has very beautiful, large, frilled flowers. It is distinct from the Loderi group.

Lord Roberts—x, H–3. Here we have a variety rating only x following one which rates xxxx, but each has its own particular place. This variety seems to be a little hardier than its rating of H–3 indicates. It is a dark red, with a black center blotch, and blooms in late midseason. It is grown rather widely across the country because of its general adaptability.

Mars—xxxx, H–2. This is another late midseason red. It is a deep, true red, and the light-colored stamens make an interesting pattern on the rather full, upstanding truss. It makes a rather slow growth, reaching about 4 feet in ten years. This is one of the better varieties of this hardiness rating. It is grown, and well liked, in the Northwest, and can also be grown in all except the very cold areas of the East Coast.

May Day G.—xxxx, H–3. Although not usually considered a dwarf, 'May Day' is slow-growing, reaching about 3 to 4 feet in ten years. Its growth as a young plant is rapid, but it soon begins to blossom freely, and the shoot growth becomes less and less. It tends to spread, so that a plant is likely to be considerably broader than its height. The color is a bright scarlet. This variety, like many others of which *R. griersonianum* is a parent, has a rather lax truss, with the flowers tending to hang down rather than stand upright. It is a group variety, and several forms have been distributed.

Medusa G.—xx, H–4. This is of the 'Fabia' type, having resulted from a very similar cross. In my experience it has been a little better than most of the forms of 'Fabia.' It has a little more orange, or vermilion, running through the petals in threads of color, giving the flowers a richer appearance. It is a little better grower and, based on one or two test years, it is somewhat hardier than 'Fabia.' However it does have the same type of lax truss, and if you do not like 'Fabia' you will probably not like this one. It is a group variety, but I know of only one clone being grown.

Mother of Pearl—xxx, H–4. Very few rhododendron varieties have arisen from bud sports or mutations. This is reputed to be a sport of 'Pink Pearl,' opening blush and turning snow-white. As a white variety it is a good one, although some of the newer ones may possibly excel it.

Mrs. A. T. de la Mare—xx, H–3. This is another white, characterized by a distinct green spot at the center of the flower. It is relatively free-growing and will reach about 5 feet in ten years. Although not a pure white, because of the green throat, it is a desirable landscape variety.

Mrs. Charles Pearson—xx, H–3. The flowers of this variety open a blush mauve with brownish spots, and fade to a light pinkish white. The leaves are large and dark green, and the entire plant gives an appearance of lush, free growth which makes it attractive the year round. It is probably a little hardier than the rating would indicate.

Mrs. E. C. Stirling—xx, H–3. This is a vigorous-growing variety which starts to make an upright growth and then tends to spread out and develop a fairly desirable shape. It opens blush pink and becomes a very light pink, with a rather tall, upstanding truss.

Mrs. Furnival—xxxx, H–3. This has often been compared with 'Mrs. G. W. Leak,' to which it has a faint resemblance. It is light pink with a sienna blotch, and will reach about 4 feet in ten years. It is a very fine variety which has always been in rather short supply.

Mrs. G. W. Leak—xxx, H–4. The flowers are pink with a brownish-purple blotch. It is free-growing and will reach about 6 feet in ten years. It blooms somewhat earlier than 'Mrs. Furnival,' with which it has been compared and confused, largely because of the somewhat similar color pattern. A plant in full bloom makes a beautiful appearance, and its popularity in the Northwest year after year is well deserved.

Mrs. Lindsay Smith—xx, H–3. One of the taller-growing varieties, this should reach at least 7 feet in ten years if conditions are right. The rather large flowers are produced in late midseason. Although it is listed as a white, it is spotted red on the upper lobe and gives an impression of being a rather delicate pink. I consider it a very desirable variety.

Mrs. P. D. Williams—xxx, H-2. This is a late midseason variety which grows rather slowly, reaching about 4 feet in ten years. The color is ivory-white with a golden-brown spot. A plant in full bloom is a beautiful sight. Possibly the root system is not quite as vigorous as might be desired, as sometimes young plants seem to blow over fairly easily, although once well established, this should not be a drawback.

Mrs. Tom H. Lowinsky—x, H-3. This is a late-flowering plant, the flowers opening blush, with reddish-brown spots. As they become fully open, they become lighter, and the appearance at a little distance is of a white-flowered variety with a large brown blotch. It is vigorous-growing, free-blooming, and should become more popular. It is not new but was only comparatively recently introduced from England. In my opinion it should rate a little higher in quality, and is perhaps a little hardier than the rating would indicate.

Mrs. W. C. Slocock—xxx, H-3. There are two other somewhat similar varieties which have *R. campylocarpum* as one parent—'Unique' and 'Souvenir of W. C. Slocock.' This one opens, as do the others, apricot pink shaded to yellow. The leaves are rather small and rounded, and the bush is quite compact, reaching about 4 feet in ten years.

Naomi G.—xxx, H-2. This is one of those group varieties which, like 'Loderi,' has produced a number of similar but very desirable clones. It is a comparatively recent introduction to this country, and should become more popular, although it is slow to propagate. The color is pink, some clones running to a rich salmon pink. A dozen or so selections of the group have been named. At the present writing I cannot do better than recommend any one of them, as all with which I have had any contact seem to have some merit. The variety 'Glow' has been very attractive in the test garden at Portland. The hardiness rating was based primarily on behavior in the Northwest at the time of the 1955 freeze. How 'Naomi' or its various clones will do in the East is still largely to be determined.

Odoratum—0, H-3. There must be a good reason to suggest, in a list of this type, a variety which has a quality rating of 0, which usually indicates that it is generally unworthy of being grown. However this azaleodendron, probably one of the oldest named varieties in existence, does have one very valuable characteristic, and that is strong fragrance. The flowers are rather small and pale lilac; the leaves are somewhat small, but the bush will grow to about 4 feet in ten years and make a neat, fairly attractive plant. The only place I would recommend it is for the garden where fragrance is particularly desired in a rhododendron planting. A plant or two of 'Odoratum' somewhere in the background will, under the right conditions, scent a whole garden.

Penjerrick G.—xxx, H–5. I was told by a well-known English rhododendron fancier that he considered 'Penjerrick' to be the finest variety which had ever been produced. Certainly in the milder parts of England it makes magnificent plants. It has been grown to some extent in the Northwest, although very cold winters may hurt it. It is my feeling that it should become a valuable variety in parts of California, or elsewhere where mild winter temperatures prevail. Unfortunately it is one of those group varieties of which several different clones have been distributed, ranging from pink through yellow to white. The one I have especially observed is a creamy yellow with large flowers, and very beautiful. This would certainly be a variety for the beginner, only in very mild climates, but is one with which the advanced amateur might well experiment, in various parts of the Northwest.

Pink Pearl—xx, H–3. Probably the best-known rhododendron, partly because of its euphonious name and partly because it does have considerable merit, 'Pink Pearl' opens a good rose pink, but tends to fade to a blush which is less attractive. The plant is rather free-growing and should reach around 6 feet in ten years. The foliage tends to be a little light in color and the plant rather open, so that I would not consider it a very good landscape plant so far as foliage is concerned. Many rhododendron fanciers tend to look down on this variety, but it has a great deal of merit where properly used. Do not plant it in front of low windows. It will be a beautiful sight from inside the house for a year or two, and then will be just too big for such a location.

Princess Elizabeth—xx, H–2. This is a rather late-flowering, crimson-colored rhododendron, which has a rather attractive flower and truss, but is a very leggy and relatively unattractive plant. It is worthy of trying where weather conditions do not permit the growth of better reds.

Purple Splendour—xxxx, H–2. Of all the purples this is, in my opinion, quite the best. It is a deep, royal purple with a black spot. The growth is rather compact, spreading after the plant reaches a few years of age, but it should grow to about 4 feet in ten years. Because of the very dark color, this variety should be grown where it can be seen from nearby. At a distance, as with any other dark-colored variety, it would be hard to distinguish the flower from the dark-green leaves. Where a lighter-colored sort such as white, or particularly yellow, can be grown near 'Purple Splendour,' it tends to set off the color to considerable advantage. This variety is proving relatively hardy, although sometimes the buds may be injured by cold. It is being grown or tried pretty much wherever rhododendrons will thrive, except in their extreme northern range.

Radium G.—xx, H–3. This is a free-growing, blood-red variety, which really stands out when it is in full bloom. It will reach 4 or 5 feet in ten years. The leaves are rather long and narrow, as is true of many hybrids of *R. griersonianum*. It has been reported as very satisfactory in parts of California.

Sappho—xx, H–2. For those who want a heavily spotted variety, which will grow to about 5 feet in ten years, this is worth growing. It is white with a very large, conspicuous, purplish blotch. Growth is rather open, and the plant itself not particularly graceful when young. Compare with the description of 'Hyperion.'

Sarita Loder G.—xx, H–4. This is a late midseason, pale salmon-pink variety which will reach about 6 feet in ten years. It is one of the *R. griersonianum* hybrids and, like so many of that parentage, may be somewhat on the tender side, but where it will grow it is a beautiful thing.

Scandinavia—xx, H–3. This is a late midseason, scarlet-crimson variety with reddish twigs. It is not very well known, but is worthy of being tried.

Snow Queen G.—xxx, H–3. Where it can be grown in light shade this makes a magnificent sight. It is a pure white variety with large flowers.

Sunrise G.—xx, H–4. This is a free-growing light pink variety, opening late midseason. It will reach a height of approximately 6 feet in ten years where growing conditions are satisfactory. It produces a very beautiful flower, with delicate and attractive coloring.

Tally Ho G.—xxxx, H–5. This is a late-flowering, bright scarlet hybrid of *R. griersonianum*. It would be very fine if it were a little hardier, but where it can be grown it is a good choice as a bright-colored variety in the red field. It will grow to about 5 feet in ten years.

The Hon. Jean Marie de Montagu—xxxx, H–3. At the present writing this is close to being the most popular standard variety in the Northwest. It is bright crimson, blooming in midseason, and will reach 4 or 5 feet in ten years. It is extremely floriferous, and the beautiful flowers are well set off by very dark-green, attractive foliage. It is being grown some in the East, in areas which would indicate that it may be hardier than H–3. For the beginner who likes plants with bright red flowers, this could hardly be surpassed as the first rhododendron to be purchased.

Trilby—x, H–2. Here we have a deep crimson variety with a dark blotch, blooming in late midseason, and reaching a height of about 5 feet in ten years. It does not have quite the flower quality of a number of other red varieties, as indicated by the rating of x, but it is a good, free-growing, and rather attractive variety. It is well distributed in the trade, and if your nurseryman or garden center has it in stock, you would not go wrong by planting it.

Unique—xxx, H–3. This is sometimes described as a pale yellow, but that is rather deceiving. The bud is pink when it opens, and the color is more of an ivory or cream than a yellow. It is a beautiful variety, on a bush which can hardly be surpassed, but it should not be purchased by those who are looking for a definitely yellow flower. The leaves are rather small and rounded, and the growth is quite compact, the height reaching to between 3 and 4 feet in ten years. This is a very fine rhododendron, liked by practically everyone who has grown it.

Unknown Warrior—x, H–4. This is an early-blooming, bright, light-red variety, which has been grown quite a bit in California. It is attractive when it first opens, but the blooms tend to fade to a color not so desirable. It will reach about 5 feet in ten years.

Vulcan G.—xx, H–3. A seedling of 'Mars' x *R. griersonianum,* this shows distinct inheritance from both parents. The bright, brick-red blooms come in late midseason. Sometimes, under certain growing conditions, the rapid shoot growth may tend to obscure the flowers. The height runs to about 4 feet in ten years. 'Vulcan' is listed in the International Register as a clone, but at least two forms have been distributed.

White Swan—xxx, H–4. White, suffused with delicate pink, blooms are produced by this variety in late midseason. It will reach about 5 feet in ten years.

THE OLD HARDY HYBRIDS

The practice of naming group varieties did not become common until after the old hardies had been introduced and, as far as I know, they all started as clones. However over the years, seedlings of similar parentage were raised, and it was almost inevitable that some confusion should arise. The practice of giving Latin names to clonal varieties added to the confusion. So it is not surprising that more than one clone may be found under a given name and, in some cases, it is difficult, if not impossible, to determine which is the original and correctly named form.

America—x, H–1. This is considered by various writers as being about the best of the very hardy red varieties. It blooms midseason and should grow to about 6 feet in ten years.

Boule de Neige—x, H–1. This is a very hardy white, the flowers being of medium size, but the trusses give the impression of large snowballs. The leaves are fairly large and so, although a small, slow-growing variety, it is not usually listed with the dwarfs. The plant is very compact and rounded in appearance and it should reach 3 or 4 feet in height in ten years.

Catawbiense Album—x, H–1. This is a vigorous-growing, very hardy, white variety, reaching about 7 feet in ten years. For those localities where temperatures are mild, there are better whites, but for colder climates this will give a good show where a rather large plant is desired. If a low-growing plant is wanted, 'Boule de Neige' would be more desirable. However, it blooms early, and 'Catawbiense Album' blooms late.

Charles Dickens—x, H–1. This is a very hardy red, blooming in midseason and reaching about 6 feet in ten years.

Cunningham's White—x, H–2. Gardeners looking for a white variety would not choose this if they could grow some of the larger-flowered, more tender varieties. However, 'Cunningham's White' does have good bush characters, being slow-growing, dense and with fairly small, shiny, dark-green leaves. It is better as a landscape shrub than as a specimen.

Dr. V. H. Rutgers—x, H–2. With flowers of aniline red, this is a midseason and fairly free-growing variety, reaching about 6 feet in ten years.

Everestianum—x, H–2. This is rosy lilac, blooming in midseason and making a rather large, rounded bush to about 6 feet in ten years. It is considered one of the old hardy hybrids, or one of the ironclads, but not quite as hardy as some of the others.

Lee's Dark Purple—x, H–2. Where 'Purple Splendour' is not quite hardy enough, this should be a fairly acceptable substitute for a purple rhododendron. It is over a hundred years old, but still useful in its place.

Mrs. Charles S. Sargent—x, H–1. This rose-red, yellow-spotted, very hardy variety has been spoken of as the best of the old hardies in the pink shades. It is quite old, but nevertheless still worthy of planting in areas where hardiness is a very important factor.

Roseum Elegans—x, H–1. This is a free-growing, midseason rhododendron with flowers of soft rose or rose-magenta color. Although it was introduced as a clone, several similar types have gotten into the trade during the one hundred years or more since 'Roseum elegans' was first distributed. I have been told that the original clone is best. It might be well to see this one in bloom, if possible, before purchasing it, in order to be sure the clone is what you desire from the standpoint of color.

THE DWARF VARIETIES

The following varieties are usually considered to be dwarfs, although some of them may reach 4 or 5 feet in height at maturity. Most of them have rather small leaves and are relatively slow-growing. Obviously the distinction between the dwarfs and the larger-growing varieties is rather indefinite, but the following are listed as dwarfs by most writers.

Much could be said about the use of dwarfs, but in any event they must be used close to where the garden visitor is standing, and not somewhere in the distant background. That means they should be fairly conspicuous, in a rock garden or as an edging for a larger border or a pathway, where they will be under close scrutiny the year round. Although some of the large growing varieties may be valued for their beautiful flowers, in spite of a rather awkward-looking, unattractive bush, dwarfs must make a reasonably attractive plant to be worthy of inclusion in most gardens.

Arthur J. Ivens—xxx, H–2. One parent of this variety is *R. william-sianum*, which is a nice thing in itself, having small, almost round leaves, a rather beautiful, coppery bronze-colored new shoot growth in the spring, and flowers that are pink and bell-shaped. The seedlings of this species all have certain characteristics in common, including the rounded leaves and the bell-shaped flowers. This one is pale pink, and in ten years will grow to at least 3 feet in height. Its hardiness makes it worthy of consideration for a rather wide area.

Augfast G.—xxx, H–3. This is one of several small-leafed types, with blue-violet flowers borne in profusion fairly early in the season. The height in ten years would be about 3 feet.

Blue Diamond G.—xxx, H–3. Another small-leafed hybrid, 'Blue Diamond' has a rather upright growth. The color is listed as blue, although it has a slight violet tinge. It is one of the best dwarfs where a fairly upright and not too symmetrical growth is desired. It is probably hardier than most of the blue-flowered dwarfs.

Blue Tit G.—xxx, H–3. The plant of 'Blue Tit' grows very much like 'Augfast,' and has occasionally been confused with that variety in the market. However the flowers are a lighter and truer blue in color. This is a group variety, but the ones I have seen in the Northwest are apparently all of one clone. It might reach 3 feet in ten years.

Bow Bells G.—xxxx, H–3. A plant of this variety which has become well established, and grown for a few years, is a beautiful thing. However the young plants are a bit tricky to grow under some conditions. At ten years, 'Bow Bells' should reach about 4 feet, which is as large as some of the varieties not considered to be dwarfs. However the slightly smaller flowers, the smaller, rounded leaves, and the generally slow growth cause this variety to be so listed. The flowers are bright pink in color, and are produced in early midseason. Athough this is a group variety, I do not know of more than one form.

Bric-a-Brac G.—xxx, H–3. This is somewhat similar to 'Cilpinense,' which is from a slightly different cross. The color is white with dark-brown anthers. The principal value of this variety, and its principal hazard, is that it is extremely early in blooming, about a month before 'Cilpinense' in the Northwest. Although the plant is fairly hardy, open flowers will be blackened by a freeze or severe frost, and at that time of the year such frosts are not uncommon. However a shrub as beautiful as this, blooming in February, is a beautiful sight, even if it is only enjoyed for a day or two before being cut down by frost. The type of growth is rather spreading, open, and distinctive, rather than being compact and mound-shaped, typical of so many of the dwarfs.

Carmen G.—xxx, H–4. This is a beautiful little rhododendron for the rock garden, with very dark-red flowers. It blooms in late mid-season, is spreading rather than upright-growing, and after ten years would do very well to reach 2 feet in height. It is not as easy to get started and established in the garden as some of the other dwarfs.

Cilpinense G.—xxx, H–4. The buds of this variety are pink, but usually fade to white or a very light pink as the flowers open. It resembles 'Bric-a-Brac,' but blooms about a month later. It is, on that account, somewhat more likely to miss frosty periods, and so may be considered a more reliable bloomer, although it still blooms much earlier than most rhododendrons. It is a group variety and several clones are in the trade, varying mostly in the amount of pink on the unopened buds.

Conemaugh G.—xx, H–2. This is a dwarf variety originated by Mr. Joseph Gable of Pennsylvania. The flowers, which appear very early in the season, are fair-sized for a dwarf, and lavender pink. The first growth is inclined to be upright and somewhat open. For early bloom, especially where hardiness is a factor, this is one to consider.

Elizabeth G.—xxx, H–4. Of all the dwarf varieties, this is probably the most striking when in full bloom. The bright, blood-red flowers are quite large for such a small plant, in fact as large as the flowers on many standard varieties. It is a comparatively recent introduction from England, and has become widely grown in the Northwest during the last few years. 'Elizabeth' makes a rather rapid growth the first year or two, and then settles down to blooming, and will get no higher than 2½ to 3 feet in ten years. It has not been around long enough to be thoroughly evaluated as to its adaptability to various climatic conditions. I have heard that it is likely to show scorched leaves in California, although in other parts of the same state—especially if it is in light shade—I believe it may do fairly well. It is such a fine variety where it grows well that it is worth trying almost anywhere, if winter temperatures are not too low. There are several forms of this group variety, but they are quite similar.

Humming Bird G.—xxx, H–4. This is another seedling of *R. williamsianum,* which produces the rather symmetrical, rounded bush previously described as typical of this species and its seedlings. It is early midseason, produces pink, bell-shaped flowers, shaded with vermilion. It will reach about 2 feet in height in ten years, but will be considerably broader than that. The small, rounded, shiny, dark-green leaves make it an attractive foliage plant throughout the year. It doesn't bloom quite as promptly as some of the other dwarfs, but once well established, it produces a good show.

Jock G.—xxx, H–3. This dwarf produces rather large flowers, in this case rose pink. It is a graceful and open grower, for a small plant, with leaves smaller than those of most of the larger varieties, but not as small as those of many of the dwarfs. It has not been widely tried as yet, but would seem to be very worth while for trial in most rhododendron areas.

Moonstone G.—xxxx, H–3. This is probably the best of the dwarf yellows, although some might feel that it is a little large for the rock garden and that certain other yellows, particularly species, might be better there. 'Moonstone' is another *R. williamsianum* hybrid, making a nicely rounded bush up to about 2 feet in height in ten years. It produces, in early midseason, a multitude of cream-colored flowers, slightly edged with pink. It is a very nice plant indeed, and can be used wherever a rather low, spreading rhododendron is called for. There are said to be cream, ivory, and pink forms within the group, but the only one I have seen in the Northwest is a good light yellow.

Praecox G.—xx H–3. This variety has rosy lilac flowers that would be considered mediocre, except for the fact that they are produced very early in the season. At that time color in the garden is scarce, and the rather small flowers, borne amidst the dark green leaves, are quite attractive. It will reach about 3 feet in ten years. Although young plants are inclined to be rather stiffly upright, this stiffness is lost as the plants get larger and spread out more gracefully.

Racil—xxx, H–3. An early-flowering, shell pink, this variety is inclined at first to make rather open, leggy growth. However it can be trained to make a more compact, spreading growth, or can simply be left as nature intended it, to provide a striking accent early in the spring. Once it gets settled down to blooming, it will not grow nearly so rapidly, reaching perhaps 3 feet in ten years.

Ramapo—A hybrid produced by Mr. Guy Nearing of New Jersey, 'Ramapo' does not at this time have A.R.S. ratings. However for the person who wants a dwarf rhododendron which is adaptable to fairly low temperatures, this might be one to try. The leaves are small and the flowers fairly small, of a pinkish-mauve color. It is a neat-appearing plant, although the color is not as good as that of some of the more tender varieties.

Sapphire—xxx, H–3. Of several dwarf blue rhododendrons, it seems to me that 'Sapphire' is one of the best, because of its very good blue color and the small neat leaves, with a slight blue-green cast. It will reach about 2 feet in ten years unless in some shade, in which case it will grow taller. The foliage has a very spicy, aromatic odor, noticeable when one brushes against or crushes a leaf. In some gardens in the East it has been shy about setting buds, although it is very floriferous in the West.

Temple Belle G.—xxx, H–3. Another *R. williamsianum* hybrid, this resembles to some extent 'Bow Bells' and 'Arthur J. Ivens.' The color is pale rose to a deep rose pink. It will make a broad little mound some 2 to 3 feet high in ten years.

Thomwilliams G.—xx, H–4. This is still another *R. williamsianum* hybrid, growing much the same as those previously described. The flowers are deep rose pink, produced rather early in the season on a plant reaching some 2 feet in height in ten years.

MANY OTHER GOOD VARIETIES

There are doubtless many other varieties that various gardeners would add to the preceding list. Some would be more or less local sorts, so perhaps a word should be said about varieties produced by breeders in your own locality. It is surprising how many rhododendron and azalea breeders are to be found, scattered pretty much throughout the United States, except in the Great Plains area and in the mountain and desert country of the West and Southwest. In most cases the varieties produced by these local breeders will be especially well adapted to the conditions under which the selections were made. Usually, therefore, a gardener would not go wrong by trying a variety selected and named in his own general climatic area.

Space will not permit a discussion of all breeders who are doing very worth-while work, but it might be well to mention two who have been working for a great many years. These are Guy Nearing in New Jersey and Joseph Gable in Pennsylvania. Both have produced and named a number of clones. Both have been breeding and selecting particularly for hardiness, trying to produce for their own localities varieties just as hardy as the old ironclads, but with better flower or plant characters. We have already mentioned 'Ramapo' of Mr. Nearing and 'Conemaugh' of Mr. Gable. Each has a number of other varieties to his credit, some of which will undoubtedly be more widely grown.

In the Northwest we have a number of breeders who have developed exceptionally fine things, and some of these will be mentioned in Chapter 13. However Northwestern gardeners have had a wide range of English and Dutch varieties to choose from, and so the need for new introductions has not been as urgent as in colder parts of the country.

CHAPTER 12

Azalea Varieties

There is no doubt but what azaleas are more widely grown than other rhododendrons, especially in the South. The plants usually sell at a somewhat lower price than other types of rhododendrons, and almost invariably they begin blooming at a very early age. As a matter of fact a large percentage of azaleas, as well as rhododendrons, are sold when they are in flower, or at least displaying flower buds. Although azaleas have the same general peculiarities of adaptability to soil and climatic conditions and other environmental factors as do rhododendrons, the latter seem to be somewhat more fussy. Whether this means that azaleas can actually withstand unfavorable conditions better than rhododendrons, or just that the proper rhododendrons have not yet been bred, or at least not yet been introduced to those areas, is something we do not know.

Certainly for the gardener who has never grown either, and who does not know much about them, and who does not know of any in his immediate vicinity, it would seem wise to start with azaleas and, if they do well, then go on to plant other rhododendrons. This does not mean that rhododendrons and azaleas can be used interchangeably in the garden, although to some extent they can. Still, azaleas have a place of their own, based on their low, spreading growth and profusion of brightly colored flowers, excelled by no other temperate zone shrubs.

MANY SPECIES AND VARIETIES

As we have already seen, all azaleas are grouped together as one series of the over-all rhododendron group or genus. However there are between seventy and eighty species of azaleas now considered to be distinct, and several thousand varieties have been named. Of course not all of these are available from present catalogues, or even in existence, but at least several hundred varieties are currently listed. This may be surprising to many gardeners, as in some localities only one or two are generally grown. In some areas this might be the deciduous Mollis type, and in others an evergreen clone, perhaps

'Hinodegiri,' or a few of the more tender varieties found in the South.

Nearly all azaleas with non-Latin names are actually clones, the result of asexual propagation from one original seedling. While such varieties are usually spoken of as having "English" names, many azaleas have Japanese names, which are simply written in English in a manner to approximate the sound of the Japanese word. Other varieties have Dutch, French, or German names, depending on the nationality of the originator.

SOME STILL GROWN AS SPECIES

Quite a few azaleas are still available only in the species form, no clonal varieties having been named or propagated. Examples might include *R. schlippenbachi, R. calendulaceum, R. occidentale,* and others. The plants of these are grown from seed, and each plant will be a little different from any of the others; and although in many cases the differences will be extremely small, with some species the range will be from very fine plants to those distinctly inferior. Therefore, it is best, if possible, to see the plant you expect to buy, when it is in bloom. When buying a cutting-grown, named variety, it might be sufficient to have seen the variety in a neighbor's garden or in a show, or even to have read a detailed description.

AZALEAS SOLD AS HYBRID GROUPS

Other types of azaleas may be hybrid in nature, but still sold as seedlings or as a group. One of the best examples of this is the so-called Mollis azalea, which has resulted from the hybridization of at least two original species. Since the Mollis hybrids come fairly true from seed, that is to the extent that there are usually not too many inferior seedlings, it has been the custom to sell seedling plants. The gardener would be well advised to see a Mollis azalea bloom before he buys it, as there is enough variation to make some difference in the value of the plant—color, for instance, ranging from yellow to a tawny apricot. One reason why they are usually sold as seedlings is that they are difficult to grow from cuttings. Some superior forms have been named, and introduced in the form of grafted plants or plants raised from layers, but that is a more expensive method than seed propagation.

As we have already seen, the British custom, for a time at least, was to give English names to a group of rhododendron seedlings from a particular cross. Fortunately that situation has not occurred to any great extent with azaleas. It is true that a few group names have been given, but so far as I know seedlings are not now being sold as "named varieties" under group names in this country.

It can be seen that there is enough variation in the way azaleas are propagated and sold that, for his own protection, the beginner should learn something about names and what they mean. Also one likes to be reasonably intelligent about a variety he owns, in case he might be discussing it with another gardener.

TYPES OF AZALEAS

Rhododendrons other than azaleas, as we have seen, are usually divided, for the convenience of gardeners, into two rather poorly defined groups—the large or standard type, and the dwarfs. It would be possible to handle azaleas in the same way, but they are usually divided into a larger number of different, and more or less distinct, groups. In some cases the group is based on parentage, as all the varieties are the result of a certain type of cross. Such varieties may resemble each other fairly closely, so that a general discussion of the characters and cultural requirements of the group might be useful, as what is said could be applied more or less to each individual clone.

In other cases an azalea group represents the varieties originated by one man, or one working group. He may have done a great deal of intercrossing and backcrossing, so that a large number of species are involved in the parentage of his selections, which may be of several different types. However for purposes of general information and better understanding, considering one man's introductions as a group may be desirable. For instance we frequently hear of the "Gable" azaleas. These are selections from the breeding of Mr. Joseph Gable of Stewartstown, Pennsylvania. The parentage may include many different types and varieties, but Mr. Gable has for many years been breeding for increased hardiness. When one speaks of the Gable azaleas, it may not bring to mind a particular color or form so much as a group of relatively hardy varieties, originating in a specific locality, as the contribution of one individual.

Perhaps the first basis for breaking up the hundreds of varieties of azaleas into understandable groups would be to consider them as either evergreen or deciduous. All the smaller groups fall in one of these two types, although it is entirely possible that we might eventually have a group, based on one man's breeding, which would include both types. So far, to my knowledge, that is not the case. In general the evergreen types have been somewhat more tender, and so are grown in the southern part of the country, thus far more or less to the exclusion of the deciduous varieties. The deciduous types being hardier, they are naturally grown to the northern limits of rhododendron culture. In most southern gardens one rarely sees a deciduous azalea, and in most northern ones there are very few evergreen varieties. The large group of gardeners living in the broad central climatic zone can choose either or both types, each of which has its advantages.

The following discussion of azalea groups is not intended to be a scientific analysis of that subject, for which I would refer the reader to other and more technical publications. The groups are discussed as a means of helping the beginner to become familiar with varieties and their relationships. Azalea varieties have not yet been rated by the American Rhododendron Society, although some have been given ratings by the Royal Horticultural Society, using somewhat the same system as that previously described for rhododendrons.

My approach to the discussion of groups and varieties is made in a spirit of humility, as I have had less experience in this field than with the other rhododendrons. The information about the various groups is more or less standard, appearing in a number of books in this field.

The choice of varieties to list, or briefly describe, under each group was based partly on personal experience, partly on the literature. On the whole they were not selected as the best in the group, except where so indicated. The "best" are often new and hard to obtain, and what is best in one locality may be mediocre in another. For the beginner, perhaps ease of culture, availability of plants, and "good" quality rather than "best" are most important, and the selections were made on that basis in full knowledge that lists prepared by others might be somewhat different. But the most expert would probably disagree among themselves, so what I have attempted is a useful list, and I hope it is that.

EVERGREEN AZALEAS
• KURUME AZALEAS

This is a group of evergreen azaleas, originating about 150 years ago in the area of Kurume, a Japanese industrial city. The first introduction to this country was at the time of the Panama Pacific Exposition at San Francisco in 1915. Some of the plants exhibited there were bought by nurserymen in this country, and additional importations were made. A few years later, Mr. E. H. Wilson, one of the famed plant explorers, visited Kurume, and a year after that sent to the Arnold Arboretum fifty selections which he felt to be outstanding. These have since been known as the Wilson Fifty. Later, additional importations were made by the Department of Agriculture, so that perhaps a hundred varieties of this type have been introduced from Japan. The Kurumes are variable as to size, but they are generally upright, rounded, and usually dense and shapely. Old plants spread in a very picturesque and attractive manner. The flowers are single, unless otherwise mentioned, and range from ½ inch to 1½ inches in width.

Hinodegiri—This is probably the best-known evergreen azalea and a comparatively hardy one. The color is a bright, vivid crimson, tending towards violet as it fades. It is undoubtedly a striking and useful variety, but has occasionally been used to excess. It is probably as good as any for the beginner.

Coral Bells—A low, spreading variety, with hose-in-hose flowers.

Hinomayo—Fairly tall, early midseason, with single soft pink flowers.

Ward's Ruby—This is a good, bright-red sort, but somewhat more tender than the others mentioned.

• KAEMPFERI HYBRIDS

In 1892, Professor C. S. Sargent of the Arnold Arboretum sent back seeds of this azalea from the Kirishima mountain area in Japan. Mr. E. H. Wilson maintained that this was a form of *R. obtusum,* in which species the Kurume azaleas are presumed to have had their origin. Later experience leads to the conclusion that *R. kaempferi* is a good species in itself.

The Kaempferi hybrids are rather upright-growing, and may eventually reach a height of 8 feet. They are somewhat hardier than the Kurumes. The flowers are single, with some hose-in-hose, and in general larger than most of the Kurumes. Breeding in this group was carried on by certain Dutch nurserymen, including P. M. Koster, and C. B. vanNes and Sons, both of Boskoop. Plants are occasionally found in nurseries under the name Kaempferi. These may be plants of the original species, but more often they are hybrids, as this group crosses readily with *R. obtusum,* from which the Kurumes were derived. There is some opinion that *R. kaempferi* may also have been involved in the ancestry of the Kurume group.

'Annamaria' and 'John Cairns' are said to be good selections of the Kaempferi hybrids.

• PERICAT HYBRIDS

These azaleas are the result of breeding work by Alphonse Pericat at Collingdale, Pennsylvania. The parentage is not definitely known, but they may be hybrids between the Kurume and Belgian Indian types, produced primarily for greenhouse forcing. They are, however, hardier than many of the forcing types, and are considered to be satisfactory as outdoor plants from Washington, D.C. south.

Flanders Field—Late midseason, orange red in color.

Madame Pericat—Hose-in-hose, pink with a lighter center, late midseason.

• KOREAN AZALEAS

Known botanically as *R. poukhanense,* this is the hardiest of the evergreen azaleas in common cultivation. This is not so much a "group" as it is a single species, with its various seedlings and chance hybrids. It has been used in breeding by Gable and others. Most of the plants available are seedlings, although a few might be accidental hybrids. There is one double form known as 'Yodogawa.' Although this is considered to be an evergreen species, it loses a good part of its leaves during the winter, in colder climates.

• GABLE HYBRIDS

Mr. Joseph B. Gable of Stewartstown, Pennsylvania, has for many years been breeding both rhododendrons and hardy evergreen azaleas. Since a number of different species were involved in the parentage, the Gable hybrids represent a rather miscellaneous group, but hardiness has been a dominant factor. Species used as parents include *R. poukhanense, R. kaempferi,* and various named varieties of *R. obtusum* and other species.

Among the Gable hybrids are the following, from a total list of perhaps fifty:

Big Joe—Early midseason, spreading, medium height, single flowers to about 2½ inches. Reddish violet in color.

Caroline Gable—Flowers to 1¾ inches. Red.

Elizabeth Gable—Late-blooming, single flowers, frilled, 2½ inches. Red with darker blotch. Very hardy.

Purple Splendour—Probably the best purple in the azalea field, although not nearly so dark and rich as the 'Purple Splendour' rhododendron.

Rosebud—This is a low-growing, dense, late-flowering variety with double flowers. Violet rose in color.

Cameo—Late-flowering, hose-in-hose, flowers about 1½ inches. Shell pink in color.

• INDICA AZALEAS

Japanese hybridizers have given us a group of very late-flowering varieties, derived from *R. indicum,* sometimes known in the trade as the Macrantha type. This group is known in Japan as the Satsuki azaleas, and certain forms have been in cultivation for some 300 years. Most of the flowers are large; some are frilled. Most varieties are fairly hardy, at least as far north as Washington, D.C.

A group of azaleas brought into this country by the Plant Introduction Section of the U.S.D.A. came from the Chugai Nursery, and are sometimes known as the Chugai hybrids. They include plants of the Indica type, and some hybrids between that type and others, particularly the Belgian Indian varieties. Some forty or fifty varieties were brought in but probably not all are now available in the nursery trade. Certain clones, known as Gumpo, seem to belong to a subspecies known as the dwarf Indica, or possibly to be seedlings of that species crossed with some other. The Gumpo clones, available in at least white and pink, are very low-growing, spreading, with relatively large and attractive flowers, and are hardy in the New York City area.

Jindair—Very late, white.

Keisetsu—Orange red with a white throat and variegated leaves, late.

Waraigishi—Deep rose with a darker blotch, single to semidouble, late.

• RYUKYU GROUP

Several species are involved in this group which came from the Ryukyu Islands south of Japan. The species most widely grown is *R. mucronatum.* This has been under cultivation in Japan for more than 300 years, and is still available in the nursery trade as 'Indica Alba,' or 'Ledifolia Alba.' It is a spreading, medium-tall plant, with single, pure-white flowers some 3 inches in diameter, hardy as far north as Long Island, New York. The leaves are somewhat hairy and tend to hold the mud splashed onto them during rains or during the winter. A similar clone is 'Sekidera,' essentially the same as the type except that the flowers are blotched with violet red in a very striking, contrasting pattern.

• BELGIAN INDIAN HYBRIDS

In the early 1800s, a number of breeders in Belgium, and to a certain extent in other European countries, used plants of several species including the Ryukyu types to produce forcing varieties. They were not interested in hardiness, as the varieties were considered solely for forcing. It has been said that this program held back the development of hardy garden azaleas for many years, as garden-minded people came to think of this group of plants as too tender to be considered as outdoor subjects. It is true that these Belgian Indian hybrids include what are probably the most beautiful flowered azaleas in existence. Some are double and some beautifully frilled, with a wide range of clear and attractive colors.

Although some of these forcing varieties are very tender, others have sufficient hardiness so that they may be grown out of doors, in the southern states at least. As a matter of fact, some often sold farther north have just enough hardiness to be tantalizing. Potted plants are given as presents during holiday seasons, especially at Easter, and the recipient naturally wants to keep them and plant them outside. Very often they will persist for a year or two, but gradually succumb to the rigors of outdoor climate. It is not the purpose of this book to instruct in the growing of forcing azaleas. They have been brought in incidentally, as the problem so often arises as to what to do with such forcing azaleas received as gifts.

• SOUTHERN INDIAN HYBRIDS

Another reason for mentioning the Belgian Indian varieties is the fact that they have been a factor in the development of the so-called southern Indian hybrids, or Southern Indicas. These are the magnificent old plants found in the famous azalea gardens of the South, first introduced into this country close to 100 years ago. Essentially they are the hardier clones of the Belgian Indian hybrids which have proven satisfactory outdoors in the South.

Most of the Southern Indian clones are too tender for growing anywhere but the far South, although a few do reasonably well as far north as Washington, D.C. Whether they would grow in the Northwest is a question as, so far as I know, it has never been seriously attempted. Very little breeding has been done with these azaleas in the South, presumably because the original importations, so many years ago, proved to be so desirable and so well adapted to local conditions. It is somewhat surprising that, for a long time, these varieties were largely confined to a few of the great azalea gardens, and were not used to any extent in personal gardens of the smaller type. Gardeners in the southern states naturally should try these among the first, if they are at all interested in planting azaleas. Because the varieties were introduced so many years ago, and records are scanty, the actual identity of many of the plants is difficult to determine. The best advice perhaps would be to see the plant in flower before purchasing.

• GLENN DALE HYBRIDS

This is the largest group of evergreen azaleas now available to the gardening public. The various clones were grown and selected by Mr. B. Y. Morrison, formerly of the Plant Introduction Section of the U.S.D.A. The original seedlings were grown at the Plant Introduction Station at Glenn Dale, Maryland, hence the name. The original aim was to produce varieties which would be hardy and happy in the climate of Washington, D.C., although some of them will thrive far beyond that area. From some 70,000 seedlings over 400 clones have been named—a rather unfortunately large number, as the azalea lover has been faced with the monumental task of deciding which ones of these numerous varieties are suited to his conditions and meet his esthetic requirements.

Some of these clones were introduced almost twenty years ago, but we still do not have ratings or lists of the best of the group for various climatic conditions. However a number are emerging as hardier or more adaptable than the rest, and eventually will take their place in the azalea world. The parentage of the Glenn Dale varieties is quite varied, including the Indica azalea, the Chugai selections, *R. kaempferi,* and a number of named varieties as well as additional species. The plants are mostly of average size, some upright, some spreading, and most have large and rather attractive single flowers, although there are some doubles.

It is certain that, for the environment of Washington, D.C., the gardener can find a wide range of plants with beautiful flowers and attractive bushes. Gardeners in other areas who are just beginning with azaleas will probably have to rely on the experience of their local nurserymen, or order plants from a distance by catalogue description and hope for the best. In the Pacific Northwest there seems to be somewhat more interest in rhododendrons than in azaleas, and so there has not been enough experience accumulated to make possible the compilation of a recommended and tested list.

Aztec—Low, red with a white throat, late.

Ballet Girl—Early, flaming, orange red.

Cordial—Pink, late midseason.

Crinoline—Pink, about midseason.

Cygnet—Early, low-growing, white.

Driven Snow—Late, low-growing, white.

Eros—Low-growing pink, blooms very late.

Glacier—White, late midseason.

Joya—Early midseason, pink.

Pearl Bradford—Low-growing, very late, deep rose pink.

Tanager—Late midseason, orange red.

Wildfire—White-throated red, late.

OTHER EVERGREEN GROUPS

There are several other groups not listed here for various reasons, including the matter of space. The varieties with which the beginner should start mostly fall within the above mentioned groups. But there will be further fields to conquer for those who really love azaleas and set out to become familiar with all the various types.

DECIDUOUS AZALEAS

There are several groups of azaleas which lose their leaves in the winter and, possibly because of that, are somewhat hardier than most of the evergreen types. Gardeners wanting azaleas in the yellow shades will have to find them here. These deciduous plants are extremely colorful and beautiful while in flower, and in addition many exhibit autumn coloration, running through the yellows to bright red to deep maroon. However in midwinter they are unmistakably bare, and that must be considered in using them in the landscape.

• GHENT HYBRIDS

Breeders in Ghent, Belgium, beginning in the early 1820s, worked with some of the native American species and the native deciduous azalea of southeastern Europe, commonly known as the Pontic azalea, or *R. luteum*. The group of varieties resulting from their work is usually known in this country as the hardy Ghent hybrids, and in Holland as the Pontica azaleas. Some are single and some double.

Colors run through yellows to orange-red. As deciduous flowering shrubs, they are difficult to match for brilliant color, graceful form, and autumn coloration. The plants generally are rather upright-growing while young, but later spread to form fairly well-balanced bushes. Some are said to have survived 25° below zero. The flowers are only medium in size, with a long tube, and frequently possess some fragrance.

Coccinea Speciosa—Reddish orange in color, over 100 years old but very striking.

Nancy Waterer—Golden yellow, midseason variety with rather large flowers.

Gloria Mundi—A tall-growing variety, producing single, frilled flowers in late midseason, orange with a yellow blotch.

The Ghents, long popular in the deciduous azalea field, have been replaced or superseded, to a considerable extent, by some of the groups to follow.

• MOLLIS HYBRIDS

This is a rather complex group, including at least two Asiatic species. The breeding began close to a hundred years ago in Belgium and Holland. A rather large number of varieties have been named, but not all of these were clones. A few types came fairly true from seed, and the seedlings were sold under a variety name, after odd-colored or obviously different plants were held out. These azaleas are rather difficult to propagate by cuttings, and layering is slow and tedious. Varieties can be grafted, but the experience has not been especially satisfactory, as grafted azaleas have not been as resistant to drought and cold as plants on their own roots. Furthermore, the understock, usually *R. luteum,* frequently sends up shoots, and the result is a mixture of the bright, yellow-flowered understock with whatever type of flower is produced by the scion variety. The result has been that seedlings have been sold in large numbers, just as Mollis hybrids. As a general rule the Mollis seedlings are not quite as large in flower or as pure in color as some of the named varieties, which are sometimes rather difficult to find. The seedlings are usually of two colors, light yellow or a reddish apricot. Occasionally deeper reds or especially good yellows are found.

Adriaan Koster—A good deep yellow.

Aureum Grandiflorum—This is said to be the correct name of the rather striking orange yellow, frequently sold under the name of 'Altaclarensis,' which is white with an orange blotch. 'Aureum Grandiflorum' is sometimes listed with the Ghents but presumably has *R. molle* as one parent. The white 'Altaclarensis' is listed as a Ghent hybrid.

Christopher Wren—A seedling of 'Aureum Grandiflorum,' and superior to it. Large yellow flowers with an orange blotch.

Dr. M. Oosthoek—Reddish orange with a lighter blotch.

Koster's Brilliant Red—Reddish orange.

• OCCIDENTALE HYBRIDS

Koster's in Holland and John Waterer Sons & Crisp of England during the latter part of the last century crossed the native western azalea, *R. occidentale,* with Mollis hybrids and produced a number of very fine deciduous varieties, usually considered under the name Occidentale hybrids. They do not, however, have the large flowers to be found in the following group.

Graciosa—Orange yellow, suffused with red, with a yellowish orange blotch.

Irene Koster—Late midseason, with scented flowers, white-flushed red.

• KNAP HILL HYBRIDS

Beginning about 1870, Anthony Waterer, one of the leading English nurserymen, crossed a Chinese species, *R. molle,* with the native American azalea, *R. calendulaceum.* Additional crosses were made, bringing in other American species, and later the western species, *R. occidentale,* until there are probably seven or eight species involved if we consider the whole Knap Hill group.

Eventually plants were furnished by Waterer's Nursery to the Slocock Nursery, and to the late Edgar Stead at the Ilam Estate in New Zealand, and to the late Lionel de Rothschild at Exbury, near Southampton, in England. Each of these individuals made further crosses and created further improvements. Their plants have been introduced under the group names Knap Hill, Slocock, Ilam, and Exbury. Certainly they are all somewhat different, but in view of the fact that they are all based on the original breeding at the Knap Hill Nursery, and as they all have some characters in common, the tendency now is to call them all Knap Hill azaleas. In this group are to be found varieties which have larger and more spectacular flowers, more beautiful shades of coloring, and in general a more attractive floral display than in any of the other azalea groups. Some show attractive autumn coloration, and some are quite fragrant.

These, like all the other deciduous azaleas, have proven to be rather difficult to grow from cuttings. They have been grown in England by layering, as being more satisfactory than grafting. However, this is a slow process, and results in plants which, while young, are rather poorly shaped, and need to be grown in the nursery row for a couple of years to develop a bush of pleasing form. Many nurserymen have been interested in growing these varieties by cuttings, and a great deal of progress has been made, so that in the near future we may look forward to seeing named, cutting-grown varieties available.

In the meanwhile nurserymen and azalea fanciers in general were faced with the problem of having some very beautiful varieties in their possession with no very rapid means of multiplication. As they do produce seed rather freely, and the seedlings are easy to grow, a great many seedlings, some of controlled crosses and others open-pollinated, have been produced. The results have been quite remarkable from the standpoint of general average quality—considerably better than is usually obtained from sowing seed of cultivated varieties of other ornamental plants.

Some varieties were found to come fairly true to type, and others produced a very miscellaneous lot of seedlings. At one time there was a trend toward selling seedlings under the name of the female parent which, of course, was undesirable. Several nurserymen in the Northwest have been growing relatively large numbers of seedlings and selling them in bloom simply as unnamed seedlings. This permits the gardener to select a plant which he likes, and one which no one else has in exact duplication. The difficulty is that he may want another plant, or a friend might want one, and it is simply not available. It will be better for all concerned when these plants are freely grown from cuttings, although the seedlings have given rise to a large number of very fine individuals. Some have been named, and others will be named, and propagated asexually.

As might be expected from such a varied ancestry, the hardiness of the various varieties and unnamed seedlings varies considerably. Quite a number have been found to be extremely hardy. Among the varieties available in this country, and at least partially proven in the Northwest, are the following:

Balzac—A fragrant orange-red variety.

Berry Rose—Orange red with a yellow blotch.

Flamingo—Tall-growing with large carmine-rose flowers, very definitely a flamingo pink.

Golden Oriole—Upright, early, tall; a large yellow flower with a deep-tangerine blotch.

Goldfinch—Rather tall, the flowers yellow with a deeper yellow blotch.

Marion Merriman—This is a rather low-growing, spreading variety, blooming in late midseason, with large flowers of greenish yellow flushed with orange yellow.

Strawberry Ice—Rather tall-growing, peach pink.

White Throat—This is a rather low-growing, spreading variety, blooming in midseason, with pure white, double flowers about 2 inches in diameter.

Persil—Large-flowered white with a pale-yellow blotch.

Satan—Bright scarlet.

SPECIES AZALEAS

Some of the species of the azalea series are very fine garden subjects. In some cases there are hybrids, which carry some of the desirable species characteristics, but others are available only in the species form.

R. schlippenbachii—This so-called Royal azalea from Korea has apparently not been used to any extent in hybridizing. Perhaps the hybridizers have looked at its large white to pink flowers, some as large as 4 inches across, and have wondered what could possibly be crossed with it to make it more beautiful or more desirable. It produces a rounded plant to 10 or 12 feet in height, perhaps 4 to 5 feet in ten years, and is quite hardy. It is true that there is considerable variation in seedlings, and so it is always desirable, if possible, to propagate from a plant of known characteristics. However, almost any *R. schlippenbachii* seedling will produce a beautiful and useful garden plant.

There are other azalea species from the Far East which will no doubt eventually be more frequently used than they now are. At present they are not as readily obtainable as *R. schlippenbachii,* and on the whole are perhaps not as spectacularly effective in the garden. We might mention three other very fine deciduous azaleas worth trying, if you can find them: *R. albrechtii, R. quinquefolium,* and *R. reticulatum.* We have already mentioned the evergreen sorts,

R. kaempferi and *R. mucronatum,* to which we might add *R. oldhamii,* all of which make excellent garden plants.

NATIVE AMERICAN SPECIES

It has been stated that several of our native American species were involved from the beginning in the development of the Ghent hybrids, with which were combined, over a period of years, certain other American species, to produce eventually the Knap Hill type, with its very large and beautifully colored flowers. These flamboyant varieties are a far cry from the more modest and retiring species, which, however, were responsible for many of the best characteristics of the Knap Hills. There might be some who would question whether there is need for the original species plants, now that we have the far superior named varieties, selected, during a century and more of breeding, from thousands and thousands of seedlings of dozens of different crosses.

As previously stated with respect to rhododendrons, the tendency for the beginner is to desire the largest-flowered and brightest-colored of the hybrid varieties. Later he begins to appreciate the species rhododendrons because of their refined and well-balanced appearance—not only for their bloom, but for their individual and unique characteristics of leaf, twig, and bush shape. In the same way the native azalea species bring to the garden plants with real character and individuality. Some are outstanding for color in mass, others for fragrance, others for blooming at the time when flowers in the garden are scarce, and others just for inherent qualities of gracefulness and attractiveness.

The real problem is where to secure these desirable shrubs. Very few nurserymen are raising them from seed. Still fewer have selected outstanding specimens and propagated them from cuttings or layers. There are superior individuals, and there are natural hybrids occurring rather frequently in the wild, so that we may certainly look forward to being able, eventually, to secure fine forms of these native shrubs. How then can one, and especially a beginner in this field, find plants for his garden?

There are some plants collected in the wild and listed in nursery catalogues. If properly handled, these may be reasonably satisfactory, although the plants are usually collected while dormant, hence include the poor seedlings with the good ones. The ideal way to collect these azaleas would seem to be in the form of seed from individual plants that are outstanding because of their size, color, vigor, or other desirable characteristics. A large segment of our population lives in the Southeast, where the species are at their height as to number of types, number of individuals, and adaptability to growing conditions. The seedlings are not too difficult to grow, as indicated in the chapter on propagation. By planting a number of seedlings together, perhaps in a shrub border, there will be opportunity to weed out the less desirable forms as they come into bloom, so the final result should be several plants of good to excellent quality.

Far be it from me to recommend the digging of wild azaleas, although I have an idea the average gardener would be at least as circumspect as the professional collector. Certainly plants should not be dug from parks or other restricted areas, and the removal of large specimens should usually not be attempted. These might be transplanted safely, but only by careful digging with a large ball of soil, which is usually out of the question, or at least very difficult, where plants are growing in uneven terrain and mixed closely with other trees and shrubs.

There are places, of course, where the digging of a few small seedling plants would harm no one and would preserve for human delight plants which might never survive in the wild, or which might be in the way of road developments or other natural or man-made catastrophes that would effectively prevent the seedlings from growing to maturity in their native habitat. If you are going to take them up, however, please don't yank them out of the hard ground and leave most of the root system in the soil. Dig them carefully with a good root ball, keep them shaded and moist, and plant them as quickly as possible where conditions are suited to their needs.

The following list does not include all of our native azaleas, or even all the desirable ones but, rather, a few which are most likely to be available and useful in your garden. They are all deciduous.

R. arborescens—This is a late-flowering species, which at maturity becomes a rather large, spreading shrub. The white, sometimes flushed pink, flowers appear after the leaves are out. It is rather important for garden purposes to use selections which have large flowers and glossy, attractive foliage. This is a very hardy species, native from New York and Pennsylvania south to Georgia.

R. bakeri—Apparently synonymous with *R. cumberlandense,* this species is somewhat more compact than the following, but resembles it in color range, blooming somewhat later. It is found at high elevations from Kentucky south to Georgia and Alabama.

R. calendulaceum—Of all the southeastern azaleas, this one, known as the Flame azalea, has probably been recognized as a fine ornamental for the longest period of time. It has been used freely in breeding, but there has not been too much progress in the introduction of very fine forms of the species itself. It is an upland grower, found from Pennsylvania to Georgia. The colors range from yellow to orange to brilliant red, through apricot and other intermediate shades. This species produces a vigorous plant to 10 or 12 feet in height, and is especially effective in the edge of a woodland, or growing up through other shrubs and small trees.

R. canadense—This is a very hardy, deciduous species, growing from the east coast of Labrador and Newfoundland south to the northern part of New Jersey. It makes an upright little bush, reaching perhaps 3 feet in height. It has grayish-green foliage and rosy purple flowers. There is a white form which is especially nice. This species was at one time placed in a separate genus, *Rhodora,* but is now considered an azalea. For the northern gardener with acid soil, this little plant may permit inclusion of the genus in gardens where the more common types of rhododendrons would be completely out of the question.

R. nudiflorum—An early midseason, pink-flowering azalea, this species makes a fine garden subject because of its very free flowering and sweet, spicy fragrance. It is known as the Pinxterbloom or Honeysuckle azalea. It grows in the wild from Massachusetts to North Carolina, and hence must be considered reasonably hardy. With this, as with the other native species, it is important to find good specimens. It has been said that the difference between the best and poorest of these native species "is often the difference between platinum and tin."

R. occidentale—This is the only azalea native to the West Coast, where it is called Oregon azalea, or just Western azalea. It is found from Southern California north to the State of Washington, with its greatest development along the coast, near the Oregon-California border. Plants grow to 8 or 10 feet in height, and greater than that in spread, and produce beautiful, sweet-scented, creamy white to pink flowers with a yellow, or orange-yellow, blotch. This beautiful species has not been satisfactory as a garden plant in the East or in Europe, but has been a valuable parent in the development of our modern garden azaleas, especially the Knap Hills and similar groups. It is a very desirable garden shrub in those areas of the West where it appears to be naturally adapted.

R. roseum—Quite attractive in its best color forms, this species varies from almost white to deep pink, approaching red. It is very hardy, occurring in the wild from New England west to Indiana, and south to the Virginia Blue Ridge.

R. speciosum—This species must be considered as somewhat less hardy than the preceding, as it comes from the lowlands of Georgia and South Carolina. It is especially notable for its fine flower color, ranging through yellows to bright, incandescent reds, with softer types intermediate.

R. vaseyi—This Pink Shell azalea from western North Carolina is a beautiful thing, grown to some extent in Europe, but all too scarce in American gardens. The best forms are deep, rich pink in color, although a good white form has been selected. It is somewhat hardier than its southern origin might indicate.

CHAPTER 13

Rhododendrons and the Plant Breeder

As first outlined, this chapter was to be headed "What the Plant Breeders Have Accomplished." That would be covering a great deal of territory, considering we have some 10,000 named varieties of azaleas and rhododendrons, all probably rated as accomplishments by the persons who named them. Then as the chapter developed, it seemed important to say something about what is still needed and likely to be forthcoming in this field. Some might say that the plant breeder need not be mentioned at all in a book for the beginner, as it will in no way improve the quality of his gardening. But it may increase his interest and general knowledge of a very large and farflung group of ornamental plants, and that usually results, in some way, in a more successful garden. So we'll touch a bit on rhododendrons and the plant breeder, both past and future. And I would be willing to gamble that some of the beginners reading this will, before many years have passed, succumb to the lure of the unknown, and be looking over their own seedlings in search of that bigger, better, and most unusual plant, always just around the plant breeder's corner.

AZALEA BREEDING IN JAPAN

Relatively early in the garden history of rhododendrons, the plant breeders set to work to improve on the original species. Quite possibly the first breeders were Japanese gardeners of some 300 years ago or more. At least there is evidence that a great many named varieties were in existence at that early date. They could have been just open-pollinated seedlings, but their range of types and forms indicate a planned development.

AZALEA BREEDING IN BELGIUM

Serious breeding, involving a number of collected sorts, began in Belgium about 1820. This was a lapse of a hundred years, since some of the species had been imported into England, but in those days things moved relatively slowly. There had to be time for the seeds, which were imported, to germinate and grow into plants. These had to be evaluated by the gardeners of the day. Additional seedlings had to be raised, or layers made, or some of the original plants transported across the Channel to the Belgian breeders.

It is always a little difficult to look back and explain the reasons for development along certain lines, or lack of development along other lines. Certainly the American azaleas were beautiful in their own right. However they apparently did not strike any responsive chord among the gardeners of that day, except to indicate to a few dreamers that they might be of value for crossing, to produce flowers with larger size.

One sometimes wonders what the rhododendron and azalea situation would be today if the breeders had not become interested, as they did. With certain other shrubby material, we find the species growing in gardens for centuries with apparently no particular interest on the part of plant breeders. Perhaps the beauty and desirability of the American azaleas were appreciated when they were first introduced, and perhaps they were grown in gardens more than our present knowledge would indicate. Perhaps also their very desirability and superior qualities as garden plants simply stimulated the azalea fancier—plant breeders of the day, who proceeded to make some wonderful plants even better by their distribution of pollen.

An account of the breeders who had a part in improving azaleas makes very interesting reading, and can be found in various publications. It is hardly a function of this book to go into that history, except from the standpoint of results. This has already been traced, to some extent, in the azalea field, by mention of the Ghent hybrids, coming from that very early work in Belgium through the efforts first of Mr. P. Mortier, a Ghent baker. A few years after he began his work he sold out to another breeder in the same city. Slightly later, breeding began in England, and soon there were hybrid plants to distribute and to use as a basis for still further breeding.

ANTHONY WATERER BRINGS IN MORE SPECIES

As more and more species were sent to Europe by the plant explorers, they were used to introduce various additional and desirable characters. This proceeded in a rather desultory way up to 1870, when Anthony Waterer, one of a long line of nurserymen in his family, began to improve the Ghent hybrids by bringing in *R.*

molle, and our own western azalea, *R. occidentale,* and the eastern *R. arborescens.* These added additional characters, increasing size, fragrance, and range of colors. The work of the breeders of that day is not set down in detail, and many of them were wary of disclosing the parentage of their seedlings. As a consequence there are many older varieties the parentage of which is unknown.

It is difficult adequately to evaluate the contribution made by any one of these breeders, as that evaluation would depend on our own personal likes and dislikes. Certainly size of flower was greatly increased, although to some this may be a doubtful improvement. Certainly it is accurate to say that the range of characters available for further breeding was extended to a remarkable degree. Whether everyone would agree that all of these new varieties were better than the first hybrids, or even better than the species, is problematical. However, the number of gardeners was increasing, and the number of types which these gardeners would prefer probably increased in about the same ratio. Gardeners are like that. So the breeding did give a great deal more variety, and choice as to blooming season, color, size, fragrance, bush characters, and all the rest.

Another factor of some importance, even in the early days, was hardiness. We may think of England as a more or less subtropical country, if our experience has been in Cornwall, or along the southern coast, or even parts of the west coast of England, Wales, or Scotland. However, there are areas on the east coast and inland where hardiness is a very important factor. In the early days not so much was said about it. If one's seedlings were hardy in his own neighborhood, he was satisfied, and did not worry much about whether they would survive in a more rigorous climate. Transportation was relatively primitive, and in many cases, perhaps, there was no thought of widespread distribution.

IMPORTATION OF R. CATAWBIENSE

The era of plant breeding of rhododendrons, as of azaleas, was based on the importation into England of certain hardy species from America, particularly *R. catawbiense.* The first importations were about 1850, and to the best of my knowledge at least one of the original plants is still growing at the Knap Hill Nursery, where I had the privilege of seeing it a few years ago. As with the azaleas, there is a question as to whether the American species, when first brought into England, created any particular furor insofar as their use as garden plants is concerned. Here again there is much we do not know about the subject, but in the famous old gardens where rhododendrons are featured, *R. catawbiense* is certainly not usually pointed out. The English have apparently had something of a dislike for the mauve or magenta colors, and perhaps rightly so. However, *R. catawbiense* did have two characters which recommended it to the attention of the plant breeder. These were extreme hardiness as compared to other species, and relatively good plant characters, including vigor of growth.

Again the name Waterer appears—Anthony Waterer, that is— as the breeder and nurseryman who combined *R. catawbiense* with other species. This breeding apparently began before 1850, and by 1865 we find some of his varieties have been grown and developed far enough to receive a first-class certificate from the Royal Horticultural Society. The other parent used with *R. catawbiense* is, in many cases, unknown, as Anthony was a close-lipped breeder, following the traditions of the day. In some cases the parentage can be guessed.

THE ASIATIC SPECIES COME TO ENGLAND

The bright, clear colors in whites, yellows, pinks, and reds which we now enjoy in many rhododendron varieties come from various Asiatic species. One of the first of these, introduced by Sir Joseph Hooker, was *R. arboreum*. Another, a little later, was *R. griffithianum*. Then came *R. fortunei* and its associates. These brought not only additional colors and, in some cases fragrance, but also more varied foliage and plant characters. Soon there was a deluge of new species, brought in by various plant-hunting expeditions. This was a bonanza for the breeders.

At the beginning there was some inclination to cross these new and exciting species with *R. catawbiense,* or the old hardy hybrids. Strangely enough, many of these newly introduced things from high, cold elevations in the Himalayas and surrounding hills and mountains were not nearly so hardy as their original location would seem to indicate. On the other hand, most of the species found in western China and the Himalayan foothill area did have enough hardiness to make them satisfactory as garden plants in the more favored parts of England, and along the west coast of the United States. The plant explorers worked down into Burma and eventually into the East Indies, where species tender to the slightest touch of frost were discovered. As might be expected, with such a profusion of spectacular species to choose from, the breeders have produced varieties of outstanding merit with respect to everything except hardiness, and in many cases with a considerable degree of that.

Breeding in this era of plant exploration was carried on, to a large extent, by a very few nurserymen and certain wealthy estate owners who had participated in the financing of the original expeditions which brought in the Asiatic species. They were, for the most part, located in southern England, or at least in the milder parts of England, so that hardiness was of somewhat secondary concern. From their breeding efforts came the varieties now being grown most extensively in the Pacific Northwest. Fortunately some have proven hardier than the rest, and may be of value in parts of the country somewhat colder than the Pacific Coast areas.

HARDINESS CONSIDERED FOR EXPORT

The English nurserymen, particularly the Waterer family group, with an eye to sales over a relatively wide area did not neglect the hardier species, and brought out varieties intermediate between the old "ironclads" and those just mentioned as being grown on the West Coast. Probably 'Pink Pearl' was one outstanding result of this breeding, or at least it has received more attention than the others.

Early in the twentieth century Dutch nurserymen became interested in producing varieties primarily for export. Partly because of their own climatic situation, and partly because the plants were to be shipped to England and other European countries and to the United States, hardiness was considered as being one of the most important characters. Most potential American buyers were from the East Coast, where hardiness was essential. In general, the Dutch varieties have ranged from the hardiness of the old Waterer "ironclads" down to that of the somewhat later English types, such as 'Pink Pearl.'

THE DWARF RHODODENDRONS

Relatively little interest was evidenced in the breeding of dwarf rhododendrons during the early days, partly because some of the finer dwarf species were not available at that time, and partly because the private breeders were interested in large and striking plants which would grow to an immense size, for the widespread and sweeping vistas favored by the landscape designers of the time. The ranch-type house was non-existent, as a style of architecture, and dwarf rhododendrons had no place against the foundation of a two-and-a-half-story house. Furthermore the small home owner had, for the most part, not yet become garden conscious. Rhododendron buyers were estate owners, and their requirements set the style for the breeders.

With the advent of some of the better dwarf species, such as *R. williamsianum, R. forrestii,* and others, breeders turned their attention to these plants. At the same time there developed a trend toward smaller gardens on the part of the relatively wealthy, and a greater interest in gardens on the part of the average person, who formerly was not considered as being of any particular moment in the gardening world, unless he happened to work as a gardener for some wealthy individual. More recently the changing times have brought in the low, sprawling type of house with no basement, consequently lower foundations, and windows almost down to ground level. Here the dwarf rhododendron and azalea can be used with wonderful effect.

What, one may ask, were American plant breeders doing while the English, the Dutch, and the Belgians were hybridizing the new introductions as they were received? The answer is fairly obvious. During the early part of the nineteenth century there were few landed estates in this country sufficiently large to maintain a corps of gardeners, and plantings which could make good use of rhododendrons. Gardening on the small estate and the city lot, as we now know it, was then almost unheard of. To be sure, knowledgable gardening for the small home was yet to be developed in Europe also. American species of both azaleas and rhododendrons that were collected and sent to Europe at first went primarily as specimens to enrich the collections in botanical gardens, rather than to decorate the home garden.

The first real impact of rhododendrons, as decorative garden plants, came to the American public at the time of the Philadelphia World's Fair in 1876. The Waterer Nursery sent over some 1500 *R. catawbiense* hybrids which were much appreciated by the fair visitors. Many of these plants were bought by nurserymen and distributed to gardens in the Philadelphia area.

THE FIRST AMERICAN BREEDERS

Mr. E. S. Rand, in his book previously mentioned, which was published in 1871, stated that thousands of seedlings were being grown in the Parson's Nursery, owned and operated by Mr. Samuel B. Parsons at Flushing, Long Island. Apparently Parsons imported large numbers of seedlings, probably small plants, from which he named some two dozen varieties. These were catawbiense hybrids, similar to others named and introduced by Waterer himself. Just how many of the varieties named by Parsons were from his own breeding and how many from Waterer is unknown. At least his work could be considered as an extension of the Waterer breeding and not of tremendous importance on its own, except as being the first selecting and naming of rhododendrons in America.

BREEDERS OF THE 1920–30 DECADE

We hear little of American breeders in this field until the 1920s, when several rather widely scattered people began breeding work. Those who started in this decade would include Joseph Gable of Stewartstown, Pennsylvania; Mr. C. O. Dexter of Sandwich, Massachusetts; Mr. James E. Barto of Junction City, Oregon; Mr. Guy Nearing of Ramsey, New Jersey; Mr. Frank L. Abbott of Saxtons River, Vermont; Mr. John Bacher of Portland, Oregon; Dr. Clement Bowers of Maine, New York; Mr. Frank Morgan of Hoquiam, Washington; Mr. Julian Pot of Chesterland, Ohio; and possibly others.

The objectives of these widely scattered rhododendron and azalea breeders were extremely varied. Some were working primarily for their own gardens. Others were thinking of a contribution to the gardening world, and probably most were driven by that mysterious urge which causes the plant breeder to make crosses "to see what will happen," and with the perhaps subconscious idea that he may better the lot of mankind by producing more beautiful plants for his gardens. Certainly one of the primary objectives of the eastern breeders was greater hardiness. The westerners were interested in producing outstanding plants for their own area, where hardiness was not the most important factor.

Of the varieties produced by these early breeders, those originated by Joseph Gable, especially his azaleas, have probably been distributed more widely and have had more of an impact on American gardening than most of the others. Gable and Nearing have worked closely together, freely exchanging plant material and ideas. Guy Nearing's work has been conducted in a rigorous climate and he has been most careful to save only plants which are quite hardy. A flood in 1945 practically wiped out his nursery and put him out of the rhododendron breeding field for several years, and undoubtedly has delayed the time when his varieties will be more generally distributed and grown in the gardens of America.

MORE RECENT BREEDERS

Since 1930 tremendous interest has arisen in the improvement by breeding of rhododendrons and azaleas.

The Glenn Dale azaleas, mentioned in the preceding chapter, are the result of hybridizing by Mr. B. Y. Morrison, starting about 1935. This is the largest breeding project in the entire rhododendron field, in recent years at least. We know little about the numbers of seedlings raised by the early European breeders, but at least none named so many new varieties—well over 400. Azalea breeding was carried on for a number of years in another branch of the U.S.D.A. by Mr. Guy Yerkes and, after his death, by Mr. R. L. Pryor, and several selections have been named.

As good varieties have become more generally available, they have in turn stimulated gardeners to do something about still further improving them. A writer is on dangerous ground in attempting to pick out breeders whose work is outstanding enough to warrant its being mentioned, whereas others are not mentioned. Perhaps even now there are, in the gardens of the unmentioned breeders, varieties better than any of those now available, either in the trade or in the gardens of those whose names we do mention. Still the following, all of whom have several named clones to their credit, should be named, because of the comprehensiveness of their work and the wide range of crosses made: Rudolph Henny, Brooks, Oregon; Ben Lancaster, Camas, Washington; Halfdan Lem, Seattle, Washington; Endre Ostbo, Bellevue, Washington; Lester Brandt, Tacoma, Washington; A. M. Shammarello, Euclid, Ohio. And there are many others, some very good friends of mine, who have made real contributions and will make more. To them I extend my apologies. An appreciation of their work will appear, I am sure, in a more complete account of American rhododendron breeders. Most are undoubtedly carrying on their breeding work for pleasure, and in a spirit of public service.

If we were to sum up the accomplishments of the plant breeders to this time, it could probably be pretty well indicated by saying that they have increased beauty and combined it with hardiness. In some cases, perhaps, there has been an increase in variety and number of types rather than any tremendous increase in total beauty, although there are many exceptions.

WHAT OF THE FUTURE?

It might be of interest to speculate for a moment on the future accomplishments we may expect, more or less confidently, from the breeders. Whether this will be of interest to the beginner depends, more or less, on how long he remains a beginner. I have seen people become so interested in a new garden plant that within two or three years after they started growing their first specimens they were already making crosses, or at least they were figuring out a breeding program of their own in order to create, for their own gardens, plants particularly adapted to them, and, for their own enjoyment, things which particularly satisfy their fancy.

There is no limit to possible improvement in hardiness. At least not until we have good varieties, hardy enough to grow anywhere in the United States, even during test winters. They may never be found, but it does seem certain that we will more nearly approach that goal as time goes on, and the breeders continue their efforts. For some people increased hardiness may be the most important goal. For others it is a secondary matter, depending altogether on the accident of residence. Just as important as resistance to cold I would place resistance to, or greater tolerance of, heat, drought, and alkalinity. Actually rhododendrons are hemmed in on the south by a barrier just about as effective as the one to the north. We should probably include, with these things, greater tolerance to soils that are heavy in texture and inclined to be poorly drained during the winter. Some species in the wild and some named varieties seem to be more tolerant to these unfavorable conditions than others. This is all the plant breeder needs to give him a lead as to how crosses might be made, to increase resistance.

Rhododendrons and azaleas in general have not shown great susceptibility to insect or disease damage, although there are pests of some kind prevalent in all growing areas, and difference in susceptibility of varieties has been observed with respect to nearly all of the ordinary pests. So far as I know, breeders generally have not been particularly interested in this problem, but in the future more of them will be.

BREEDING TO EXTEND THE SEASON OF BLOOM

We now have rhododendrons blooming from very early in the spring—or practically all winter in milder climates—to late summer. However, most of the finer varieties bloom in midseason. That means that there is an opportunity to breed not earlier-flowering rhododendrons, but better varieties, which will flower as early as some we have now. Somewhat the same thing can be said for late-blooming varieties. Some may feel that after a gardener has had a couple of months of concentrated rhododendron blossoming, he would be willing to have some other kind of shrubs bloom during midsummer and late summer. I doubt that this is entirely true. Once a person becomes interested in rhododendrons, he would usually like to have them in bloom over as long a period as possible. Visitors will drop in late in the summer, hoping to see rhododendrons in bloom. If there were a few varieties which would open good blooms in late summer and hold them for a reasonable length of time, it would be a distinct addition to our gardens. One of the problems is that the hot, dry weather of midseason is hard on the blossoms, and tends to cut down the time during which they remain in good condition. Along with lateness of blooming, therefore, we must have better substance and keeping quality.

BETTER COLORS POSSIBLE

The amateur gardener who decides to make a few crosses for his own amusement probably will be thinking more of color of flower than almost any other factor. The more experienced breeder, on the other hand, will probably be thinking more of good plant characters and certain physiological factors, such as hardiness and resistance to other unfavorable conditions. It is true, however, that there could be considerable improvement in color, especially with the yellows and the blues. So many of the yellows are very pale—actually more cream or ivory than a good rich yellow. Recently introduced varieties are getting nearer the ideal, but are not yet close enough. There are a few good blue varieties, especially in the dwarfs, and among the selections of R. *augustinii*. Even with these, the blues could be purer and more intense. There are no good blues among the azaleas, or in the larger plants of what we might call the standard rhododendron varieties. There are several which give a hint of an over-all bluish color, and are sold under that name, but they leave much to be desired.

Better substance, or keeping quality, of flowers has been mentioned in connection with the late-blooming types, but varieties throughout the season could stand improvement in this particular character. The only double or semidouble rhododendron generally available has been that century-old variety known as 'Fastuosum Flore Pleno.' Recently breeders have been making a little progress in this direction, but still there are not any really good doubles generally available. For my part, I am satisfied with the flowers as they are, as I think they have greater grace and character than any double ones could have. However, there are people who like double flowers of any kind, and there is no reason they should not eventually be able to have them in rhododendrons of various sizes and colors.

PLANT CHARACTERS RECEIVING MORE ATTENTION

It is coming to be realized in the rhododendron world that the plant characters of a variety are just as important as its flower characters—more so, in some cases. Better shape and character of bush, coupled with foliage which is of nice texture and decorative in itself, in addition to remaining relatively free of wind and sun damage, would do much to increase the landscape value of any rhododendron group.

Many of the dwarf species have not been used at all in breeding work, and there is certainly tremendous improvement to be anticipated in this very interesting and useful group. When we have a whole range of dwarfs of various seasons, foliage patterns, and colors, with flowers as large and as good as those of 'Elizabeth,' or 'Moonstone' at their best, then we will feel that the dwarf rhododendron has received the attention it deserves.

Perhaps the above sounds somewhat like a youngster's want list at Christmas time. However, improvement along all these lines, if not actual fulfillment of all the goals, can be anticipated with confidence. In many cases great improvement has already been made, or is even now in the making. The gardener just starting with rhododendrons might well consider this in looking for varieties to fill a specific need in his garden planting plan. The fact that a local nurseryman may not have anything suitable does not mean that he should stop looking at that point. There are many fine varieties available, but which are not found at every retail nursery. The beginner, possibly after he has two or three rhododendrons or azaleas and has become really interested, might well look into the whole variety situation and find out what has really been accomplished in providing plants tailor-made to fit specific needs in the garden.

CHAPTER 14

Planting Lists for Many Places and Purposes

The variety is the basis for success in any horticultural enterprise. The fruit grower does not plant just an apple tree or a peach tree, but varieties that he knows will be productive in his soil and climate, and produce fruit of a type that his customers will desire. So with rhododendrons and azaleas. There are varieties to be recommended for all sorts of conditions. Of course that does not mean that every conceivable condition can be matched by a variety which will do well in that situation. However some will undoubtedly do better than others, and that is the purpose of these lists.

Perhaps your neighborhood nurseryman may not have any of the varieties included in one of the lists which supposedly fits your requirements. These lists are necessarily short, and in most cases do not include nearly all the varieties which could be recommended for a particular set of conditions. Your nurseryman has undoubtedly considered local growing conditions when ordering his plants, hence his suggestions should bear weight. However if you want a particular variety from one of these lists, he will, in all probability, be able to secure it for you. Please do not be worried if varieties you already have are not included in the lists, as they may be just as satisfactory for your conditions as the few that are listed.

The first group of suggestions will be for rhododendrons other than azaleas.

FOR COLD CLIMATE
The "Ironclads"

Some of the old *R. catawbiense* hybrids, which have been grown for almost a hundred years, and certain others of similar breeding, which were developed later, are often considered together as the "old hardies," or the "old ironclads." They are to be seen as large bushes in many plantings around Philadelphia, New York, and vicinity. They are the hardiest of the available named varieties, and should be satisfactory where temperatures do not go below -25 degrees. Of course one must remember that an unseasonable freeze—that is, very early or very late in the season—may cause damage even to these varieties, at temperatures well above what they will normally withstand. These are all rated H–1.

Boule de Neige—Early white.

Catawbiense Album—White, pink buds.

Charles Dickens—Crimson red.

Mrs. C. S. Sargent—Rose red.

Roseum Elegans—Rose.

A Second List of "Ironclads"

The following are usually included among the old hardies, but are rated only H–2, hardy to -15 degrees, although some will undoubtedly withstand still lower temperatures if the plants are well matured.

Album Grandiflorum—Almost white.

Atrosanguineum—Red.

Dr. V. H. Rutgers—Red.

Everestianum—Rosy lilac, frilled.

Lee's Dark Purple—Purple.

Other Very Hardy Varieties

There is another group of hardy varieties, perhaps not quite in the class of the "old ironclads," but resulting from the work of Dutch and English breeders, sometimes with *R. catawbiense* in the parentage, sometimes not. These varieties are being grown in the Northwest, where some are considered to be quite on a par with other good modern varieties. There is a greater color range, and the colors are inclined to be somewhat clearer and purer than in the "old ironclads." 'Jean Marie de Montagu' and 'Madame de Bruin' are rated only H–3, but I believe they should rate H–2, as do the others.

Blue Peter—Pale lavender blue, deep blotch.

Goldsworth Yellow—Apricot yellow, spotted green.

Jean Marie de Montagu—Bright crimson.

Madame de Bruin—Cerise red.

Mrs. P. D. Williams—Ivory white, golden brown spot.

FOR HOT CLIMATES

We probably have less information about varieties adapted to conditions of extreme heat than about those adapted to extreme cold, largely because not enough varieties have been tested in the hotter areas to give full information. However, we can list certain varieties that we have heard reported as doing well in the areas where summer climate is relatively hot.

Broughtonii Aureum—H–3, azaleodendron, soft yellow with orange spots.

Cornubia—H–5, blood red, early.

Jean Marie de Montagu—H–3, bright crimson.

Pink Pearl—H–3, soft pink, fading to blush white.

Unknown Warrior—H–4, bright, light red, early.

For Very Dry Conditions

Rhododendrons require plenty of moisture during the summer. This can be given in most places, by irrigation, if not from rainfall. However where the humidity is very low also, it may not be so easy to provide good growing conditions. Frequent syringing or sprinkling will help, unless the water is very alkaline, although it will not completely take the place of a higher humidity. As a general rule high temperatures and low moisture are associated, and the preceding varieties would be ones to consider. In addition we might suggest the following.

Cilpinense—H–4, very early, pinkish white, dwarf.

Cynthia—H–2, rosy crimson, tall.

Doncaster—H–3, scarlet crimson, rather low-growing.

Forsterianum—H–5, white.

Fragrantissimum—H–5, white, tinged pink.

Varieties for Alkaline Conditions

This situation is usually correlated with hot and dry climate, so the preceding recommendations should be about as close as we can come to it. It must be realized, of course, that any considerable degree of alkalinity is likely to be fatal to most varieties of rhododendrons, and that if one is gardening under such conditions, it is not a matter of finding varieties which will tolerate them. The conditions must be changed to provide at least a reasonable degree of acidity for the rhododendrons. Under extreme conditions this may mean growing them in planters, or raised beds. There is some circumstantial evidence that many azaleas are somewhat more tolerant of alkalinity than are rhododendrons. The following rhododendron species are supposed to be somewhat more tolerant of alkalinity than others.

R. chartophyllum—H–3, pinkish to nearly white, spotted.

R. davidsonianum—H–4, pink, spotted red.

R. fargesii—H–3, pink.

R. oleifolium—H–3, pink to almost white, rather dwarf.

R. rubiginosum—H–2, rosy lilac, spotted brown.

FOR AVERAGE CLIMATIC CONDITIONS
Rhododendrons for Shade

The importance of shade varies somewhat with climatic conditions. In our own locality most varieties can be grown satisfactorily in full sun, if they have plenty of moisture during the summer. Even here, however, we occasionally have a very bright and relatively hot day during early summer, when the young shoots are making soft growth. For a period of three or four hours, loss of water by transpiration may be more rapid than it can be taken in through the roots. The soft new growth will wilt, and frequently there will be "burning" or browning of these young leaves on some of the more susceptible varieties. If we can keep sprinklers going over the plants during this period, they will not be damaged. This may indicate that shade, for many varieties, is not so much a necessity in itself, but that it cuts down on transpiration during periods of moisture stress. In other localities, especially farther south, where there are many hot days during the summer, shade is more important, as it would hardly be practical to keep rhododendron leaves covered with moisture continuously during the hours of excessive transpiration. In most areas and for most varieties a partial shade, sometimes called dappled shade, or shade during the middle of the day is desirable. Continuous dense shade usually results in leggy growth and poor blooming. For a planting site which is in fairly deep shade throughout the day, the following varieties are suggested:

Azor—H–4, soft salmon.

Betty Wormald—H–3, rose pink, pale purple blotch.

Diane—H–3, primrose yellow.

(Loderi G.) King George—H–4, blush white.

Snow Queen—H–3, pure white, poor foliage in full sun.

Varieties to Grow in Full Sunlight

Many of the dwarfs need to be in almost full sun if they are to maintain that low, compact type of growth which is just one reason we grow them. Of the larger-growing varieties, the following seem to be somewhat more resistant than others to full sun, although even these will be subject to burning under certain conditions of extremely low humidity and bright sun.

Cynthia—H–2, rosy crimson.

Jean Marie de Montagu—H–3, bright crimson.

Lady Clementine Mitford—H–2, peach pink, deeper margin.

Mrs. T. H. Lowinsky—H–3, blush, fading to white, brown spots.

Purple Splendour—H–2, deep purple, black spot.

Varieties for Attractive Foliage

In this particular group we are thinking of varieties which bear leaves of pleasant texture and appearance, usually maintained in good condition throughout the year and carried in an attractive way on the plant. One of the prime requirements for a good landscape plant is that it be attractive twelve months of the year. There are some varieties, of course, which are grown primarily for their foliage, with leaves exceptionally large or brightly colored, or covered with an attractive indumentum on the underside. Many of the dwarfs have attractive foliage. The following varieties are normally grown for their flowers, but also have attractive foliage:

Bowbells—H–3, pink; small, rounded leaves.

Gomer Waterer—H–2, white, blushed; glossy, dark-green leaves.

Mrs. T. H. Lowinsky—H–3, blush, brown spots; dark-green, convex leaves.

Sir Charles Lemon—H–4, white flowers, brown indumentum on underside of leaves.

Unique—H–3, pale yellowish pink; neat, rounded leaves.

VARIETIES FOR EASTERN CONDITIONS WITH GOOD SOIL AND CLIMATE

In this and the following three sections are included varieties which should do well in various parts of the country, in those gardens where conditions are reasonably satisfactory for the area.

Antoon van Welie—H–3, carmine pink.

Blue Peter—H–2, pale lavender blue, deep blotch.

Jean Marie de Montagu—H–3, bright crimson.

Madame de Bruin—H–3, cerise red.

Mrs. Furnival—H–3, light pink, sienna blotch.

VARIETIES FOR IDEAL CONDITIONS IN THE PACIFIC NORTHWEST

Many, many good varieties are available, so this is somewhat of a tossup, with some attention to an assortment of colors. The (Loderi

G.) 'King George' is only for good growing conditions, with partial shade and plenty of room, and it can be magnificent.

Betty Wormald—H–3, rose pink, pale purple blotch.

Carita—H–3, primrose.

Jean Marie de Montagu—H–3, bright crimson.

(Loderi G.) King George—H–4, blush white.

Purple Splendour—H–2, deep purple, black spot.

VARIETIES FOR IDEAL CONDITIONS IN THE SOUTHEAST

Strangely enough some of the old hardies or "ironclads" are reported as doing well in the mild climate of the southeast. Not so strange, perhaps, when we stop to realize they have *R. catawbiense* as one parent, and that it is native to the highlands of Georgia, Alabama, and the Carolinas. The following have been mentioned as doing well in Georgia·

Dr. Dresselhuys—H–2, aniline red.

Everestianum—H–2, rosy lilac.

Lee's Dark Purple—H–2, purple.

Mrs. C. S. Sargent—H–1, rose.

Roseum Elegans—H–1, rose.

Information as to the behavior of the more modern varieties in the Southeast is not plentiful. The following have been reported as doing well:

Betty Wormald—H–3, rose pink, pale purple blotch.

Cynthia—H–2, rosy crimson.

Pink Pearl—H–3, rose pink, fading to blush.

Purple Splendour—H–2, deep purple, black spot.

Vulcan—H–3, brick red.

VARIETIES FOR IDEAL CONDITIONS IN CENTRAL CALIFORNIA

Countess of Derby—H–3, rose pink.

Fragrantissimum—H–5, white tinged pink.

Gill's Crimson—H–5, blood crimson.

Jean Marie de Montagu—H–3, bright crimson.

Unknown Warrior—H–4, bright red.

EARLY-FLOWERING VARIETIES

In most climates the very early-flowering varieties are not completely reliable year after year. No matter how hardy they are in plant, and even in flower bud, there are no varieties that I know of that will stand a hard frost while in flower, without the petals' turning brown. However, when few other flowering plants are decorating the garden, even two or three days of bloom from an extra early rhododendron are worth while. Because of the fact that so few are extra early-blooming, there have been relatively few seedlings from which the breeder could select desirable plants. The general level of flower size, color, and general attractiveness, therefore, is understandably somewhat less with some of these early-flowering varieties than it is for those blooming in midseason. There are some excellent early-flowering dwarfs which will be named in another list.

Christmas Cheer—H–2, blush pink; blooms in winter in mild climate.

Cornubia—H–5, blood-red.

Dame Nellie Melba—H–3, pink.

Dr. Stocker—H–4, ivory-white.

Unknown Warrior—H–4, bright red.

VARIETIES FOR MIDSEASON

The beginner will probably be well advised to start with varieties of this season, which would include the best there are, because this is where a great majority of varieties bloom. The following are chosen partly for color range:

Carita—H–3, primrose.

Jean Marie de Montagu—H–3, bright crimson.

Lady Chamberlain—H–4, salmon pink.

Loder's White—H–4, white, frilled.

May Day—H–3, scarlet.

VARIETIES FOR VERY LATE BLOOM

As with the very early varieties, the late-blooming ones, being fewer in number, include fewer which are outstanding because of flower characters. Especially where midsummer is likely to be extremely hot and dry, the late varieties will be at a distinct disadvantage, but the rhododendron fancier, at least, will want them to round out the blooming season and give it a maximum length. The beginner might be interested in them for some special reason. For instance, a summer home, occupied after mid-June, might be landscaped with

Near the end of footbridge to the ''Island'' at the Test Garden in Portland.

Walk flanked by azalea collection at the Test Garden.

Rhododendrons across path from Japanese maple for contrast of color and texture.

Rhododendrons border garden path under fir trees.

A water vista in the Portland Test Garden of the American Rhododendron Society.

Broad grass paths help to show off rhododendrons in border planting.

A restful area in the Rhododendron Test Garden in Portland.

R. williamsianum, at right, is perfectly at home in area mostly occupied by azaleas.

The beginning of the rock garden at the Test Garden.

Rhododendrons, like other shrubs, require a reasonable expanse of lawn to show them off at their best.

The early-blooming, large-leafed species, *R. calophytum*, shows off well against the lake.

R. degronianum at the base of a fir tree greets the visitor near the entrance to the Test Garden in Portland.

Rhododendrons seem very much at home near water, be it stream or lake.

Water vista adds to over-all picture at the Test Garden.

Rhododendrons used effectively in street planting in a modern shopping center. Provision for adequate watering should be made when azaleas or rhododendrons are used in this way.

A mass planting of white azaleas used effectively on state capitol grounds, Olympia, Washington.

rhododendrons which would bloom while the owners are present, rather than earlier, while no one is there to enjoy them.

Azor—H–4, salmon pink.

Grenadier—H–3, deep blood-red.

Mrs. T. H. Lowinsky—H–3, blush, reddish, brown spots.

Polar Bear—H–3, white.

Tally Ho—H–5, bright scarlet.

TALL-GROWING VARIETIES

There are always places in the garden where shrubs somewhat taller than the average are especially desirable. The more rhododendrons one has, I suppose, the more need there is for variation in height in order to provide the attractive differences in contour that make a garden planting varied and interesting.

A. Dedford—H–3, lavender, dark eye.

Beauty of Littleworth—H–3, white, brownish dots.

Cynthia—H–2, rosy crimson.

Faggetter's Favorite—H–3, slivery pink.

Mrs. Lindsay Smith—H–3, white, suffused peach.

VARIETIES OF MEDIUM HEIGHT

Antoon van Welie—H–3, carmine pink.

Betty Wormald—H–3, rose pink, pale purple blotch.

Carita—H–3, primrose.

David—H–3, blood red.

Loder's White—H–4, white, frilled.

LOW-GROWING VARIETIES

There is no clear-cut dividing line between what might be called low-growing standard varieties and dwarf varieties. However by low-growing, in this case, we mean those which in ten years in full sun, or nearly so, would reach a height of 3 or 4 feet. These all have fairly large leaves. Some, such as 'Bow Bells,' may reach this height, but have smaller leaves, and are usually classed, more or less arbitrarily, as dwarfs.

Britannia—H–3, bright crimson red.

May Day—H–3, scarlet.

Medusa—H–4, orange salmon, flushed vermilion.

Purple Splendour—H–2, deep purple, black spot.

Unique—H–3, light pink, suffused yellow.

DWARF VARIETIES FOR EARLY BLOOM

Actually some of the varieties usually considered as dwarfs may reach a height as great as, or greater than, that of those in the preceding group. However they are plants with very small leaves, rather slow-growing, and usually with smaller flowers.

Bric-a-brac—H–3, white, earliest.

Cilpinense—H–4, pinkish white.

Conemaugh—H–2, lavender pink.

Racil—H–3, shell pink.

Tessa—Not rated, probably H–3, rosy lilac.

DWARF VARIETIES FOR MIDSEASON BLOOM

Elizabeth—H–4, light blood-red.

Humming Bird—H–4, pink, shaded vermilion.

Jock—H–3, rose pink.

Moonstone—H–3, cream- or light yellow-edged pink.

Sapphire—H–3, blue; aromatic foliage.

RHODODENDRON VARIETIES FOR FRAGRANCE

It might be nice for all rhododendron flowers to be fragrant, but such is not the case. Ordinarily we purchase plants largely for the size, color, and attractiveness of their flowers. If they are fragrant, that is a bonus. Many have a slight fragrance which one can appreciate at close range. In the following list I have included some with unusual fragrance—enough to make that character a factor in securing them. Note that some are relatively tender.

Forsterianum—H–5, white.

Fragrantissimum—H–5, white-tinged pink.

Lady Alice Fitzwilliam—H–5, white.

(Loderi G.) King George—H–4, blush white.

Odoratum—H–3, pale lilac; azaleodendron; fragrance its main asset.

RHODODENDRONS FOR CUT FLOWERS

Relatively few gardeners have enough rhododendron plants so that they can cut them freely for use in the house as cut flowers. There is, however, nothing much more striking than a large vase or bowl with large flowering branches of rhododendrons, attractively arranged. Probably few rhododendron beginners will select varieties on this basis, as it involves a fair number of plants if the cutting is not to be too evident in the garden. The ideal way would be to plant a few varieties, especially suitable for cutting, in an inconspicuous place where they could be pruned heavily when desired for house decoration. Attractive foliage character should not be forgotten, as leafy branches may be used all winter, as greenery with cut flowers of other types, or just as a vase or bowl of green leaves. The keeping quality of the foliage of some of the leathery-leafed varieties is remarkable.

Blue Peter—H–2, pale lavender, deep blotch, foliage a bit thin.

Fastuosum Flore Pleno—H–2, mauve, double.

Fusilier—H–4, scarlet.

Mrs. G. W. Leak—H–4, pink with brownish purple blotch.

Mrs. T. H. Lowinsky—H–3, blush, reddish brown spots.

VARIETIES FOR FORCING IN THE GREENHOUSE

There are a good many gardeners in the colder parts of the country who have a little greenhouse space. They might use some of this for actually forcing certain varieties into bloom in early spring, or simply for storing, for two or three months of the winter, those varieties which are not quite hardy enough to stay outside under the prevailing temperature conditions. These latter might be just any varieties that the gardener is trying to grow north of their normal zone. The following, however, are ones which might be more satisfactory than most for actually forcing into bloom before their normal season. All varieties can be forced, to a certain extent, but some will break into bloom much earlier, under forcing conditions, than will others. The following were reported as relatively satisfactory after extensive tests in Holland:

Dr. Arnold W. Endtz—H–3, carmine.

Mrs. Charles Pearson—H–3, blush mauve, spotted burnt sienna.

Peter Koster—H–3, crimson.

Pink Pearl—H–3, rose pink, fading to blush.

Purple Splendour—H–2, deep purple, black spot.

VARIETIES FOR GROWING IN POTS AND TUBS

In extremely alkaline areas the only feasible way to grow rhododendrons may be in planters or containers of some kind. They are excellent for the patio or outdoor living room. The tall varieties are occasionally grown in large tubs or boxes, for use in parks, or for hotel decoration, but for the home the smaller plants are suggested, at least to begin with.

Arthur J. Ivens—H–2, pale pink, rounded leaves.

Blue Tit—H–3, light blue, small leaves, compact.

Cilpinense—H–4, pinkish white, early-flowering.

Elizabeth—H–4, bright red, large flower on small plant.

Unique—H–3, pinkish yellow, larger leaves than the above, compact.

RED-FLOWERED VARIETIES

The following suggestions for various color groups include, primarily, those considered as standard sorts, hence relatively well tested and available.

Britannia—H–3, bright, crimson red.

David—H–3, blood-red.

Jean Marie de Montagu—H–3, bright crimson.

Mars—H–2, deep, true red.

May Day—H–3, scarlet.

PINK-FLOWERED VARIETIES

Antoon van Welie—H–3, carmine pink.

Betty Wormald—H–3, rose pink, pale purple blotch.

Cynthia—H–2, rosy crimson.

Dame Nellie Melba—H–3, pink.

Mrs. Furnival—H–3, light pink, sienna blotch.

WHITE-FLOWERED VARIETIES

Beauty of Littleworth—H–3, white, brownish spots.

Loder's White—H–4, white, frilled.

Mother of Pearl—H–4, blush, turning snow white.

Mrs. A. T. de la Mare—H–3, white with green spot.

Snow Queen—H–3, pure white, needs shade.

VARIETIES WITH YELLOW OR CREAM FLOWERS

Broughtonii Aureum—H–3, azaleodendron, yellow.

Canary—H–3, bright yellow.

Carita—H–3, primrose.

Idealist—H–3, pale yellow.

Unique—H–3, pale pink, suffused light yellow.

VARIETIES WITH BLOTCHES OR CONSPICUOUS SPOTS

Hyperion—H–3, lilac, deep blotch.

Mrs. G. W. Leak—H–4, pink with brownish purple spot.

Mrs. P. D. Williams—H–2, ivory white, brown spot.

Sappho—H–2, white, large brownish purple spot.

Trilby—H–2, deep crimson, dark blotch.

BLUE-FLOWERED VARIETIES

Blue flowers are more frequently found among the dwarfs, or certain species, than among the standard varieties, so we give only three, and of those only one, 'Blue Peter,' is generally available.

Blue Ensign—Pale lavender blue, black spot.

Blue Peter—H–2, pale lavender blue, deep blotch.

Electra—Violet blue.

RHODODENDRON SPECIES

For Use as Specimen Plants

The following species are reasonably easy to grow, and will make beautiful specimens, rather large plants, with large leaves except *R. wardii,* which is of medium size.

R. calophytum—H–3, light pink, deep blotch, early.

R. discolor—H–3, light pink, late.

R. macabeanum—H–4, yellowish white, blotched, early.

R. sutchuenense—H–3, pale rosy lilac, very early.

R. wardii—H–4, light yellow, midseason.

For Background Planting

As flowering evergreen shrubs for background planting, certain rhododendrons are very satisfactory. They grow rather tall, up to 6 feet or more in 10 years, and the flowers, although rather small, are very numerous.

R. augustinii—H–3, lavender rose to blue.

R. davidsonianum—H–4, pink, spotted red.

R. desquamatum—H–3, mauve, spotted crimson.

R. rubiginosum—H–2, rosy lilac, spotted brown.

R. yunnanense—H–3, pinkish white, spotted red.

Low-growing Shrubs

This group of species will make attractive small shrubs some 2 to 3 feet high in 10 years.

R. carolinianum—H–2, white to rosy purple.

R. degronianum—H–3, pink, sprawling.

R. neriiflorum—H–4, bright scarlet.

R. racemosum—H–2, white to pink, small flowers, easy to grow.

R. smirnowi—H–2, purplish rose to pink.

For the Rock Garden

Some of the low, spreading rhododendron species make ideal plants for the rock garden, attractive even out of bloom for their neat evergreen leaves.

R calostrotum—H–3, bright magenta purple.

R. campylogynum—H–2, rose purple, small nodding bells.

R. chryseum—H–2, bright yellow.

R. keleticum—H–2, purplish crimson, very low growing.

R. radicans—H–3, purple, prostrate, creeping.

AZALEA VARIETIES

Suggestions as to azalea varieties are made on the basis of climatic adaptation rather than for specific planting purposes. There are relatively large numbers of varieties of some types available in certain parts of the country, the variation within the group, in many cases, being primarily one of color. The following varieties might be used as a starting point although there are many others available.

EVERGREEN AZALEAS

Azaleas for Cold Climates

Evergreen azaleas as a group have not exhibited as great hardiness as the deciduous varieties. This list, therefore, is suggested for the northern range of evergreen azaleas, and not for the extreme northern part of the country. For the most part, evergreen azaleas, except the hardiest sorts, should not be planted where temperatures much below -5°F. are to be expected.

Othello—Kaempferi hybrid; brilliant red.

Purple Splendour—Gable; hose-in-hose, orchid purple.

Rose Greeley—Gable; white, sweet scented.

Springtime—Gable; pink, upright.

Stewartonian—Gable; bright red.

Azaleas for the Latitude of Washington, D.C., South to the Gulf States, and for the Pacific Coast

This is a rather large territory, and there will be small areas included where the climate is probably too rigorous for the varieties suggested. In general, however, it does include one great azalea-growing section of the United States, the Gulf states being the other. The available varieties are numerous—in the hundreds.

Balsaminaeflora—Macrantha; orange red, double, low, spreading, late.

Crinoline—Glenn Dale; pink, ruffled, midseason.

Hexe—Hose-in-hose, violet red.

Indica Alba—*R. mucronatum,* single, pure white.

Joya—Glenn Dale; brilliant rose pink, early midseason.

Azaleas for the Gulf States

This is the area where the so-called Indian azaleas, an offshoot from the Belgian forcing type, have been making a spectacular show for many years in the large azalea gardens. My information in this field is not extensive. The following names have been taken from the literature, and would at least indicate to the beginner varieties known to be adapted to Gulf state conditions. They belong to the group know as the southern Indian Hybrids

Alba Maculata—White, spreading, late midseason.

Cavendish—Rose with white edges, low-spreading, late.

Duc de Rohan—Orange red, medium height, early midseason.

Elegans Superba—Deep rose pink, tall, late midseason.

Triomphe de Ledeberg—Orange red, spreading, late.

Azaleas for Forcing

These are the Belgian Indian hybrids, not hardy outside, except for a few in the far South. These are not suggested as the best varieties for commercial use, but suitable for the amateur gardener who has greenhouse space available and would like to work with azaleas.

Albert-Elizabeth—White with orange-red edging, semidouble frilled.

Eri Schaeme—Orange red, white margins.

Jean Haerens—Rose, double, frilled.

Mme. van der Cruyssen—Pink, frilled.

Paul Schaeme—Light orange, double.

White-flowering Varieties

This, and the next two lists, includes varieties hardy at least as far north as Washington, D.C. They are arranged in order of blooming, early to late.

Cygnet—Glenn Dale; white, early, dense bush.

Samite—Glenn Dale; pure white, hose-in-hose.

Glacier—Glenn Dale; white with green tone.

Driven Snow—Glenn Dale; pure white, large flowers.

White Gumpo—Satsuki; white, very low and very late blooming.

Red-flowering Varieties

Ballet Girl—Glenn Dale; orange red, hose-in-hose.

Beacon—Glenn Dale; nearly scarlet.

Fortune—Pericat; red, semidouble.

Waraigishi—*R. indicum;* rose red, semidouble.

Aztec—Glenn Dale; peach red, white zone at base.

Pink-flowering Varieties

Bopeep—Glenn Dale; white, tinted rose pink.

Pink Profusion—Yerkes-Pryor; pink, hose-in-hose.

Sherwoodi—Kurume (Sherwood); reddish violet.

Crinoline—Glenn Dale; pink, ruffled margin.

Eros—Glenn Dale; pink, low, spreading, very late.

DECIDUOUS AZALEAS

As previously mentioned, most of these are relatively hardy compared to the evergreen types. The following lists are based on the literature, and in some cases on experience. They should provide a starting point for the beginner.

Hardy Varieties

For the gardener who is on the northern limit of the azalea-growing territory, the following are among the hardier varieties of the deciduous type. They belong to the Ghent hybrid group.

Coccinea Speciosa—Reddish orange.

Corneille—Pink, double, late midseason.

Narcissiflora—Yellow, double, late midseason.

Pallas—Orange red, early midseason.

Raphael de Smet—White, edged orange red.

Varieties for the Central and Southern Parts of the Azalea-growing Territory

So far as I know, there are no particularly desirable deciduous azaleas, which are quite tender, and which might be grown only in the southern states, and not farther north. The following list, therefore, might be considered as worth trying in all the regions where the deciduous azaleas normally grow. These varieties belong to the Mollis group.

Christopher Wren—Yellow, large.

Directeur Moerlands—Golden yellow, darker throat.

Dr. M. Oosthoek—Reddish orange, lighter blotch.

Hugo Koster—Reddish orange, orange blotch.

Spek's Brilliant—Orange red.

Knap Hill Hybrids

This group includes varieties from Exbury (Rothschild) and the Slocock Nursery, as well as from the Knap Hill Nursery. The finest of the deciduous azaleas, from the standpoint of color and size, many are extremely hardy, probably as hardy as the Ghents previously listed under hardy varieties. They have been slow to propagate. If you buy a named variety, be sure it has been propagated by cutting or layer, and not from seed.

Red-flowered Varieties

Balzac—Exbury; orange red.

Bullfinch—Knap Hill; deep red.

Firecracker—Waterer Sons & Crisp; currant red.

Satan—Slocock; scarlet.

Tunis—Slocock; red, orange blotch.

Pink-flowered Varieties

Beaulieu—Exbury; pink with orange blotch.

Berry Rose—Exbury; carmine, yellow blotch.

Flamingo—Knap Hill; flamingo pink.

Strawberry Ice—Exbury; peach pink.

Sylphides—Knap Hill; light violet red.

Yellow-flowered Varieties

Basilisk—Exbury; cream, yellow blotch.

George Reynolds—Exbury; yellow.

Golden Oriole—Knap Hill; yellow.

Goldfinch—Knap Hill; yellow.

Marion Merriman—Knap Hill; greenish yellow, flushed orange.

White-flowered Varities

Crinoline—Exbury; white, flushed pink, frilled.

Nancy Buchanan—Exbury; white, yellow blotch.

Oxydol—Exbury; white.

Persil—Slocock; white, pale yellow blotch.

White Throat—Knap Hill; white, double, low, spreading.

AZALEA SPECIES

Native American Species

There are some very fine azaleas which can be obtained only as species, no named varieties being available, except of hybrids which are so different that they do not take the place of the species. These American species in general are hardy and desirable, for woodland planting, for fragrance, or just plain attractiveness.

R. arborescens—White, fragrant, tall, late.

R. calendulaceum—Yellow to red, tall, midseason.

R. nudiflorum—Pink, midseason, fragrant.

R. roseum—Light to deep pink, midseason, fragrant.

R. vaseyi—Pink, early midseason.

• ASIATIC AZALEA SPECIES

R. kaempferi and *R. mucronatum* are usually available as named clones, but they are occasionally sold under the species name, hence are included in this list.

R. albrechtii—Deep rose, deciduous, hardy.

R. kaempferi—Salmon rose, partially evergreen, hardy.

R. mucronatum—White, several clones, as 'Indica Alba.'

R. poukhanense—Reddish violet, one of the hardiest of the evergreen azaleas.

R. schlippenbachii—Pink, deciduous, very hardy, large flowers.

CHAPTER 15

Rhododendrons and Azaleas
As Hobby Flowers

Never before have so many people been so interested in the different kinds of flowering plants. This is amply evidenced by the large number of "single plant" societies now functioning in this country. In addition to these there are many garden clubs and horticultural societies—national, district, and local. The total number of horticultural organizations is tremendous and seems to be increasing every year—one of the very desirable and promising developments of our time, when there are so many interests of doubtful value.

The raising of flowering plants and the collecting of varieties or types of specific groups have for centuries been hobbies, even though the word hobby, as we now use it, is a rather modern concept. Until our present century, activity in this field was largely confined to the wealthy or leisure class. There were exceptions, of course—probably many exceptions, of which we have no record. Some plantsmen are remembered only because they wrote a book, or an article for a magazine, and others because they became interested in improving their favorite flower, and created new varieties to commemorate their names.

SOME PLANTS OF SPECIAL INTEREST

It is a bit difficult to understand sometimes, at least for the person who is not specifically interested, just why certain groups of plants seem to attract an unusual number of people, and why those people band together in organizations to further the cause of those particular plants. Presumably beauty and usefulness in the garden or in the home are primary factors. Then there is the matter of challenge. Plants which are very easy to grow may be considered by some gardeners almost as weeds; if there is no challenge there is no interest. Another factor, undoubtedly, is the number of types, species, or varieties in existence, and which can be obtained and grown in this country. The average American has a great instinct for collecting. Some of the most important hobby groups in other fields are based almost entirely on collecting—as, for instance, the stamp collectors, coin collectors, and collectors of old glass, buttons, and many, many other things. The collecting of plants not only satisfies the collecting instinct, but may also provide everything which ornamental plants imply: beauty in the garden, usefulness in many phases of the landscape, and enhanced value of the home.

RHODODENDRONS AS HOBBY PLANTS

There is probably no group of plants which offers more to the plant hobbyist than rhododendrons and azaleas. Of course I admit to being prejudiced, but here we have an extremely large genus, with over eight hundred species described. And there are undoubtedly valuable species yet to be found, in the now unapproachable areas of western China and other Himalayan foothill regions. Probably no single collector could hope to grow all of the known species, and even if he had them, there would always be the tantalizing glimpse of species not yet introduced, but hinted at by some traveler's note in an obscure publication. There have been over 10,000 horticultural varieties named. Presumably many of these are not now available, but the number of obtainable species, varieties, and types is somewhere in the thousands, and certainly enough to challenge the collecting instinct of any gardener.

While this group of plants, as we have tried to show, is not especially difficult, in much of the United States, yet it is certainly enough so to provide a challenge to the gardening ability of anyone, even in especially favored localities. And yet once established with reasonable attention to their specific requirements, these shrubs will live for many years, increasing in beauty and charm, without having to be started anew each spring or dug and replanted annually. Opinions vary as to the desirability of various types of flowers and shrubs, yet I have never heard of anyone who particularly disliked rhododendrons or azaleas, or who was entirely impervious to their charms. On all counts, therefore, this group of flowering shrubs comes as near to being the perfect hobby plant as any I can call to mind.

THE AMERICAN RHODODENDRON SOCIETY

Among the single-flower societies is one devoted to rhododendrons and azaleas. The rhododendron organization, although not quite as old as some of the others, has had an impressive and progressive career. Founded in 1944 as the American Rhododendron Society, it began with a small group in and around Portland, Oregon. Since that time it has expanded until, at the present writing, there are eighteen chapters, including one in British Columbia, and extending from Seattle in the Northwest to Oakland, California, Asheville, North Carolina, and New York City as central points of the most widely spread chapters. Anyone interested in this group of plants and wishing to join the society usually affiliates with one of the chapters, if there happens to be one in his general vicinity. The chapter organization permits groups in many localities to meet for discussion of rhododendron problems, to share their experiences, and to stage exhibits and displays of various kinds.

The purpose of the society is to give service, in any way possible, to its members, who have the common bond of an intense interest in rhododendrons or azaleas, or both. The society serves as a clearinghouse for information, and has developed special services, such as awards to new and outstanding varieties, presentation of medals to outstanding personalities in the rhododendron world, the holding of shows, and other affairs such as regional and international rhododendron conferences. It publishes a quarterly bulletin and certain books and leaflets.

RATINGS ESTABLISHED

With the extremely large number of rhododendron and azalea varieties and species available for garden use, and with the great differences in appearance, in hardiness, and general adaptability, it is easy to understand that one of the prime functions of a national organization is to develop and disseminate information about varieties and species. The society has developed ratings for hardiness and for plant and flower quality, ratings which are used in this book as indicated by symbols following the variety names. Official A.R.S. ratings have been published for some 200 varieties and about 150 species.

Test gardens and display gardens have been established by the society, or its chapters, in order to secure preliminary information about newly introduced varieties, and additional information about species and the older varieties. Special awards may be given to new varieties that are determined, by a group of competent judges, to have reached a certain stage of perfection. The National Test Garden of the American Rhododendron Society is located in Portland, Oregon, surrounded by the Crystal Springs Lake Golf Course. It is on an island of some four acres lying within the lake, plus some adjacent land along the lake. Several of the chapters have established test gardens or display gardens for the benefit of their members and the gardening public.

Another group, not affiliated with the American Rhododendron Society, is the Washington Rhododendron Society, with headquarters at Tacoma, Washington. It is a successor to the Tacoma Rhododendron Society, formed several years ago. This group also has meetings, discussions, and publications in the field of its special interest.

It might seem somewhat farfetched to mention an organization in another country as being of some help to rhododendron fanciers in the United States. The Royal Horticultural Society, with headquarters in London, England, is an old and honored organization, which has been in existence for over 150 years. It is not devoted exclusively to any one plant group, but in the publications of the society rhododendrons have, for many years, had a prominent place. A good many American rhododendron fanciers are members of the R.H.S.

There are other national rhododendron organizations, including those in Germany, New Zealand, and Australia, which might be of interest to gardeners who become seriously interested in this field.

RHODODENDRON SHOWS

One of the best places for a beginner to learn something about varieties is at the various flower shows. Of course in many parts of the country general flower shows do not attract rhododendron exhibits, either because they are at the wrong season, or because rhododendrons are not grown in that particular area by people who are interested in exhibiting them. They are, however, appearing in more and more flower shows, either as entries in special classes or in garden exhibits put on by nurserymen.

The American Rhododendron Society and several of its chapters have been holding special rhododendron shows for some time. These shows normally provide classes for varieties and species, both as cut flowers and as entire plants. As rhododendrons transplant so easily, a gardener or a nurseryman can dig a plant, wrap the root ball in burlap, and plant it in a bank of peat moss at a show. It may be left there for three or four days and, if kept reasonably moist, can be returned to the garden from which it came, replanted, and continue to grow almost as if it had not been moved.

Most of the exhibits in the shows are of cut trusses, a truss being the cluster of flowers which come out of one bud. There may be classes for individual varieties, or for groups of varieties. Thus one may see flowers of a number of the best pink sorts displayed on a table in one group, so that comparisons can easily be made as to number of flowers in the truss, general size and character of the truss, the size of the flowers, their color, and even their keeping quality. To obtain such information otherwise might necessitate visits to a number of gardens. Even then it is difficult to carry in one's mind, from garden to garden, the detailed characteristics of the flower of a particular variety for purposes of comparison. Quite often a person may see a flower and be very much pleased with it. However when he sees it side by side with a better variety, the difference is immediately obvious, and the gardener has learned something about the relative desirability of the two varieties.

In rhododendron shows the rule is that certain leaves should be present around the flower truss. This will give the viewer an idea of their size, color, and anything special about them, such as colored indumentum on the underside of the leaf. However these leaves, adjacent to the flower heads, are sometimes undersized or mis-shapen, so that they do not convey an accurate idea of the appearance of the bush. Bush characters are very important and should always be considered when selecting varieties to plant. A comparison of the exhibits at a show does give the prospective grower a great deal of help, and also an incentive to go out and see the nature of the bushes from which especially fine cut trusses had been taken. Usually the name of the exhibitor is on the entry card and, judging from my experience with rhododendron growers in the past, the exhibitor would be glad to have interested persons come and see his plants, or to tell them where plants of a particular variety may be seen in other gardens.

In some of the larger rhododendron shows there are classes calling for landscaped gardens of various sizes. Such garden exhibits are usually designed and entered by nurserymen, who bring in blooming-sized plants, balled and burlapped. This provides an excellent opportunity for the show visitor to study varieties and their use in the landscape.

PUBLIC RHODODENDRON GARDENS

Public collections of rhododendrons offer the prospective gardener an opportunity to enjoy a beautiful shrubbery planting, to make comparisons between varieties, and to study detailed varietal characteristics such as season of bloom, length of blooming season, and the general color and character of the flower. Public parks, in areas where soil and climate are favorable, use rhododendrons and azaleas rather freely in mass plantings in their general landscape plan. Unfortunately the plants are too often unlabeled, so that the names of varieties can be learned only by consulting the park superintendent, or planting plans in his office.

There are several very wonderful and well-known azalea gardens in the Southeast, along the Atlantic and the Gulf coasts. These are open to the public on payment of an admission fee. They provide a wonderful opportunity to see what a mature and well-cared-for azalea planting can be like. In many cases, unfortunately, the varieties are not labeled.

There are well arranged collections of these plants, usually properly labeled, in a number of botanic gardens and arboretums in various parts of the United States. A list of species and varieties being grown in such public gardens is being prepared, and will be published by the American Rhododendron Society. In some cases the botanic gardens are located in areas where practically no rhododendrons are grown in private gardens. The fact that interested gardeners in many localities can go to an arboretum, within driving distance perhaps, and see plants of various types in bloom should be worth knowing, and so it is hoped that that information can be made generally available.

Although I do not know of all such collections, there are some I feel should be mentioned. It would certainly be desirable for beginners to visit one of these collections, or to determine whether there is one in their own neighborhood.

In Portland, Oregon, the Test Garden of the American Rhododendron Society contains one of the finest collections of rhododendron varieties in the country. There are between two and three thousand plants, including nearly all of the standard or commonly grown varieties, and many which are comparatively rare. There are also a great many species, including representatives of all the forty-three series, into which the hundreds of rhododendron species are divided. This collection is open to the public during the day from early in the spring until the end of the summer, covering the blooming season of nearly all varieties.

At Seattle, Washington, the Arboretum of the University of Washington contains a very fine collection of species and of named varieties of both rhododendrons and azaleas.

There is an extensive collection of rhododendrons in the Golden Gate Park at San Francisco. In this collection are found some of the relatively tender varieties not hardy in the Pacific Northwest. At the Huntington Botanic Garden, associated with the Huntington Library in Pasadena, California, there are several varieties but no extensive collection. The outstanding thing here is that rhododendrons are growing well under conditions sometimes thought to be completely unsuitable. It simply shows what can be done, in the way of providing suitable conditions for these plants, to offset heat, drought, and alkalinity. There are also a few plants in the Los Angeles County Arboretum, again a small indication of what can be grown, with attention to specific requirements.

In the East there is a collection of a limited number of varieties at the New York Botanic Garden in the Bronx, and at the Morris Arboretum in Philadelphia. At the Arnold Arboretum, Jamaica Plains, Massachusetts, rhododendrons have been given consideration for many years. A large number of introductions have been made from other countries and from the various exploring expeditions, but the rigorous climate has eliminated all but the very hardiest types. This, of course, is valuable information, as it is important to know which ones are too tender for a given climatic area.

In the National Arboretum at Washington, D.C., are located specimens of all, or almost all, of the Glenn Dale azaleas. These azaleas originated in that area, and are especially well adapted to it. In addition there are extensive collections of Dutch azaleas and various types of rhododendrons.

In the Southeast, the Biltmore estate of Asheville, North Carolina, which is open to the public for a fee, has a very fine collection of azaleas native to the Southeast. To this collection have been added many other azalea varieties, and some rhododendrons.

The above mentioned are only a very few of the places where rhododendrons can be seen. There are many private collections and collections owned by nurserymen, most of which can be seen upon application.

RHODODENDRON PUBLICATIONS

Rhododendron fanciers are about as varied as the plants which absorb their interest. Some obtain a few plants and are enthused about them, but never go further in developing a hobby. Others may do a great deal of reading and studying before obtaining even the one first plant. However a relatively large, and increasing, proportion of gardeners are interested in both growing and reading about their favorite plants. The officers of the American Rhododendron Society realized this, and so a quarterly bulletin has been published since the society was first instituted. This bulletin gives up-to-date information about things going on in the rhododendron world, and has numerous articles about culture, varieties, control of pests, classification, and other things of special interest.

The *Journal of the Royal Horticultural Society* has already been mentioned as a source of considerable rhododendron information. There are a number of garden magazines in this country and in England which feature rhododendrons from time to time. Leaflets published by the Australian, German, New Zealand and Washington societies of course are important parts of the rhododendron literature.

The American Rhododendron Society and the Royal Horticultural Society have published yearbooks from time to time. The current series by the R.H.S. is combined with camellias to give the *Rhododendron and Camellia Yearbook*. The American Rhododendron Society published a yearbook for a few years, then switched to a book about every five years, as it was felt that there would be much more valuable information available to include in a book at the longer intervals. The first five-year book was published in 1956. These books contain ratings of varieties and species, information about new varieties, cultural methods, and many other phases of rhododendron and azalea growing.

There are a number of books devoted primarily or entirely to rhododendrons, most of them given in the following list, and the reader is urged to consult them for more detailed information than that included in this book for beginners. It is hoped that the reader will have become sufficiently interested to include one or more rhododendrons or azaleas in his garden, and to continue his reading to learn more about this fascinating group of plants.

WHERE TO GET FURTHER INFORMATION ABOUT RHODODENDRONS

There are many brief articles in various garden magazines, too numerous to list here. Most of them touch only a small segment of the entire range of cultural and varietal problems. Therefore the following list includes publications devoted primarily to rhododendrons and azaleas. Many of them are out of print but could be secured from the larger city, state, or college libraries.

PERIODICALS, YEARBOOKS

Quarterly Bulletin. American Rhododendron Society. 1947.

Rhododendron. Successor to *The Bulletin*, Tacoma Rhododendron Society. 1951—

Rhododendron und immergrune Laubegeholze Jahrbuch, Rhododendron-Gesellschaft. Bremen. 1937–42, 1953.

Yearbooks. American Rhododendron Society. 1945–49.

Yearbooks. The Rhododendron Association, London 1929–39.

Yearbooks. Rhododendron. Royal Horticultural Society, London. 1946–53.

Yearbooks. Rhododendron and Camellia. Royal Horticultural Society, London. 1954—

BOOKS ABOUT RHODODENDRONS AND AZALEAS

Bowers, C. G. *Rhododendrons and Azaleas*. New York: Macmillan Co., 1936.

Bowers, C. G. *Winter-Hardy Azaleas and Rhododendrons*. Boston: Massachusetts Horticultural Society, 1954.

Clarke, J. Harold ed. *Rhododendrons*. American Rhododendron Society, 1956.

Cowan, J. M. *Rhododendron Leaf: A Study of the Epidermal Appendages*. Edinburgh: Oliver & Boyd, Ltd., 1951.

Cox, E. H. M. *Rhododendrons for Amateurs*. New York: Charles Scribner's Sons, 1924.

Cox, E. H. M. and Cox, P. A. *Modern Rhododendrons*. New York: Thomas Nelson & Sons, 1956.

Fletcher, H. R. *The International Rhododendron Register*. London: Royal Horticultural Society, 1958.

Gould, N. K. and Synge, P. M. eds. *The Rhododendron Handbook*. 2 vols. London: Royal Horticultural Society, 1956.

Grootendorst, H. J. *Rhododendrons en Azaleas.* Boskoop: Nereniging voor Boskoopse Culturen, 1954.

Hanley, John ed. *Handbook of Rhododendrons.* Seattle: University of Washington Arboretum Foundation, 1946.

Hooker, J. D. *Rhodendrons of Sikkim Himalaya.* London, 1851.

Hume, H. H. *Azaleas and Camellias.* (rev. ed.) New York: Macmillan Co., 1953.

Hume, H. H. *Azaleas, Kinds and Culture.* (reissue) New York: Macmillan Co., 1954.

Johnson, A. T. *Rhododendrons, Azaleas, Magnolias, Camellias and Ornamental Cherries.* London: My Garden, 1948.

Lee, F. P. ed. *The Azalea Handbook.* Washington D.C.: American Horticultural Society, 1952.

Lee, F. P. *The Azalea Book.* New York: D. Van Nostrand Co.

Millais, J. G. *Rhododendrons and the Various Hybrids.* New York: Longman's, Green & Co., (vol. 1), 1917; (vol. 2), 1924.

Morrison, B. Y. *The Glenn Dale Azaleas.* U. S. Department of Agriculture. Monograph 20, 1953.

Rand, Edward Sprague. *The Rhododendron and American Plants.* Boston: Little, Brown & Company, 1871.

Schurlinck, H., en anderen. *Tuinbouw Encyclopedie I. De Azalea indica L.* Antwerp, 1938.

Steffen, Alex. *Azalea und Erica.* Ludwigsburg, 1951.

Stevenson, J. B. ed. *The Species of Rhododendron.* Edinburgh: Edinburgh University Press, 1947 (2d ed.).

Street, Frederick. *Hardy Rhododendrons.* London: D. Van Nostrand Co., 1954.

Street, Frederick. *Azaleas.* London: Cassell & Company, Ltd., 1959.

Ward, Francis Kingdon. *Rhododendrons for Everyone.* London: Gardeners' Chronicle 1926.

Ward, Francis Kingdon. *Rhododendrons.* London: Latimer House.

Watson, William. *Rhododendrons and Azaleas.* Edinburgh: T. C. Jack, 1911.

Wilson, E. H. and Rehder, A. *A Monograph of Azaleas.* Cambridge: Cambridge University Press, 1921.

INDEX